Secret Agenda

Secret Agenda
The Mormon Plan For America

Timothy J. Flanders

ISBN-13: 978-0615704050
ISBN-10: 0615704050

Library of Congress Control Number: 2013940122

Published by Veritas Press

First Printing October 2012
Second Printing June 2013

www.veritaspress.us

Printed in the United States of America

Note to the Reader

To preserve the accuracy of the historical record, there has been no attempt to correct misspellings or grammatical errors in any of the original reference material quoted throughout this book. I know I am stepping into uncharted territory by purposely choosing to eliminate the common usage of [sic] in my references, but I feel strongly this unconventional approach will result in a more powerful experience for the reader. I am also well aware of the personal criticism I may have to endure from academic circles for this radical departure from what is considered normal practice within the literary world, but it is a price I am willing to pay if by doing so my readers can easily identify with and relate to the historical persona's depicted throughout this book.

Therefore in keeping with my decision to depart from the accepted norm, all quotes, captions and excerpts have been reproduced exactly as they were originally recorded with absolutely no attempt to correct obvious misspellings.

I would like to encourage the reader who is interested in the subject of early Mormon history to continue studying the wealth of information currently available. Although every author will undoubtedly present their own unique literary style and point of view when approaching the topic of Mormonism as a whole, a much broader historical picture may be gleaned by the reader who is willing to engage in a thorough and comparative research of the written material available. Do yourself a favor and do not limit yourself to a single authors point of view.

While I am proud of my literary accomplishment and feel it is a privilege to present this information to the general public, there will undoubtedly be many who will unfortunately perceive the overall scope of my work to be somewhat narrow and limited. Admittedly the history of Mormonism in America can and often does spill over into a broad range of topics. Because of the many areas of society that were affected by the emergence of the Mormon Church, I will concede it is difficult to distill their history into a single category and even more difficult to condense the study of Latter-day Saints into one genre. However convoluted the history of Mormonism in America continues to be, my focus is squarely on the political agenda of the Mormon Church.

I feel obliged to inform you that in order to paint a historically accurate picture regarding the political agenda of The Church of Jesus Christ of Latter-day Saints, I felt it necessary to include a brief retelling of an intricate history most American's are simply unaware of. Regretfully the time I had allotted for this project did not allow for a more thorough examination of all relevant historical events in connection to the subject matter. Therefore only a brief synopsis of the Mormon Church's fascinating history could be conveyed in the pages of his book.

A large portion of the evidence presented in this book is based upon information that has been handed down from generation to generation in the form of personal diaries and family stories. From the early days of the Mormon Church my ancestors have proudly served the Church by openly proclaiming the truth of the restored gospel, while privately they were instrumental in carrying out its more sinister ambitions behind the scenes where prying eyes were not welcome. It is because of the majority of their activities are not known to the world, that this book was written. The truth must be laid bare for all humanity to witness.

All statements attributed to the leadership of The Church of Jesus Christ of Latter-day Saints and persons of authority within the hierarchy of the Mormon Church have been verified as historically accurate. All other statements are either conclusions based upon facts in evidence or the opinion of the author.

Great effort was taken to ascertain factual and historically accurate dates for each of the events reported in this book, but in some cases conflicting dates have been recorded either through second-hand accounts or by simple human error. When a conflicting date appears in the historical record, such as entries in personal diaries or newspapers reporting contradictory dates for the same event, I have taken every effort to list the date that my research proved to have the broadest evidentiary support.

Contents

Acknowledgments

I would like to express my heartfelt appreciation to those nameless souls who supported me as I gave voice to these words. Their constant encouragement was a critical component in finishing this project, especially when I ran out of steam and wanted to throw in the towel.

A big thank you goes out to Bobby Gilpin of UK Partnerships For Christ. Bobby graciously gave me permission to reprint a portion of a post on his blog www.mormonisminvestigated.co.uk.

Of course we cannot forget to mention Chris Ralph the valiant individual who composed the rousing letter I quote from.

Preface

One of the most difficult hurtles an author faces when they start researching and tabulating factual data regarding secret plots and hidden agendas is how to avoid an almost certain knee jerk reaction from their intended audience. This, shall we say, situation becomes increasingly more complicated when the heart of your subject matter deals with the secret plans of an organization that has been shrouded in mystery for well over one hundred fifty years. And to top it off, you must first convince your audience you are not some nut job with an overly active imagination sitting around your living room wearing a tin foil hat waiting for the mothership to land.

Compounding the complexity of the situation I currently face is the simple fact I am presenting evidence of a “secret agenda.” Of course people will say, “I am not sure I can believe your story. I have never heard anything like that before.” My point exactly! A vast majority of my audience will most likely have never heard about any of these events, precisely because they were kept secret. The veil of secrecy was put into place deliberately as a sort of covert counter measure to any avoid public embarrassment, which of course could become very costly for a religious institution. Also Church leaders had every intention to evade, at all costs, the inevitable prolonged scrutiny which would have undoubtedly followed had all of the facts and details been disclosed to the general public. We need not ask but a single question when attempting to discern whether or not The Church of Jesus Christ of Latter-day Saints is culpable in what appears to be an ongoing organized deceit. What is the LDS Church hiding from the American people?

Any further investigation is superfluous. That one single, solitary question itself is sufficient to break the dam and allow the floodgates of information to burst open. One seemingly innocent question unlocks a massive vault of potentially damaging data that has surreptitiously been concealed for well over one hundred years. I find it a little odd and somewhat disturbing that any Church would find it necessary to hide and keep their activities secret. That alone should be enough to raise a red flag.

Can you say, "Houston, we have a problem?"

Anyway, moving on. I know I am facing a particularly rough road. I will just have to be patient and find the strength to persevere. I know how hard it will be to have my voice heard above the din of the crowd shouting "conspiracy" and "paranoia." Members of The Church of Jesus Christ of Latter-day Saints will flock to the rescue and accuse me of any number of crimes against God and their beloved church, but I am more than willing to bear the brunt of their disdain if I can reveal to the American people the truth of my words. Lastly others who hear of my message will simply turn a blind eye to any evidence I have gathered, no matter how well documented, because after all very few American citizens actually want to know just how deep the rabbit hole goes. Nobody wants to openly admit they fell prey to the machinations of a charismatic charlatan, let alone while under the spell of religious fervor they became the willing victims of an organized deceit.

By now you may have guessed I have taken on the monumental task of talking about the colossal elephant in the room. Are you ready to begin?

One minor detail I would like to clarify before we dive headlong into the text is the various ways I will identify The Church of Jesus Christ of Latter-day Saints and its founding Prophet. First the reader should be aware The Church of Jesus Christ of Latter-day Saints has officially changed its name three times. Originally the Church founded by Joseph Smith, Jr. in 1830, was called The Church of Christ, later the name was changed to The Church of Latter-day Saints and finally it would be known as The Church of Jesus Christ of Latter-day Saints, but that name would also be altered slightly to the modern stylized typeface displayed on the various websites owned and operated by the LDS Church.

Now that we have that small little detail out of the way and everything is clear as mud, let us proceed. In an attempt to spare you, the reader, from the almost certain drudgery of having to read the same name an inexhaustible number of times throughout the text, I have adopted the following format:

1. Joseph Smith, Jr., the first Prophet of The Church of Jesus Christ of Latter-day Saints, will be referenced throughout this book as Joseph Smith, Jr., Joseph Smith and or lastly as Joseph. So as to avoid any confusion his father will always be referred to as Joseph Smith, Sr.

2. The Church of Jesus Christ of Latter-day Saints will also be referenced as The Church of Christ, The Church of Latter-day Saints, The Church, The Mormon Church, The LDS Church and finally by its official name The Church of Jesus Christ of Latter-day Saints.

3. Converts to The Church of Jesus Christ of Latter-day Saints will be referenced as members of the Church,

> church members, converts, followers, pioneers, Saints and finally by the official term preferred by the LDS Church — Latter-day Saints.

I hope this will create a more pleasant and satisfactory reading environment for everyone involved.

OK, let us continue...

As bizarre, distasteful, odd and unorthodox many of the religious practices and doctrines associated with the faith of Mormonism appear to be to adherents of mainstream Christianity, the purpose of this work is not to besmirch The Church of Jesus Christ of Latter-day Saints, but to reveal and disclose the unspoken political agenda of top leaders within the Church.

Beginning with the early history and foundation of the LDS Church, my research will not only reveal a concerted effort to deceive the American populace — but will also show how an elite hierarchy of Church leaders have kept their own members in the dark and largely unaware of their political motives. Lastly, the evidence collected will demonstrate how various members of the Church's own ruling hierarchy of General Authorities have from the early, humble formation of the Church used covert and illicit activities to cover up their real motivation and how a handful of privileged individuals have continued to operate The Church of Jesus Christ of Latter-day Saints in a fashion quite similar to Joseph Smith and his successors.

The goal of world domination envisioned by the early Mormon prophets has been perpetuated right up to the present day.

Much to the dismay of witnesses worldwide, whether they be idle curiosity seekers or individuals in search of a spiritual home, officials within the LDS Church have, over the years, decidedly tried to distance the modern faith of Mormonism from a number of questionable activities endorsed and committed by early church leaders. While, in my opinion, no religious institution can stand up to the prying eyes of an outsider without appearing somewhat odd — this seems to be especially true of the Mormon faith.

Whether or not most members of The Church of Jesus Christ of Latter-day Saints choose to be willfully ignorant of the political aims of the Mormon Church is a matter that cannot be decided here in these pages, but it is a question that must be asked. What appears to be glaringly obvious to one segment of the population may in all likelihood go completely unnoticed by other citizens. To that point, the same events that act as the catalyst for outrage and righteous indignation in some people, may not get so much as a second glance from others.

The task which now lays before me is to set the stage, gather the audience and let the historical facts speak loud and clear. Never has there been a harsher mistress than a forgotten history lurking in the shadows of the past, pensively waiting to be fully exposed in the full light of day.

It quite literally may be near impossible to delve into the hidden history of the Latter-day Saint movement without acknowledging some level of manipulation and deceit by the leadership of the LDS Church over the past one hundred eighty-two years, but the simple fact is the Mormon Church has managed to finagle its way into the policies and politics of the American people unbeknownst to most citizens of the United States.

Whether you stand "for" or "against" past and present church policy is entirely up to you and has little to no bearing at all on this work, but every citizen has the right to know exactly what has been taking place under the guise of religion and my intention is to make sure the truth is revealed. Make no mistake, your personal freedoms are being threatened.

Everyone is entitled to their own personal beliefs, so let me be perfectly clear. The goal of this book is not to challenge or change your religious beliefs, but to merely present a series of events. The facts collected in this book are presented as a historical record which hopefully will create a chain of irrefutable evidence.

By and far, the content of this book should make for some interesting reading. The subject of Mormonism in America is without a doubt fascinating to say the least.

To put all of this into perspective let us consider two separate but equally important timelines:

1. The founding of the United States of America.
2. The rise of The Church of Jesus Christ of Latter-day Saints to a position of prominence within the wider Latter-day Saint movement.

Notwithstanding any personal beliefs you may hold regarding the purpose, goals and aims of the Mormon Church, there is little use in debating this once obscure little religious community founded in upstate New York during the Spring of 1830, by Joseph Smith, Jr. has both captured the imagination and raised the ire of many American citizens.

Regardless of what you may know or think you may know concerning the rise to prominence and the religious practices of the members of The Church of Jesus Christ of Latter-day Saints, the facts as preserved by a fairly lengthy written history speak volumes. Personal beliefs are irrelevant to this treatise, so let us cast those aside for the moment as we sift through the evidence with discerning eyes. The indelible mark of their past deeds, combined with a healthy examination of their present conduct, will be our barometer and ultimate touchstone as we traverse the history of the Mormon Church in search of clues.

We may yet discover the true purpose of the LDS Church and in the process reveal a long sought-after plan the Church hopes to implement in the not too distant future.

I cannot say for certain what the future may hold for each of us as American citizens, but I can confirm the ultimate goal and plan of The Church of Jesus Christ of Latter-day Saints is to dominate world politics by establishing a theocratic government.

Although 1830, appears to be far removed from the founding of our great nation, we must remember the U.S. Government was still at that time very much in its infancy. Let us go back in time to the end of the Revolutionary War and retrace those first few tenuous steps. After a little less than a decade of guerilla warfare on the American continent, citizens were just beginning to relish the idea of personal and political freedom. A government by the people and for the people had been established, but the Articles of Confederation proved ineffective. Individual states seemed more interested in their own self promotion than building a strong cohesive nation. And so the dream that was to become America floundered in the early hours of its birth.

I firmly believe we hit the ground running, yet the idea of a democratic self-governing nation was only starting to seep into our collective consciousness. The United States of America had only begun to get its feet wet.

Despite the fact we took a stand against tyranny and declared ourselves citizens of a free and sovereign nation in 1776, the Constitution of the United States of America had barely seen the 40th anniversary of its full ratification by all thirteen states before the Mormon Church burst onto the scene. Like it or not one simple little fact will always remain a part of our history. The Church of Jesus Christ of Latter-day Saints is nearly as old as the governing body of the United States of America.

I guess you could say, the LDS Church is the pesky little brother to an older, wiser and much more mature sibling.

The Author

Secret Agenda
The Mormon Plan For America

Historical Record

Throughout this book I will be presenting a series of historical events, which when viewed as a body of interrelated actions, will show a linear progression along a well documented timeline. In this essay no single event can be viewed as a solitary and independent occurrence, to be judged solely on its own merit. Even seemingly insignificant and unrelated events are connected in some fashion one to another — either in response to a preceding event or appearing in the context of a natural progression. By taking this particular approach I will build a body of evidence to support my claim The Church of Jesus Christ of Latter-day Saints has for generations been steadily progressing toward their goal of political domination.

More than one hundred sixty-eight years ago a handful of leaders within the Mormon Church hatched a plan to establish a theocratic government within the borders of the United States in an effort to gain dominion over America and its legislative bodies.

Their goal was to have key members of The Church of Jesus Christ of Latter-day Saints strategically ensconced on the bridge of America's political ship and patiently wait for the day when political and social unrest would grip our country. Having loyal followers already in seats of power was critical to the master plan. Once all of the key elements had fallen into place, members of the Mormon priesthood, on orders from the Church President, would seize control of the massive political beast and steer the ship through the turbulent waters.

As I lay out and make a case for what I will be referring to as the hidden agenda of the Mormon church, I want to be absolutely clear regarding the historical facts. These events did in fact take place and subsequently have been recorded into the written history of our fledgling country. This much cannot be ignored. Furthermore the story of America and the emergence of the Mormon faith cannot be separated — they are inexorably tied one to the other.

If we are to give any credence to the most often paraphrased quote by George Santayana, "Those who do not learn from history are doomed to repeat it" then we must cautiously assume there is possibly no greater potential threat to our continued advancement as a nation, regardless of its policies, than a history swept aside and foolishly forgotten.

No matter how unsettling the past may be, we cannot afford to wipe from our collective memory the misdeeds of a few, for it is in our forgetfulness that we become slaves once again.

These historical events are not the made up fantasies of an individual with an over active imagination, but actual events which took place and which will unequivocally confirm and attest to the long standing political aspirations of the leadership within The Church of Jesus Christ of Latter-day Saints.

So why am I leading you back into the past instead of moving forward into the future? It is my intention to show a very real and distinct pattern of behavior from the inception of Mormonism. I will demonstrate in no uncertain terms how the LDS Church has over the course of nearly two centuries built a vast multi-national conglomerate under the guise of religion. One key element which has consistently reared its ugly head throughout the course of my research points directly at how The Church of Jesus Christ of Latter-day Saints from the first pangs of birth has operated as a corporate entity rather than a religious institution.

What truly breaks my heart is how the vast wealth accumulated by the Mormon Church and controlled by their corporate oligarchy was amassed through the beguiling of innocent people.

And so we begin...

- Joseph Smith, Jr. received his first vision of God the Father and His Son Jesus Christ in the spring of 1820.
- Joseph Smith, Jr. was arrested on March 20, 1826, for disorderly conduct.
- The Book of Mormon was published and first sold on March 26, 1830.
- The Church of Christ was formally established by Joseph Smith, Jr. on April 6, 1830.
- Joseph Smith, Jr. received a revelation in September of 1830, to preach the gospel to the world in preparation for the coming millennial reign of Christ.
- During the month of December in 1830, Joseph Smith, Jr. and Sidney Rigdon received a revelation commanding The Church of Christ to move to Ohio.
- A revelation is received in February of 1831, confirming only the Prophet Joseph Smith, Jr. can receive revelation for God's people.
- Joseph Smith, Jr. received a revelation on February 9, 1831, commanding the Prophet to establish the Law of Consecration throughout the Mormon community.

- By 1831, converts to Joseph Smith's newly formed Church of Christ began to settle in Jackson County, Missouri in order to establish the City of Zion. Saints are promised they will inherit the land held by current residents.
- Construction of the first Mormon Temple was started in Kirtland, Ohio in 1833.
- Amidst growing tensions, Mormon settlers are driven from Jackson County, Missouri forcing Latter-day Saints to flee their homes and leave their farms behind in October of 1833.
- The name of the church was changed on May 3, 1834, to the Church of the Latter-day Saints. The name of Christ remained conspicuously absent from the Church for more than four years.
- Despite failing to acquire a charter for banking on two separate occasions, Joseph Smith, Jr. created the Kirtland Safety Society in 1836.
- Avoiding warrants for their arrest on charges of illegal banking, Joseph Smith, Jr. and Sidney Rigdon fled Kirtland, Ohio, on January 12, 1838.
- In 1838, Joseph Smith, Jr. received another revelation to officially change the name of his church to The Church of Jesus Christ of Latter-day Saints.
- Joseph Smith, Jr. formed a secret group of armed vigilantes known as the Danites to protect Latter-day Saints in June of 1838.
- A revelation was received by Joseph Smith, Jr. on July 8, 1838, regarding the institution of tithing.
- John Corrill, the first Latter-day Saint elected to any state office, was elected by the largely Mormon populated

county of Caldwell, Missouri as a representative to the Missouri State Legislature on August 6, 1838.

- A skirmish on the 6th of August known as the Gallatin Election Day Battle in Daviess County, ignited the 1838 Mormon War of Missouri.
- After leading an armed resistance against Federal troops during the Mormon War, Joseph Smith, Jr. was arrested and held on charges of treason on November 1, 1838.
- Escaping custody, Joseph Smith, Jr.. fled to Nauvoo, Illinois in April of 1839.
- Seeking redress for the persecution of Latter-day Saints, Joseph Smith, Jr. meets with President Martin Van Buren in 1839, and again in early 1840.
- Thomas Carlin, Governor of Illinois, signed a charter for the city of Nauvoo on December 16, 1840, granting Joseph Smith the power to create an independent militia.
- The Nauvoo Legion, an independent military militia, was organized on February 4, 1841.
- Lieutenant General Joseph Smith, Jr. of the Nauvoo Legion was elected vice mayor of the city of Nauvoo on January 22, 1842.
- Joseph Smith, Jr. received a revelation to establish The Living Constitution, also known as the Council of Fifty, on April 7, 1842.
- Mormon Endowment Ceremony was revealed by the Prophet Joseph Smith, Jr. on May 4, 1842, at Nauvoo, Illinois. Participants pledged to sacrifice all of their time, talents and possessions to build up the LDS Church.
- Nauvoo City High Council appointed Joseph Smith mayor of Nauvoo, Illinois on May 19, 1842.

- Latter-day Saint Apostle William B. Smith, younger brother of Mormon Prophet Joseph Smith, Jr., was elected to the Illinois House of Representatives in August of 1842.
- Preparing for a future theocratic rule of the Kingdom of God, Joseph Smith, Jr. organized and established the Council of Fifty on March 10, 1844.
- Joseph Smith was formally nominated for president of the United States in Nauvoo, Illinois on March 17, 1844.
- Brigham Young appointed three hundred thirty-seven elders of the LDS Church on April 9, 1844, to serve as electioneer missionaries to support Joseph Smith, Jr. in his campaign for United States President.
- Mobilizing the Nauvoo Legion and municipal police, Joseph Smith, Jr. placed city of Nauvoo, Illinois under martial law on June 18, 1844.
- Arrested on charges of treason, Joseph Smith, Jr. and his brother Hyrum Smith were imprisoned in Carthage Jail on June 24, 1844, to await trial.
- Joseph and Hyrum Smith were killed in Carthage, Illinois on June 27, 1844.
- Brigham Young added the Oath of Vengeance to the Mormon Endowment ritual in 1845.
- The Utah War began in May of 1857.
- U.S. President James Buchanan declared the Utah Territory in open rebellion against the United States of America on June 29, 1857.
- President James Buchanan appointed Alfred Cumming governor of Utah Territory on July 13, 1857.

- Brigham Young publicly discussed secession of the Mormon community from the United States in favor of an independent theocratic kingdom on August 2, 1857.
- Brigham Young declared martial law on August 5, 1857, throughout the entire Utah Territory.
- On August 29, 1857, Brigham Young instructed Daniel H. Wells to prepare a second proclamation of martial law.
- Church Prophet Brigham Young announced his plans to secede from the United States of America and establish the Mormon "Kingdom of God" on August 30, 1857.
- First attack against the non-Mormon Baker-Fancher wagon train travelling through the Utah Territory occurs on September 7, 1857, at Mountain Meadows.
- One hundred twenty men, women and children of the Baker-Fancher wagon train were killed on September 11, 1857, during the Mountain Meadows Massacre.
- Anticipating the arrival of Federal troops, Brigham Young ordered all faithful Mormons in Salt Lake City to burn their homes on March 23, 1858.
- On April 6, 1858, James Buchanan granted a presidential pardon to Brigham Young for his involvement in the Utah War and the Mountain Meadows Massacre.
- Brigham Young surrendered the Utah Territory to Alfred Cummings on April 12, 1858.
- The Utah War ended in July 1858.
- Republicans won control of the United States House of Representatives in 1858.
- Established by LDS Church leaders for the Utah Territory, the People's Party, a church run political party, emerged

in opposition to the Liberal Party early in 1870.

- Regular meetings of the Council of Fifty officially ceased on October 9, 1884, when the Council convened for its apparent final meeting.
- On October 6, 1890, Church leaders officially issued the 1890 Manifesto. The Mormon Church had abandoned the practice of polygamy in an effort to ensure the Utah Territory be granted statehood.
- The People's Party was disbanded in June 1891, in order for the Utah Territory to gain statehood.
- In 1893, the LDS Church leadership directed specific members of influential families to become Republicans.
- Congress passed the Enabling Act on July 16, 1894, which allowed the residents of the Utah Territory to form a Constitution and State Government.
- Utah granted statehood on January 4,1896, on the condition the state constitution enforced a ban on the practice of polygamy.
- Wilford Woodruff issued the Political Manifesto of 1896, requiring all leaders of the LDS Church to seek and obtain permission from the Church Presidency before campaigning for political office.
- On April 6, 1904, Joseph F. Smith, the 6th President of the Church, issued the Second Manifesto banning polygamy throughout the entire Mormon community.
- Fearing severe reprisal from the U. S. Government the oath of vengeance was removed from the Mormon Temple Endowment ritual on February 15, 1927.
- Heber J. Grant, last official member of the Council of Fifty died on May 14, 1945.

- George Albert Smith, the first non-polygamous President of The Church of Jesus Christ of Latter-day Saints assumed office on May 21, 1945.
- Ezra Taft Benson obtained permission from LDS Church President David O. McKay in 1952, to serve as United States Secretary of Agriculture under U.S. President Dwight. D. Eisenhower.
- George W. Romney was elected Governor of Michigan in November of 1962.
- Former Governor George W. Romney was appointed as Secretary of Housing and Urban Development by Richard M. Nixon on December 11, 1968.
- A politically active Ezra Taft Benson was denied permission to be the 1976, running mate of George Wallace by LDS Church President Spencer W. Kimball.
- Coleman Young, mayor of Detroit, accused Morris Udall of being racist during his 1976 presidential campaign, due to the LDS Church's policy of denying people of African descent the right to receive temple ordinances or be ordained to the Priesthood.
- On July 8, 1978, Church President Spencer W. Kimball received a revelation reversing the long standing ban on men of African descent being ordained to the Priesthood.
- N. Eldon Tanner, First Counselor in the First Presidency of the Church, presented Official Declaration—2, at the 148th Semiannual General Conference in Salt Lake City on September 30, 1978.
- On January 4, 1993, Michael Leavitt was sworn in as the 14th Governor of Utah.
- Leavitt resigned his governorship during his third term in

office to accept President George W. Bush's nomination as Administrator of the Environmental Protection Agency.

- On January 2, 2003, Willard Mitt Romney was sworn in as the 70th Governor of Massachusetts.
- On October 28, 2003, the United States Senate confirmed President Bush's appointment of Michael Leavitt as the 10th Administrator of the EPA.
- In a nod to his father, Mitt Romney, former Governor of Massachusetts, announced his first presidential campaign for the 2008 election on February 13, 2007, at The Henry Ford Museum in Dearborn, Michigan.
- Mitt Romney formally launched his 2012 Presidential campaign on June 2, 2011, in Stratham, New Hampshire.
- Although he opened his campaign headquarters on May 18, 2011, U.S. Ambassador to China, John Huntsman, Jr. formally entered the 2012 Presidential race as a Republican candidate on June 21, 2012.
- On August 28, 2012, Mitt Romney officially accepted the GOP party nomination during the 2012 Republican National Convention.
- The first Mormon candidate to secure the Republican Party nomination was defeated by Democratic incumbent President Barack Obama on November 6, 2012. President Obama's re-election win was the largest margin of victory recorded in a presidential re-election campaign since the landslide win by Franklin Delano Roosevelt in 1936.

Political Neutrality of the Church

In order to preserve an accurate timeline of historical events this section should by all rights be placed closer to the end of the book because it presents the current policy of The Church of Jesus Christ of Latter-day Saints regarding the political activities of its membership, yet I felt compelled to include it at the beginning so the reader would be aware of the official stance the Mormon Church takes on the subject of politics. You might not find it at all surprising the LDS Church has quite often violated its own policy of remaining neutral and abstaining from political involvement. This is a truly disturbing pattern which continues even to this day. When did we abandon the sacrosanct ideal of a clear and distinct separation between Church and State?

From the onset Church leaders have claimed to remain open minded, unbiased and neutral in regards to political matters, while always urging members of the Church to vote in accordance with their conscience. Joseph Smith made his views perfectly clear to his followers. Section 134 of the Doctrine & Covenants which revealed the official stance of the Mormon Church regarding government and laws in general was adopted by a unanimous vote during a general assembly of the Church of the Latter-day Saints held at Kirtland, Ohio on August 17, 1835.

The Church of Jesus Christ of Latter-day Saints publishes a set of Standard Works which it claims is the revealed word of God. Every practicing Mormon accepts the Stand Works as holy scripture which includes the Holy Bible, Book of Mormon, Doctrine & Covenants and the Pearl of Great Price. Together these scriptures comprise the official canon of Church doctrine and are the only books considered as being absolutely authoritative in regards to doctrine and therefore binding on all LDS Church members.

While you read this section bear in mind the often repeated and publicly stated pronouncement of the Mormon Church as to its non-involvement in politics and judge for yourself if these statements hold true. In this particular case the eloquent words of Shakespeare as spoken by Queen Gertrude, "The lady doth protest too much, methinks" might be a bit more apropos.

The following is the official statement from The Church of Jesus Christ of Latter-day Saints regarding its stance on politics and civil government:

The Church's mission is to preach the gospel of Jesus Christ, not to elect politicians. The Church of Jesus Christ of Latter-day Saints is neutral in matters of party politics. This applies in all of the many nations in which it is established.

The Church does not:

- Endorse, promote or oppose political parties, candidates or platforms.
- Allow its church buildings, membership lists or other resources to be used for partisan political purposes.
- Attempt to direct its members as to which candidate or party they should give their votes to. This policy applies

whether or not a candidate for office is a member of The Church of Jesus Christ of Latter-day Saints.
- Attempt to direct or dictate to a government leader.

The Church does:

- Encourage its members to play a role as responsible citizens in their communities, including becoming informed about issues and voting in elections.
- Expect its members to engage in the political process in an informed and civil manner, respecting the fact that members of the Church come from a variety of backgrounds and experiences and may have differences of opinion in partisan political matters.
- Request candidates for office not to imply that their candidacy or platforms are endorsed by the Church.
- Reserve the right as an institution to address, in a nonpartisan way, issues that it believes have significant community or moral consequences or that directly affect the interests of the Church.

In the United States, where nearly half of the world's Latter-day Saints live, it is customary for the Church at each national election to issue a letter to be read to all congregations encouraging its members to vote, but emphasizing the Church's neutrality in partisan political matters.

Relationships With Government

Elected officials who are Latter-day Saints make their own decisions and may not necessarily be in agreement with one another or even with a publicly stated Church position. While the Church may communicate its views to them, as it may to any other elected official, it recognizes that these officials still must make their own choices based on their best judgment and with consideration of the constituencies whom they were elected to represent.

Modern scriptural references to the role of government:

Doctrine and Covenants, Section 134

1. *We believe that governments were instituted of God for the benefit of man; and that he holds men accountable for their acts in relation to them, both in making laws and administering them, for the good and safety of society.*
2. *We believe that no government can exist in peace, except such laws are framed and held inviolate as will secure to each individual the free exercise of conscience, the right and control of property, and the protection of life.*
3. *We believe that all governments necessarily require civil officers and magistrates to enforce the laws of the same; and that such as will administer the law in equity and justice should be sought for and upheld by the voice of the people if a republic, or the will of the sovereign.*
4. *We believe that religion is instituted of God; and that men are amenable to him, and to him only, for the exercise of it, unless their religious opinions prompt them to infringe upon the rights and liberties of others; but we do not believe that human law has a right to interfere in prescribing rules of worship to bind the consciences of men, nor dictate forms for public or private devotion; that the civil magistrate should restrain crime, but never control conscience; should punish guilt, but never suppress the freedom of the soul.*
5. *We believe that all men are bound to sustain and uphold the respective governments in which they reside, while protected in their inherent and inalienable rights by the laws of such governments; and that sedition and rebellion are unbecoming every citizen thus protected, and should*

be punished accordingly; and that all governments have a right to enact such laws as in their own judgments are best calculated to secure the public interest; at the same time, however, holding sacred the freedom of conscience.

6. *We believe that every man should be honored in his station, rulers and magistrates as such, being placed for the protection of the innocent and the punishment of the guilty; and that to the laws all men owe respect and deference, as without them peace and harmony would be supplanted by anarchy and terror; human laws being instituted for the express purpose of regulating our interests as individuals and nations, between man and man; and divine laws given of heaven, prescribing rules on spiritual concerns, for faith and worship, both to be answered by man to his Maker.*
7. *We believe that rulers, states, and governments have a right, and are bound to enact laws for the protection of all citizens in the free exercise of their religious belief; but we do not believe that they have a right in justice to deprive citizens of this privilege, or proscribe them in their opinions, so long as a regard and reverence are shown to the laws and such religious opinions do not justify sedition nor conspiracy.*
8. *We believe that the commission of crime should be punished according to the nature of the offense; that murder, treason, robbery, theft, and the breach of the general peace, in all respects, should be punished according to their criminality and their tendency to evil among men, by the laws of that government in which the offense is committed; and for the public peace and tranquility all men should step forward and use their ability in bringing offenders against good laws to punishment.*
9. *We do not believe it just to mingle religious influence with civil government, whereby one religious society is fostered*

and another proscribed in its spiritual privileges, and the individual rights of its members, as citizens, denied.

10. *We believe that all religious societies have a right to deal with their members for disorderly conduct, according to the rules and regulations of such societies; provided that such dealings be for fellowship and good standing; but we do not believe that any religious society has authority to try men on the right of property or life, to take from them this world's goods, or to put them in jeopardy of either life or limb, or to inflict any physical punishment upon them. They can only excommunicate them from their society, and withdraw from them their fellowship.*
11. *We believe that men should appeal to the civil law for redress of all wrongs and grievances, where personal abuse is inflicted or the right of property or character infringed, where such laws exist as will protect the same; but we believe that all men are justified in defending themselves, their friends, and property, and the government, from the unlawful assaults and encroachments of all persons in times of exigency, where immediate appeal cannot be made to the laws, and relief afforded.*
12. *We believe it just to preach the gospel to the nations of the earth, and warn the righteous to save themselves from the corruption of the world; but we do not believe it right to interfere with bond-servants, neither preach the gospel to, nor baptize them contrary to the will and wish of their masters, nor to meddle with or influence them in the least to cause them to be dissatisfied with their situations in this life, thereby jeopardizing the lives of men; such interference we believe to be unlawful and unjust, and dangerous to the peace of every government allowing human beings to be held in servitude.*

Political Party Participation of Presiding Church Officers

In addition, the First Presidency letter issued on 16 June 2011 is a re-statement and further clarification of the Church's position on political neutrality at the start of another political season. It applies to all full-time General Authorities, general auxiliary leaders, mission presidents and temple presidents. The policy is not directed to full-time Church employees.

"General Authorities and general officers of the Church and their spouses and other ecclesiastical leaders serving full-time should not personally participate in political campaigns, including promoting candidates, fundraising, speaking in behalf of or otherwise endorsing candidates, and making financial contributions.

"Since they are not full-time officers of the Church, Area Seventies, stake presidents and bishops are free to contribute, serve on campaign committees and otherwise support candidates of their choice with the understanding they:

- Are acting solely as individual citizens in the democratic process and that they do not imply, or allow others to infer, that their actions or support in any way represent the church.
- Will not use Church stationery, Church-generated address lists or email systems or Church buildings for political promotional purposes.
- Will not engage in fundraising or other types of campaigning focused on fellow Church members under their ecclesiastical supervision."

Early Financial Failures

Early attempts by the leaders of The Church of Jesus Christ of Latter-day Saints to create a sustainable financial system within the growing Latter-day Saint community met with disastrous consequences. In this section we will discuss reasons why those failures may have occurred and we will look at factors that seem to have hampered the Mormon Church's desire to become financially prosperous.

Before we can begin, we need to ask two tough questions.

Did church leaders fail in their endeavors because of their inept and gross mismanagement of simple day-to-day operations? Was their failure due, in part, to a series of sinister and devious tactics used to defraud converts of their personal property and wealth? Hopefully we can answer one or both of these question. Whatever the case may be, the cold hard facts remain — all of the early financial plans of the LDS Church failed miserably.

Years before the Law of Tithing became a standard requirement of all Latter-day Saints, one of the early programs put into place by church leaders was the Law of Consecration — a system of moral reform envisioned by Joseph Smith. Communal living was a concept that would be implemented rather quickly throughout the community of Latter-day Saints. Originally founded upon the Law of Consecration, as received through the miraculous power of revelation by the Prophet Joseph Smith, these collective communities were intended to care for the poor, the building of houses of worship and for establishing a New Jerusalem.

Early adaptation to the Law of Consecration would later evolve into a more sophisticated system of economic control, known throughout the Church as the United Order of Enoch.

Named after the biblical prophet, the United Order of Enoch was commonly referred to among members of the Church by its short form — the United Order. Brigham Young would be the first Prophet of the LDS Church to achieve any level of success with the United Order. Under his direction, Latter-day Saints established several semi-successful communities living under the rule of this new spiritual communalism. Converts to the Mormon faith were told the United Order was a commandment from the Lord.

United Order of Enoch

From its inception it is quite evident church leaders anticipated all Latter-day Saint communities would be run as a form of communal collective. Members who wished to remain in good standing were expected to commit their money and assets toward supporting and establishing the goals of the Church. This was far from an intellectual concept, early church members were required to deed all real property to a hierarchy of church leaders — to be disposed of as they saw fit. Faithful followers of Joseph Smith were happy to be supporting the Lord's work by allowing all of their material possessions to pass into the hands of the Church. After all it was their duty, a task that had been assigned by their beloved Creator. How else would God establish the City of Zion?

The long protracted history of the United Order of Enoch was a strange and mysterious affair, but one fact remained constant. All members of the Latter-day Saint community were required to relinquish any and all real assets, including real estate, money, bank notes, bonds, insurance, farm implements, jewelry, cows, hens, household goods and usable clothing. Assets of any kind were to be deeded over to the Church and placed under the direct supervision of its leaders.

In order to ensure the continued success of God's church here on earth, everything was controlled by the Presiding Bishop. Although a number of early converts to Mormonism balked at this stringent financial requirement, many of God's faithful would be convinced of its efficacy. Joseph Smith explained to his followers, just as they had been born into this life with nothing, so would they be required to give up everything of material value in order to be born again into the Kingdom of God.

Was the self-styled Mormon prophet a man of faith or was he a charismatic con man with a silver tongue?

That is a question you will have to answer for yourself. I do however find it very convenient that every time a need arose, a new revelation was received. Let us consider the following example as a case in point.

Joseph Smith, Jr., Prophet, Seer and Revelator of The Church of Christ, received a divine revelation on February 9, 1831, commanding God's faithful to institute a system of communal living. Although not specifically named in the revelation, the foundation for the United Order of Enoch had been laid.

> *If thou lovest me thou shalt serve me and keep all my commandments.*
>
> *And behold, thou wilt remember the poor, and consecrate of thy properties for their support that which thou hast to impart unto*

them, with a covenant and a deed which cannot be broken.

And inasmuch as ye impart of your substance unto the poor, ye will do it unto me; and they shall be laid before the bishop of my church and his counselors, two of the elders, or high priests, such as he shall appoint or has appointed and set apart for that purpose.

Doctrine & Covenants 42:29-31

The primary focus of the United Order appears to have been the establishment and creation of an egalitarian community designed to eliminate poverty among church members and to increase the overall self-sufficiency of Latter-day Saints. In actuality however, other than the building of churches and temples, the scheme instituted by Joseph Smith benefited only a handful of leading Church authorities. In the *Teachings of the Prophet Joseph Smith*, a book compiled and edited by Joseph Fielding Smith, Jr., we find reference to the laws of stewardship and consecration.

"...a man is bound by the law of the Church, to consecrate to the Bishop, before he can be considered a legal heir to the kingdom of Zion; and this, too, without constraint; and unless he does this, he cannot be acknowledged before the Lord on the Church Book;"

Teachings of the Prophet Joseph Smith, Section One 1830-34, Salt Lake City, 1938, page 23

Furthermore in the *Doctrine & Covenants*, originally published in 1833 as the *Book of Commandments*, we find multiple verses referring to consecration and stewardship.

Nevertheless, inasmuch as they receive more than is needful for their necessities and their wants, it shall be given into my storehouse;

And the benefits shall be consecrated unto the inhabitants of Zion, and unto their generations, inasmuch as they become heirs according to the laws of the kingdom.

> *Behold, this is what the Lord requires of every man in his stewardship, even as I, the Lord, have appointed or shall hereafter appoint unto any man.*
>
> *And behold, none are exempt from this law who belong to the church of the living God;*
>
> *Doctrine & Covenants 70:7-10*

On numerous occasions the Prophet of God's one, true church preached the communal Law of Consecration to his followers. The idea of "consecrating" all of your material wealth to the Lord, seemed to have been Joseph's go to sermon for years.

> *Verily I say unto you, my friends, I give unto you counsel, and a commandment, concerning all the properties which belong to the order which I commanded to be organized and established, to be a united order, and an everlasting order for the benefit of my church, and for the salvation of men until I come—*
>
> *With promise immutable and unchangeable, that inasmuch as those whom I commanded were faithful they should be blessed with a multiplicity of blessings;*
>
> *But inasmuch as they were not faithful they were nigh unto cursing.*
>
> *Therefore, inasmuch as some of my servants have not kept the commandment, but have broken the covenant through covetousness, and with feigned words, I have cursed them with a very sore and grievous curse.*
>
> *For I, the Lord, have decreed in my heart, that inasmuch as any man belonging to the order shall be found a transgressor, or, in other words, shall break the covenant with which ye are bound, he shall be cursed in his life, and shall be trodden down by whom I will;*
>
> *For I, the Lord, am not to be mocked in these things—*
>
> *Doctrine & Covenants 104:1-6*

And again, a commandment I give unto you concerning your stewardship which I have appointed unto you.

Behold, all these properties are mine, or else your faith is vain, and ye are found hypocrites, and the covenants which ye have made unto me are broken;

And if the properties are mine, then ye are stewards; otherwise ye are no stewards.

But, verily I say unto you, I have appointed unto you to be stewards over mine house, even stewards indeed.

And for this purpose I have commanded you to organize yourselves, even to print my words, the fulness of my scriptures, the revelations which I have given unto you, and which I shall, hereafter, from time to time give unto you—

For the purpose of building up my church and kingdom on the earth, and to prepare my people for the time when I shall dwell with them, which is nigh at hand.

And ye shall prepare for yourselves a place for a treasury, and consecrate it unto my name.

Doctrine & Covenants 104:54-60

Originally intended to be "an everlasting order for the benefit of my church, and for the salvation of men until I come" the United Order failed to meet most, if not all, of its overly ambitious and lofty goals. In practice the Order was relatively short-lived during the life of the Prophet Joseph Smith. Believing however it was a divinely inspired program, several Church leaders would attempt to revive the United Order in later years.

Under the leadership of Brigham Young the United Order saw its greatest success during its comparatively short life span. And finally before giving up the ghost, under the direction of Brigham Young's successor, church members would once again attempt to live the principle of communalism with John Taylor at the helm.

Between the years of 1855 and 1858, plans were initiated to establish communal centers throughout the Utah Territory, but all of the efforts put forth by church authorities failed. Not a single community materialized as planned. Brigham Young did however manage to eventually establish more than two hundred communities under the strict confines of communal living.

Between 1874 and 1877, a score of fresh new communities would be established under the United Order of Enoch, but once again each one would fail for a variety of reasons. In the end the United Order was not a successful financial endeavor. With the ultimate failure of each new attempt, The Church of Jesus Christ of Latter-day Saints had no choice but to face the music and abandon the socio-economic experiment of communal living.

Although the first three prophets of the Mormon Church failed to establish any colonies that would ultimately stand the test of time, the idea of communal sharing managed to retain its seductive allure among members of the LDS faith.

> ***Stewardship in the Church Today.***—*A system of unity in temporal matters has been revealed to the Church in this day; such is currently known as the Order of Enoch, or the United Order, and is founded on the law of consecration. As already stated, in the early days of the modern Church the people demonstrated their inability to abide this law in its fulness, and, in consequence, the lesser law of tithing was given; but the Saints confidently await the day in which they will devote not merely a tithe of their substance, but all that they have, and all that they are, to the service of their God; a day in which no man will speak of mine and thine, but all things shall be theirs and the Lord's.*
>
> *In this expectation, they indulge no vague dream of communism, encouraging individual irresponsibility, and giving the idler an excuse for hoping to live at the expense of the thrifty; but rather, a calm trust that in the promised social order which God can*

> *approve, every man will be a steward in the full enjoyment of liberty to do as he will with the talents committed to his care; but with the sure knowledge that an account of his stewardship will be required at his hands. As far as the plan of this prospective organization has been revealed, it provides that a person entering the order shall consecrate to the Lord all that he has, be it little or much, giving to the Church a deed of his property sealed with a covenant that cannot be broken.*
>
> *James E. Talmage, Apostle of the Church of Jesus Christ of Latter-day Saints, The Articles of Faith, Salt Lake City, 1919, pages 451-452*

Once consecrated as a steward over any community living under the statutes of the United Order of Enoch, only the General Authorities of the Church could remove a bishop from his office. According to church authorities, consecrated bishops are called by direct revelation from God and are not subject to the laws of man. Sounds like a great gig, as long as you are the one in charge.

Plagued with numerous problems from day one, it would appear the principle of communal living was doomed to fail. Church administrators faced a number of seemingly insurmountable issues at various levels.

1. Poor management of assets.
2. Ineffective internal administration.
3. No real plan for equitable distribution of wealth.

Scrambling to rebound from one financial failure after another, it did not take much persuasion before Church leaders were happy to discard the divinely revealed Law of Consecration. With the hopes of establishing a formal system of collective living throughout the Mormon community dashed, the principles associated with the Law of Consecration and the United Order cooperatives ceased to be an integral part of Mormonism.

The United Order was essentially abolished from the day-to-day practice of Mormonism, but it was not forgotten by the faithful who continued to practice the ideals of the Prophet Joseph Smith.

Although not officially associated with the Mormon Church which settled in Utah under the guidance of Brigham Young, Elders of the Reorganized Church of Jesus Christ of Latter Day Saints were extolling the virtues of the Law of Consecration as late as July of 1917. A sermon preached on the virtue of consecration was printed in the July 5th edition of *Zion's Ensign*, a newspaper operated by the Reorganized Church.

Bishop R. C. Evans, one of the Apostles of the Reorganized Church of Jesus Christ of Latter Day Saints spoke out against the United Order when he referenced the newspaper article in his book, *Forty Years in the Mormon Church.*

> *It says here that they should consecrate all that they have, not a portion, not come up and consecrate something that you cannot use yourself, something that you can get along without, but God requires that you shall give it all to him, and then you are to receive back from the Bishop that which is necessary to support yourself and families, and then if he is able to make an increase, take that and bring forth a residue that in turn is to be given into the storehouse.*
>
> *Bishop R. C. Evans, Forty Years in the Mormon Church, Toronto, Canada, 1920, page 148*

Although the practical application of large scale cooperatives were never fully realized and all attempts to establish communal living was eventually abandoned by mainstream followers of the Mormon faith, the United Order still to this day remains a central tenet of the LDS Church's theology.

Despite the simple fact all communities living under the communal doctrine of the United Order eventually failed, faithful Mormons still await the day the entire world will live in accord with this divine law as administered by the leaders of The Church of Jesus Christ of Latter-day Saints.

Whether the failures of communal living were the result of poor management or an inherent flaw in the system itself is of little consequence at this time. Once the elite hierarchy of the Church realized living according to the strict doctrine of the United Order was an enterprise doomed to fail, it quickly became clear another system of financial support would be needed if the Church was to survive long enough to preach the restored gospel to the world.

Years after failing to establish a single long term community capable of sustaining a thriving economy, Church leaders eventually instituted the law of tithing as its primary vehicle for achieving a viable source of income and creating capital gains.

Banking Collapse

Between 1830 and 1836, mass droves of Latter-day Saints began immigrating to Missouri and Ohio. During that same six year period of time, the city of Kirtland, Ohio, experienced a massive population growth — rapidly expanding to more than three times its original size.

Rapid growth can be both a blessings and a curse. In a few short years the asking price of land rose markedly, primarily between the years 1832 and 1837. One of the prime reasons was attributed to wild land speculations by Joseph's debt laden church. Because of rampant land speculation by leaders of the Mormon Church, the cost per acre of land rose quickly from $7 to an unbelievably high market price of $44 by the end of 1837. As with any financial gamble, an overinflated and equally unsustainable market will eventually implode. Heavy speculation is always doomed to fail, as markets cannot sustain unlimited growth. The Kirtland land market was no different.

On the verge of collapsing under its own weight, the once booming real estate market in Kirtland, Ohio, quickly came to a crashing halt. By the summer of 1839, land speculation in Kirtland had moved from the opulence of a stately throne room to a dimly lit death bed. The surviving remnants of the real estate market would ultimately execute a series of self corrections, causing prices to plummet — eventually settling around $17.50 per acre.

After the dust had settled, the land market in and around the city of Kirtland, Ohio, began to stabilize. No worse for the wear were the early settlers and real estate investors who obviously benefitted the most. Land value had increased during the boom and a small number of speculators were able to cash out when the market was ripe. Although an increase of more than five hundred percent in the value of raw land within a very short window of time could be seen as a blessing, the real tragedy was not everyone entered the market early enough to benefit.

Savvy investors fortunate enough to cash in on the artificially created land bonanza took their money and ran. A five-fold increase in land value in just under five years was an exceptional windfall for a handful of lucky individuals, but not everyone was blessed enough to cash out. Settlers who unfortunately bought in at the ridiculously over inflated prices faced financial ruin.

Now let us take a few steps backward in time in order to put all of this into perspective.

Although the LDS Church had considerable real estate holdings, roughly $60,000 in assets, it lacked liquidity — a necessary component for future land transactions. Having to travel out of town to complete simple banking transactions was a noticeable complication that took a considerable amount of time and effort to carry out. Lacking the ability to engage in perfunctory monetary transactions was a situation that simply was just not working for the Mormon leaders. In the midst of a growing metropolitan population, it was clearly evident the residents of Kirtland and the surrounding rural areas were in need of a local bank to satisfy their daily business requirements.

After two failed attempts to procure legal banking charters from the Ohio state legislature for the LDS controlled city of Kirtland, Joseph Smith, Jr. and his cohorts, stubbornly and without legal authority, established the Kirtland Safety Society on November 2, 1836. Oddly enough, the Mormon Prophet was not granted any official position as an officer in the company, but was appointed as a cashier — allowing Joseph Smith, Jr. access to bank funds, but no real authority in banking matters. Whether this was an intentional smoke screen to isolate and protect the head of The Church of Jesus Christ of Latter-day Saints remains to be seen.

Although this ambitious enterprise was doomed to fail its from inception, by establishing the Kirtland Safety Society, leaders of the Church had given themselves a license to print money.

> *As it was projected, there was never the slightest chance that the Kirtland Safety Society anti-Bank-ing Company could succeed. Even though their economy was in jeopardy, it could scarcely have suffered such a devastating blow as that which they were themselves preparing to administer to it. ... The Safety Society proposed no modest project befitting its relative worth and ability to pay. Its organizers launched, instead, a gigantic company capitalized at four million dollars, when the entire capitalization of all the banks in the state of Ohio was only nine and one third million. Such presumption could not have escaped the notice of bankers who would have been led to examine its capital structure more closely. ... according to the articles of incorporation capital stock was to be paid in by subscription but that the amount of payments were left to the discretion of the company managers. Furthermore, total issuance of notes was not prescribed, nor was the relation of notes to capital and assets. The members, to be sure, pledged*

themselves to redeem the notes and bound themselves individually by their agreement under the penal sum of one hundred thousand dollars. But there was no transfer of property deeds, no power of attorney, no legal pains and penalties. To a banker, the articles fairly shouted: 'this is a wildcat, beware!'

Robert Kent Fielding, The Growth of the Mormon Church in Kirtland, Ohio, Ph.D. Dissertation - University of Indiana, 1957

Despite failed attempts in early January and again in February of 1836, to obtain legal charters necessary to operate a bank, Sidney Rigdon, Warren Parrish and Joseph Smith forged ahead with their ambitious plans. Reasons cited for non-issuance of a banking charter included a nationwide endemic of land speculation, wildcat banking practices and counterfeiting.

Further compounding their dilemma, Oliver Cowdery had already returned from Philadelphia after acquiring plates for printing bank notes. Unable to use the plates Cowdery had acquired for fear of committing fraud, the principal officers of the Kirtland Safety Society found themselves in a rather delicate predicament. What could they do?

On the advice from legal counsel retained from outside of the Mormon community, significant changes were made to the legal structure of the Kirtland Safety Society. On January 2, 1837, a special meeting was held with only Sidney Rigdon and Warren Parrish in attendance. During the course of this meeting, the original banking constitution was annulled, a new name of Kirtland Safety Society Anti-Banking Company was adopted and the newly re-organized company was set-up as a joint stock venture instead of being incorporated as a bank.

In a veiled attempt to side-step the law, Articles of Agreement were adopted in lieu of a formal charter. Capital stock was issued at a valuation of four million dollars, with the ability to increase the amount in circulation at the discretion of company managers. Once again, Joseph Smith, Jr. was conspicuously absent from the meeting. Legally only a two-thirds majority of members needed to be in attendance to ratify changes to the corporate structure, yet considering his status as Prophet of the Church one is left to surmise. Was this an intentional legal maneuver? Plausible deniability is a political weapon used to skirt legal issues. A tactic that has been thoroughly abused by legislative bodies throughout the history of the United States.

The plates for printing currency, obtained by Oliver Cowdery on his trip to Philadelphia, were salvaged by engraving "anti-" and "ing co." before and after the word BANK which appeared on the front of the notes. Elements added to the plates were in a different font style from the bold BANK mark which dominated the currency face. The purposefully altered plates would now produce a peculiar anti-BANK-ing note. The added type was minuscule in comparison, barely making it noticeable.

The primary cause for the banking failure in Kirtland, Ohio, was very simple. Most of the cash reserves were tied up in land investments instead of being invested in the silver commodities market as many shareholders erroneously believed. Needles to say, in spite of all their well laid plans, the Kirtland Safety Society Anti-Banking Company closed its doors in November of 1837, with $100,000 in unresolved debt.

Lawsuits and arrests warrants would soon follow the pseudo banking debacle. Joseph Smith Jr. was arrested seven times between 1837 and 1839. A total of thirteen lawsuits would eventually be brought against the Prophet. Despite the ensuing chaos caused by the bank failure, Church members were steadfastly standing behind their leader. Latter-day Saints successfully raised over $38,000, the bail required to free Joseph Smith. Bail was posted as a bond which was held at the Geauga County Court.

It was not until Warren Parrish began speaking openly of Joseph's irregular banking practices that the Prophet fought back and levied his own accusations against Parrish. Joseph claimed Warren Parrish had absconded with $25,000 of bank funds. A claim that is highly unlikely based on the insolvency of the Kirtland Safety Society Anti-Banking Company.

> *It was natural that blame for the entire situation should be charged against the Prophet. They had gathered to Kirtland at his command; the idea of purchasing housing lots in the great subdivision scheme had his full support; he had inferred that the bank would not only succeed, but would one day be the most powerful institution of its kind....the Church populace was genuinely disillusioned when the bank failed. It was difficult for them to comprehend that a man who claimed to have divine revelation in religious matters could fail so miserably in economic affairs.... No amount of shifting of blame could obscure the fact that a prophet had failed in a grand project.... As the Sheriff appeared ever more regularly with summons and as the fortunes and anticipations of one after another of the leaders faced the humiliating prospect of publicly acknowledged incompetence and bankruptcy, the discipline and sense of responsibility, which are the heart of all organizations, broke completely and plunged Mormondom into ecclesiastical anarchy.*
>
> *The Growth of the Mormon Church in Kirtland, Ohio, typed copy, pages 193-197, cited in Mormonism – Shadow or Reality? By Gerald and Sandra Tanner, page 533*

But wait the story continues...

Shortly after the LDS Church failed to obtain a bank charter from the Ohio State legislature, Joseph Smith, Jr. was attempting to purchase controlling interest in the Bank of Monroe — located in Monroe, Michigan. Controlling interest would eventually be obtained from George B. Harleston, who after selling his interest in the Bank of Monroe immediately ran for the office of Mayor. Harleston won the election.

Although Joseph Smith, Jr., along with his brother Hyrum Smith and Oliver Cowdery left Kirtland, Ohio, on February 3, 1837, and travelled to Monroe, Michigan, in order to secure controlling interest in the Bank of Monroe, it was widely speculated Joseph and his companions left town to avoid an arrest warrant on the charges of illegal banking.

At a Stockholders and Board of Directors meeting held on February 10, 1837, controlling interest in the Bank of Monroe was secured with notes from the failing and nearly defunct Kirtland Safety Society Anti-Banking Company. By either purchasing a bank outright or gaining controlling interest in a charted bank, Joseph Smith, Jr. may have hoped to avoid conviction on the pending charges of illegal banking issued by the state of Ohio.

Oliver Cowdery took over as the bank's new Vice President with a Mr. H. Smith being sustained as bank President during the stockholder meeting. With two leaders of the LDS Church at the helm, the Mormon Church had just acquired a new cash cow. Immediately upon taking over controlling interest in the Bank of Monroe, Oliver Cowdery increased its capital stock to $500,000, the maximum limit allowed by its original charter. The next day a large bank loan was arranged for the Mormon Prophet, who upon leaving Monroe went directly to Cleveland, Ohio, to cash in a sizable amount of bank notes for gold and silver coin.

For over a decade the Bank of Monroe appears to have functioned as a type of "offshore bank." Located across the Ohio state line in the territory of Michigan, residents of Ohio could avail themselves of banking services without the annoying legislative oversight of a state sponsored bank. For this reason alone, two Cleveland area banking institutions had long standing relationships with the Bank of Monroe. On his way back to Kirtland, Ohio, Joseph Smith, Jr.

stopped at the Bank of Cleveland to convert his stack of bank notes into gold coinage before travelling to the Commercial Bank of Lake Erie to do the same.

Returning to the city of Kirtland on February 19, 1837, Joseph was outraged to hear his followers have begun to doubt his calling as Prophet, Seer and Revelator. In a rousing sermon Joseph Smith rebukes church members.

> *I am still the President, Prophet, Seer, Revelator and Leader of the Church of Jesus Christ. God, and not man, has appointed and placed me in this position, and no man or set of men have power to remove me, or appoint another in my stead; and those who undertake this, if they do not speedily repent, will burn their fingers and go to hell.*
>
> *Wilford Woodruff reporting a discourse given by the Prophet Joseph Smith in the Kirtland Temple on Feb. 19, 1837 - "History of Wilford Woodruff," Deseret News, July 14, 1858, page 85*

What was so appealing about the Bank of Monroe?

At the time the Mormon Church gained controlling interest in the Bank of Monroe, Michigan had only weeks earlier been admitted into the Union as the 26th State. Joining the Union as a state meant a change in banking laws throughout the entire State of Michigan. While the full benefits sought after by the Mormon Church under the old banking charter were effectively impaired, there was a silver lining the Prophet Joseph Smith, Jr. planned to take full advantage of and capitalize on.

Still in effect was the single most useful feature of the old charter granted to the Bank of Monroe. The charter allowed the bank to suspend the redemption of bank notes previously issued for a period of sixty days. This stipulation certainly would not be included in any new banking charters issued by the State of Michigan, yet it was technically legal under the existing charter.

With precious little time to plunder as much as possible, the newly installed Vice President of the bank put a devious plan hatched by the ruling hierarchy of the Mormon Church into motion.

Charges of illegal banking still pending against Joseph Smith were further compounded by the fact the Kirtland Safety Society Anti-Banking Company was virtually worthless. How did God's Prophet fix his banking problem. He plundered another bank.

Follow along as we piece together a series of clues clumsily left behind on this trail of deceit.

As we begin, our first clue is discovered on the morning of February 24, 1837. Mr. H. Smith suddenly resigns as President of the Bank of Monroe. Exactly two weeks after buying controlling interest in the bank, the new bank President appears to have lost faith in the enterprise and resigns his post. What would prompt such a drastic action? Did Mr. Smith have prior knowledge the bank would be closing its doors within the month?

Oliver Cowdery remains in his position of Vice President just long enough to doctor the banking ledgers. On March 10, 1837, one month after the Mormon Church took control, the Bank of Monroe issued a balance sheet showing $191,330.76 in debt offset exactly by $191,330.76 in credit owed. The above statement was notarized on March 14th by Carlos Colton, Notary Public and published in The Monroe Times March 16, 1837.

Of the $191,330.76 reported in the balance sheet prepared by Oliver Cowdery, $122,565.00 were bank notes in circulation. Presumably a substantial portion of which had been converted to gold and silver coin in Cleveland by Joseph and Hyrum Smith. His duties completed, Oliver Cowdery resigned his position as bank Vice President and quietly left town.

Interesting enough throughout the entire banking debacle and subsequent trials, Joseph Smith Jr. claimed to have taken out a loan of $1,225.00 to keep the Kirtland Safety Society Anti-Banking

Company solvent, but that just happened to be the same amount of money left in the Bank of Monroe at the time they closed their doors. Maybe someone left it as a tithe.

Obviously not everyone was duped by the charismatic Prophet of the Mormon Church.

> *How have the Mighty Fallen!! -- We understand that the Mormon bank, alias the KIRTLAND SAFETY SOCIETY ANTI-BANKING CO. suspended specie payments on Saturday last, agreeably to a Revelation of the Mormon Prophet we suppose. We also learn that some particular friends of the concern who have a large amount of the Rags on hand, have become uneasy -- surprising!!*
>
> *Painesville Telegraph, February 3, 1837*

> *O. Cowdery, Secretary in the Gold Bible imposition, was chosen a Director and Vice President of the Bank. The public themselves may judge from this fact, as to the permanency of the institution. Is not the Bank controlled by men who are in the habit of borrowing ten dollars for every dollar they have to lend?*
>
> *Painesville Telegraph, February 24, 1837*

> *"I perceive by the papers that the Monroe Mormon Bank closed its doors against all demands for specie, after having for its presiding officer about three weeks the wonderful and noted Oliver Cowdery, one of the fathers and translators of the Golden Bible. A sworn statement of the said shaving mill is published in the papers, by which it appears, that it has bills in circulation to the amount of $122, 585 -- and specie on hand, $1, 208.59...." It was, no doubt, in anticipation of forthcoming reactions such as this one, that "H. Smith" exercised the prudence of resigning as President of "the said shaving mill."*
>
> *Painesville Telegraph, March 31, 1837*

By January of 1838, both Sidney Rigdon and Joseph Smith, Jr. had fled Kirtland, Ohio, to Clay County, Missouri, seeking refuge from prosecution for their banking crimes. Weeks earlier Brigham Young had also left Kirtland for Missouri.

Despite public outcry over the colossal failure of two church owned banking institutions, leaving hundreds if not thousands of unsuspecting people financially destitute, the missionary efforts of The Church of Jesus Christ of Latter-day Saints continued to attract converts to the faith.

In what may very well be the most interesting coincidence of this entire chapter of Mormon history is the curious fact that Joseph Smith, Jr. and Oliver Cowdery comprised two-thirds of the Mormon Church's Presidency. Likewise Joseph Smith, Jr. and Sidney Rigdon also constituted two-thirds of the existing Church leadership. And to add further insult to injury, the Prophet's own brother, Hyrum Smith was appointed Second Counselor in the Mormon Church's First Presidency the exact same month the Kirtland Safety Society Anti-Banking Company failed.

What are the odds that of all the people on this planet, the three individuals holding the central power of the LDS Church in 1837, would all be involved with two separate banking enterprises located in two different states and they would both become insolvent, ultimately failing at approximately the same time? Maybe it was nothing more than an uncanny coincidence.

Law of Tithing

Desperately needing to recover from the socio-economic collapse which nearly devastated the early Mormon Church, Joseph and his band of Apostles once again sought divine intervention in the form of revelation. Severe economic hardship had befallen the leaders of the Latter-day Saint community, with a significant amount of their debt stemming from two utterly disastrous attempts to establish church controlled banking institutions. Prior to that the Mormon leaders had trouble convincing their followers the Law of Consecration was of divine origin. With little cash reserves and even bleaker prospects of receiving real property from church members — LDS Church leaders unhappily discovered they were in a fairly precarious financial bind.

Joseph Smith, Jr., the mouth-piece of God, needed to find a way out of the deep financial hole he had dug for himself and his followers. Where would the necessary funds to provide for the needs of Church leaders come from? Without a steady stream of income, the Mormon Church would be unable to buy farms, run businesses, build houses of worship and temples.

If ever there was a time for divine interaction it was now. Joseph Smith's skill as a Prophet, Seer and Revelator would be put to the test. Hoping to rebound from their most recent financial failures, The Church of Jesus Christ of Latter-day Saints revealed God's law of tithing to its growing membership. Officially implemented in July of 1838, the law of tithing was given as a replacement to the Law of Consecration which Mormon leaders had failed to established throughout the church.

> *Verily, thus saith the Lord, I require all their surplus property to be put into the hands of the bishop of my church in Zion,*
>
> *For the building of mine house, and for the laying of the foundation of Zion and for the priesthood, and for the debts of the Presidency of my Church.*
>
> *And this shall be the beginning of the tithing of my people.*
>
> *And after that, those who have thus been tithed shall pay one-tenth of all their interest annually; and this shall be a standing law unto them forever, for my holy priesthood, saith the Lord.*
>
> *Verily I say unto you, it shall come to pass that all those who*

> *gather unto the land of Zion shall be tithed of their surplus properties, and shall observe this law, or they shall not be found worthy to abide among you.*
>
> *And I say unto you, if my people observe not this law, to keep it holy, and by this law sanctify the land of Zion unto me, that my statutes and my judgments may be kept thereon, that it may be most holy, behold, verily I say unto you, it shall not be a land of Zion unto you.*
>
> *And this shall be an ensample unto all the stakes of Zion. Even so. Amen.*
>
> *Doctrine & Covenants 119: 1-7*

While discussing the subject of finances and the Latter-day Saint community I must point out an interesting historical anomaly. Although Joseph Smith and all subsequent Church leaders have claimed direct revelation from God, on this particular occasion a speedy answer was not forthcoming.

Eventually the Mormon Prophet would reveal God's law of tithing to his followers and include it in Mormon scripture, but it was a long time coming. As noted below, the Prophet and his First Counselor would not receive an answer to their supplication for nearly four years. Joseph Smith, Jr. did not receive any revelation regarding the implementation of tithing until July of 1838.

> *While suffering intensely because of their debts and lack of means to meet their obligations Joseph Smith and Oliver Cowdery, November 29, 1834, in solemn prayer promised the Lord that they would give one tenth of all that the Lord should give unto them, as an offering to be bestowed upon the poor; they also prayed that their children, and the children's children after them should obey this law.*
>
> *History of the Church of Jesus Christ of Latter-day Saints, Period 1, Volume 2, pages 174-175*

From the above noted quotation cited directly from the Mormon Church's own written history, a total of one thousand three hundred seventeen days would pass in relative silence until the Lord deemed it appropriate to supply the Prophet of God's one, true church with a suitable answer.

> *Now, however, it became necessary for the law to be given to the whole Church so the Prophet prayed for instruction. (Church History and Modern Revelation, 2:90-91) The answer they received is found in Doctrine and Covenants 119.*
>
> *Doctrine and Covenants and Church History Student Study Guide, Published by The Church of Jesus Christ of Latter-day Saints, Salt Lake City, 2011, pages 135-136*

Despite seeking divine guidance from the Lord through the act of earnest prayer and fasting, God chose to remain mute in regards to their financial crisis for quite some time. Although paying a full tithe became a badge of honor and a default requirement for active membership, Apostles of The Church of Jesus Christ of Latter-day Saints have continually admonished church members to prepare for the day when God would restore the higher Law of Consecration to the righteous.

> *"The Law of Tithing was given to supersede, for the time being, a greater law known as the Law of Consecration, the object of which was and is to sanctify the Lord's people and 'prepare them for a place in the celestial world'. To that end it was designed to do away with selfishness, greed, pride, envy, poverty, and all the ills that spring from such conditions. For none of these things can be admitted into the kingdom of heaven. It was to institute an order of equality and consequent unity, in which every man, employed at that for which he was best fitted, would be 'seeking the interest of his neighbor and doing all things with an eye single to the glory of God'.... A brave attempt to practise it was made by the Latter-day Saints, soon after this Church was*

organized. But they lacked experience, and did not completely rise to the occasion. Selfishness within, and persecution without, prevented a perfect achievement. So the Lord withdrew the Law of Consecration, and gave to his people a lesser law, one easier to live, but pointing forward, like the other, to something grand and glorious in the future. That lesser law, the Law of Tithing, is as a schoolmaster, a disciplinary agent, to bring the Saints eventually up to the practise of the higher law, and meanwhile to keep their hearts open for its reception when it returns. Those who obey the Law of Tithing will be prepared to live the Law of Consecration. Those who do not obey it will not be prepared. That is the whole thing in a nut shell."

Apostle Orson F. Whitney, April 1931,
In Conference Report, pages 65-66

An exposé of a church and their financial entanglements might seem strange and out of place in a book purporting to disclose a secret political agenda hidden from the public eye for nearly two hundred years, but I postulate politics and money are kissing cousins. Where one goes the other will eventually follow. If you want to uncover the truth, you must pursue the money trail.

Throughout the entire history of the LDS Church we find continual reference to the Kingdom of God and the Church's supposed place as the temporal guardians of God's Kingdom, hence I will propose all those who remained and continue to remain loyal to the Mormon faith have from the early beginnings of the church all the way down to the present day conspired to establish a world-wide theocratic government. Conspire might sound a bit harsh, so in the spirit of fairness I will stipulate members of The Church of Jesus Christ of Latter-day Saints have willingly or unwittingly committed their support of church leaders in the act of establishing a governing body ruled by the First Presidency of the LDS Church.

Eyes on the Prize

Clearly the political ambition of the Mormon Church began to take form much earlier than the late Fall of 1839, when a disappointed Joseph Smith, Jr. unsuccessfully sought redress from President Martin Van Buren. Citing the rampant persecution of the Mormon community as the primary catalyst, Church leaders seized the opportunity created by a lack of executive action on behalf of Saints to catapult their far reaching political aspirations to even greater heights.

We must remember by this time the followers of Joseph Smith had grown to a sizeable number. Amassing a good deal of wealth along the way, The Church of Jesus Christ of Latter-day Saints owned a number of profitable businesses and managed to maintain a political stranglehold over the people of Nauvoo.

Let us not forget Joseph Smith, Jr. as the self proclaimed Prophet and leader of the Latter-day Saints, mayor of Nauvoo, Illinois, and Lieutenant General of the Nauvoo Legion steadfastly maintained a standing militia of more than three thousand men loyal to his church. Regardless of their unflinching loyalty and unquestioning willingness to take up arms against any enemy at the slightest command from the Prophet, the church militia was but a small cog in a much larger political machine.

Time and time again members of the LDS Church would consistently vote as a single political bloc to sway an election in their favor. This was usually done under the direct guidance of the Prophet Joseph Smith, Jr. or in accordance with the wishes and desires of other prominent church leaders. Church leaders seemingly unsophisticated attempts to garner political influence in communities where there were large numbers of Latter-day Saints had played a huge role in the growing resentment of the Mormon Church. Fearing an economic, political and social monopoly over regional resources, local towns folk disliked Mormons and were wary of the Church's motives.

Once again let us take a small step backward, just for a moment, to gain a little perspective on the religious fervor sweeping the nation as well as the political climate of the time, which some could argue ultimately lead to the political ambitions of the Mormon Church.

Shortly after founding the Church of Christ in Palmyra, New York, Joseph Smith, Jr. at the urging of Sidney Rigdon, a Campbellite preacher who had converted to Mormonism, uprooted his church and moved to Kirtland, Ohio in search of religious tolerance. Seeking refuge in the growing storm of religious bigotry, many lesser known religious sects had also set their sights on rural Ohio. At a time when religious intolerance seemed to be on an upward swing in American history the Mormon community was but a portion of the sum total of spiritual seekers who migrated west in quest of a more tolerant society. Vast numbers of Campbellite, Millerite and Mormon converts chose to leave the big cities of the east coast behind as hostilities mounted toward any member of a religion that was not perceived as traditionally Christian.

Largely due to constant proselytizing, the early church gained a huge following throughout Ohio and the surrounding regions. Faithful converts were pouring into the folds of the newly created Mormon faith. With its missionary efforts paying off handsomely, Joseph Smith undoubtedly saw a burgeoning potential as membership within the church continued to rise. Early church leaders most assuredly recognized both the economic and political possibilities that lay before them. Following the strength in numbers theory, Joseph decided Kirtland, Ohio was to be the place where he would establish the new headquarters of his church.

Historical events as disseminated throughout the world-wide membership of the LDS Church is often fraught with inaccuracies and bias in favor of the Church. Granted there are always two sides to a story and churches obviously want to paint their actions in as favorable a light as possible in hopes of attracting more converts, but let me pose this question. At what point does a revisionist history become a contrived deception? Case in point, the real reason the followers of Joseph Smith, Jr. left Kirtland, Ohio and settled in Missouri.

Contrary to what is commonly assumed to be fact within the greater context of early Mormon history, Latter-day Saints were not driven from Ohio because of religious persecution. Although the LDS Church would prefer for you to believe their propaganda, one of their own Apostle's effectively refutes their claim.

B. H. Roberts in his massive six-volume work *A Comprehensive History of The Church of Jesus Christ of Latter-day Saints; Century I*, rightly informs us the primary reason Latter-day Saints fled Kirtland and other parts of Ohio was because Joseph Smith, Sidney Rigdon and Oliver Cowdery were escaping a colossal financial crisis their inept handling of banking funds had created.

> *Pride and worldly mindedness among the Saints had preceded some of their financial difficulties, and when their troubles came thick upon them they accused each other of all kinds of sin*

and folly; there were evil surmisings, bickerings, fault-finding, false accusations and bitterness, until the spirit of the gospel in Kirtland was well nigh eclipsed.

Brigham Henry Roberts, A Comprehensive History of The Church of Jesus Christ of Latter-day Saints: Century I, Deseret News Press, 1930, page 402

In 1898, the House of Representatives denied Roberts, a General Authority of the LDS Church and member of the First Council of the Seventy, his elected seat in the 56th Congress due to his active participation in the Mormon marriage practice of polygamy. Apostle Roberts and his political ambitions is yet another fascinating aspect of the Mormon saga, but let us continue with this part of the story before we get too far off track.

And so without further ado...

On The Move

Relocating his newly created Church of Christ from the sleepy little East coast town of Palmyra, New York, to Kirtland, Ohio, was a calculated risk for Joseph Smith, yet he and his counselors felt confident in making the trek during the dead of winter. Packing all of your belongings into horse drawn wagons and travelling two hundred sixty miles across country by horse or foot was not an easy task to undertake, especially in 1831, when interstate roadways did not exist. Yes, it is true plenty of people moved westward to settle the more primitive frontier lands in hopes of finding a better life, but a great many of these types of journeys where usually embarked upon during the warmer spring climate and only after months of careful planning and preparation.

Which brings us to our first question. What prompted the sudden need to move? The first point of attraction which cannot be overlooked was a considerably larger financial base for the small, but growing Latter-day Saint community to tap into. With each new convert Mormon missionaries brought into the fold came the possibility of increasing the wealth and resources of Joseph Smith's fledgling church and Ohio was proving to be a wellspring of fresh converts to the faith.

An interesting side note which is almost completely overlooked by church historians was the curious little fact that late in 1830, Joseph Smith, Sr. and his family left Palmyra due to extreme financial troubles. Failing to make mortgage payments on either the land or house the Smith family was forced to move. These turn of events may or may not be related. Without concrete proof we can never know for certain if the move to Ohio was based solely on financial reasons, but what we do know is there appears to be a long history of running from debt in the early years of the Church.

Can we state unequivocally Joseph Smith's reasons for moving were purely financial? No. All of these events occurring at or around the same time may very well be nothing more than a strange coincidence, but moving across state lines certainly would have been one way to avoid satisfying legal judgments levied against the Smith family.

Whatever it was that ultimately brought the Latter-day Saints westward to Ohio we do know that within months of reaching Kirtland, Joseph received an astounding number of revelations including a calling from the Lord to build up and prepare the City of Zion for the Second Coming. Curiously enough although Joseph and his compadres had been commanded by divine revelation to establish the headquarters of his church in Ohio, Zion the city of Christ's triumphant return would not to be built in Kirtland, but was to be built nearly a thousand miles away in the town of Independence, Missouri.

At the time of the arrival of the Saints in February of 1831, Kirtland was already a thriving farming community of more than a thousand souls, yet the cryptic revelations of Joseph Smith, Jr. suggested the Saints would build a great city upon the land of this western Ohio township. A little known historical peculiarity was the township of Kirtland, established in 1803, would not be recognized as a city until the federal census of 1970, recorded a population exceeding more than five thousand residents. Kirtland was officially granted the status of city in February of 1971.

Prior to their mass migration following the Kirtland Banking debacle, the Latter-day Saint community endeavored to transform the Kirtland landscape. Between February of 1831, and March of 1836, a rising population of more than two thousand Mormons worked diligently to create a city, establish commerce and construct the first Mormon Temple.

Despite the fact a steady flow of Mormon immigrants continued to swell the population of Kirtland and its surrounding areas, the grand and glorious dream Joseph Smith had for establishing Zion, the City of God, in the lands of Ohio was a vision that never quite seemed to manifest.

Fleeing to Missouri

Desperate to settle into an urban area that would generate enough capital to support the financial aims of Joseph Smith, early church leaders roamed the western U.S. in search of a suitable home base. In addition to their desire of remaining financially solvent and building comfortable lodgings, members of the elite Church hierarchy needed a strong base of community support in order for the inner circle of Latter-day Saints to brandish their spiritual and political power over emerging congregations.

It is clearly evident it was always the goal of the LDS Church to be able to eventually exercise some level of control over the surrounding communities of non-Mormons. Church leaders also recognized the need to capture and monopolize local economies in order to finance their goals of expansion. Because their expansionist program often met with resistance, The Church of Jesus Christ of Latter-day Saints moved its base of operation no less than five times in the first two decades of its existence before finally settling the Utah territory.

Despite being brought to the Ohio valley by a revelation from the Lord, Joseph Smith sent Oliver Cowdery to Jackson County, Missouri to begin preparations for establishing the City of Zion only a few short months after his church headquarters had been relocated to Kirtland, Ohio. Once again the Saints are instructed by the Lord to buy all of the land so that the Latter-day Saints may build up the church of Christ and have an everlasting inheritance.

> *Hearken, O ye elders of my church, saith the Lord your God, who have assembled yourselves together, according to my commandments, in this land, which is the land of Missouri, which is the land which I have appointed and consecrated for the gathering of the Saints.*
>
> *Wherefore, this is the land of promise, and the place for the city of Zion.*
>
> *Doctrine & Covenants 57:1-2*

Joseph Smith, Jr. disclosed a new revelation he received on March 7, 1831, to his community of Latter-day Saints concerning the building of the City of Zion which is also called the New Jerusalem. God spoke through the Prophet Joseph Smith revealing Zion would be the gathering place for the righteous in the last dispensation. Although the Lord did not disclose to his prophet at that time where this city would be constructed.

A few months later in July of the same year it was revealed to Joseph the City of Zion would be erected in the land of Independence, Missouri, where the Lord commanded them to consecrate the land and the city to the purpose of God.

> *And it shall be called the New Jerusalem, a land of peace, a city of refuge, a place of safety for the Saints of the Most High God;*
>
> *And the glory of the Lord shall be there, and the terror of the Lord also shall be there, insomuch that the wicked will not come unto it, and it shall be called Zion.*
>
> *And it shall come to pass among the wicked, that every man that will not take his sword against his neighbor must needs flee unto Zion for safety.*
>
> *And there shall be gathered unto it out of every nation under heaven; and it shall be the only people that shall not be at war one with another.*
>
> *And it shall be said among the wicked: Let us not go up to battle against Zion, for the inhabitants of Zion are terrible; wherefore we cannot stand.*
>
> *And it shall come to pass that the righteous shall be gathered out from among all nations, and shall come to Zion, singing with songs of everlasting joy.*
>
> *Doctrine & Covenants 45:66-71*

Early Mormon settlers in Missouri fared far worse than their counterparts in Ohio. The main cause of contention between the newly arrived Latter-day Saints and the old settlers of Missouri was most certainly their odd religious beliefs, yet just as powerful were their political ideals which did not sit well with the established community. Finally the inevitable straw that broke the camel's back would be the Mormons seizing political power from the grasp of the original settlers. Because of their growing numbers, Mormon settlers were able to easily wrest power out of the hands of those who previously held political sway. Within two years of entering the land of Missouri, the Mormons were once again fleeing under threat of violence.

A full year before the founding of the Church and the publication of the Book of Mormon, Joseph Smith, Jr. dictated a revelation to his personal scribe Oliver Cowdery in which God told them to "keep my commandments, and seek to bring forth and establish the cause of Zion." The fervent belief God commanded Joseph Smith and his community of Saints to build Zion upon the American continent was first and foremost the primary catalyst for many of the actions taken by early church leaders.

Ever faithful to the founding prophets dream, the belief in the City of Zion still remains to this day a central theme of Mormonism. Although the LDS hierarchy is without a doubt actively working toward fulfilling their longtime goal of establishing their celestial city of God here on earth, it appears the home of God's righteous children will languish in the land of dreams until the Lord appoints the time and season for its construction.

Until that time Latter-day Saints worldwide will simply have to wait patiently for the Strong and Mighty One to appear and usher in the Millennial reign of Christ.

The Nauvoo Years

Eight years after Joseph Smith proudly proclaimed Independence, Missouri, as the site where he was commanded by God to erect the City of Zion, his band of faithful followers were preparing to leave the land of their inheritance empty handed. Leaving homes and property behind in the wake of the "Mormon War of 1838," the LDS community was once again on the move.

Immediately following an unsuccessful uprising against state militia Latter-day Saints faced a potential crisis. Blamed for the armed conflict, the Mormon settlers were summarily were stripped of their weapons. As a condition of surrender Church leaders agreed to the forfeiture of all property held by Latter-day Saints and the swift departure of all Mormon's from the state of Missouri.

Forced to bear the entire cost of the Missouri Mormon War by forfeiting anything of value, the followers of Joseph Smith were in effect defenseless and at the mercy of their conquerors.

With the majority of Church leaders held in Liberty Jail on a variety of charges including treason, the Mormons of Missouri were mandated to leave the state in the spring of 1839, or face the wrath of angered citizens. Without any legal protection offered on their behalf, the entire Mormon community was compelled to comply with the conditions of surrender.

Divested of personal property, thousands of disheartened Mormons sought a new home. Travelling more than six hundred miles to Quincy, Illinois, the exiled Mormons found a temporary safe haven. Sympathetic to their plight, the good towns folk of Quincy offered assistance to the Mormon refugees.

Months after his initial imprisonment Sidney Rigdon, second in command within the Mormon hierarchy, was released on a writ of habeas corpus. After his return to the main body of Latter-day Saints, Rigdon negotiated land purchase contracts for a large parcel of land from agent Isaac Galland as well as undeveloped land in Iowa, across the Mississippi river. At the same time The Church of Jesus Christ of Latter-day Saints also agreed to purchase all of the failed settlement of Commerce, Illinois.

Latter-day Saints immediately started moving west into Illinois to begin development of yet another city of promise. With the purchase of the nearly vacant town of Commerce, Illinois, added to the land Rigdon procured from Isaac Galland, the Saints would soon began the monumental task of terraforming the harsh landscape of swampy marshland into what would eventually become the largest city in all of Illinois.

> *Verily, I say unto you that ye are chosen out of the world to declare my gospel with the sound of rejoicing, as with the voice of a trump.*

Lift up your hearts and be glad, for I am in your midst, and am your advocate with the Father; and it is his good will to give you the kingdom.

And, as it is written—Whatsoever ye shall ask in faith, being united in prayer according to my command, ye shall receive.

And ye are called to bring to pass the gathering of mine elect; for mine elect hear my voice and harden not their ehearts;

Wherefore the decree hath gone forth from the Father that they shall be gathered in unto one place upon the face of this land, to prepare their hearts and be prepared in all things against the day when tribulation and desolation are sent forth upon the wicked.

For the hour is nigh and the day soon at hand when the earth is ripe; and all the proud and they that do wickedly shall be as stubble; and I will burn them up, saith the Lord of Hosts, that wickedness shall not be upon the earth;

For the hour is nigh, and that which was spoken by mine apostles must be fulfilled; for as they spoke so shall it come to pass;

Doctrine & Covenants 29:4-10

Despite the Prophet Joseph Smith receiving numerous revelations during his six month imprisonment in Liberty jail, his relationship with Sidney Rigdon was strained beyond repair as a result of the two men sharing a jail cell for months on end. Joseph and six of his fellow conspirators were confined to a tiny jail cell following their surrender at Far West, Missouri, on charges of high treason in December of 1838.

During a change of venue, Joseph Smith and the remaining prisoners would escape from their captors in April of 1839. Upon procuring his freedom Joseph immediately made his way to Nauvoo, Illinois, to resume his role as Prophet and spiritual leader of the Mormon Saints.

Although the command to preach the gospel of salvation to the world originated barely six months after the official founding of the LDS Church, Joseph and his council of twelve did not actively begin preparing to spread the word of God on a world-wide basis until June of 1837 — a full seven years after the founding of the church. Why had the prophet of God waited so long before acting upon a command given by his beloved creator?

Lack of funds to support such an endeavor could have been one contributing factor, but let us suppose just for a moment that because of the relative young age and immaturity of church doctrine Joseph Smith, Jr. was not yet fully prepared to launch a campaign of global proselytizing. Despite what historians of The Church of Jesus Christ of Latter-day Saints have put forth as official doctrine, the infancy of Joseph's church and lack of financial means most assuredly played a major role in the decisions of the Council of Twelve. Looking beyond the purported visions and revelations, the emerging Church functioned as a pragmatic organization. Missionary work could not be attempted until proper financial funds were raised.

With the ground work laid, converts to the newly created Mormon faith began to flood the United States as early as the summer of 1840. Aboard the *Britannia* more than forty Saints had left their home in England, choosing instead to relocate to the burgeoning city of Nauvoo, Illinois. Accompanying the first wave of converts immigrating from England were Elders Brigham Young and Heber C. Kimball, both men would serve the spiritual needs of emerging Mormon Saints as members of the Quorum of the Twelve. Heber C. Kimball would eventually serve the Saints as First Councilor to Brigham Young, the second President and Prophet of the LDS Church.

Despite his claims of divine revelation, Joseph Smith would throughout the course of his lifetime prove to be a poor judge of character. One such occurrence took place during the initial planning stage and building up of the city of Nauvoo. Shortly after escaping from his captors and making his way to Nauvoo, Joseph Smith removed Sidney Rigdon as his personal secretary replacing him with Isaac Galland — the land agent Rigdon had purchased vast tracts of land from. Working closely with Joseph Smith, Brother Isaac served the LDS Church faithfully by transcribing and recording all of the revelations received by the prophet during that period of time. Although Galland had been baptized into the Mormon faith and ordained an Elder by the prophet, he quickly betrayed Joseph's trust. Isaac would serve the prophet barely a year before Brother Galland would publicly denounce Smith as a charlatan and spiritual fraud.

Another example of Joseph's mediocre skill at discerning people's true character came in April of 1841. In a rather clumsy attempt to gain the goodwill of surrounding neighbors, the Prophet himself invited the editor of the *Warsaw Signal* to attend a ceremony celebrating the laying of the cornerstone for the Nauvoo Temple. Thomas Sharp was so taken aback by the excess proffered by Joseph Smith and other Church leaders that instead of gaining an ally Joseph unwittingly created an unsympathetic enemy who would publicly profess Mormonism was no religion at all, but an un-American political movement whose sole goal was the complete domination of a vast empire. Shortly after this incident occurred, the Mormon Prophet began teaching the governments of men were ineffective and that it was necessary to establish a theocratic kingdom ruled by a man of God.

But alas I digress, so let us continue on with our story...

During the six years following the initial migration of Latter-day Saints from England under the watchful eye of Brigham Young, more than thirty-four groups of Mormon converts had departed from the shores of the British Isles to undertake the voyage to America. The early English converts who travelled with Brigham

Young and Heber C. Kimball would eventual join the main party of Latter-day Saints who had migrated to the city of Nauvoo between 1839 and 1840. All total a little more than five thousand English patriots had immigrated to the United States as part of the religious migration to the land of promise.

Mormon Saints world-wide were lead to believe the city of Nauvoo would become the crown jewel of God's kingdom on earth. Nauvoo was to be the new Jerusalem, the place where God himself had ordained the resurrected Christ would rule over the modern City of Zion. With the influx of Mormon settlers from eastern U.S. states, Canada and Europe, the size of Nauvoo had swelled considerably, surpassing even that of Chicago to become the largest city in Illinois.

During this brief period of prosperity Latter-day Saints began construction of an elaborate Mormon temple. A magnificent house of worship decorated with the most splendid and costly ornaments seemed an appropriate sacrifice to demand of church members — after all the prophet of God had recently expanded church doctrine to make way for a complex cosmology. Joseph's newly expanded theology included elaborate temple rituals.

Latter-day Saints who were deemed worthy to participate in temple ordinances took oaths of silence, vowing never to reveal any portion of the Endowment Ceremony to another living soul. Church authorities informed Mormon initiates that non-member outsiders were strictly forbidden to know any of the sacred details. Joseph Smith's followers believed they were required to participate in temple rituals before the Lord would allow them access to heaven. Mormon temples are still visited today to participate in secret ceremonies.

No longer satisfied with being the spiritual leader of over 16,000 Mormon converts, Lieutenant General and Commander of the largest independent militia in the country, Mayor of Nauvoo,

Illinois, head of the municipal courts and owner of several local businesses, Joseph Smith, Jr. had also set his sights on the oval office. This seemed to be the final straw for many outsiders who believed the religious practices of the Mormon Church was an affront to their Christian sensibilities and a detriment to their way of life.

The growing rift between Mormons and non-Mormons was only exacerbated by Joseph's ambition to capture the U.S. Presidency. What makes this bid for power all the more an affront to our sensibilities as American citizens is the simple fact that by the time Joseph Smith had announced his presidential bid he had been arrested and imprisoned for charges including arson, disturbing the peace, fraud, larceny, murder, perjury and treason.

Prior to launching his presidential campaign, Joseph Smith, the self proclaimed Prophet of God, had spent a good deal of his life evading capture while running from the law. It was ultimately Joseph's status as the de facto religious, spiritual and ruling civil authority of the entire LDS community that granted Smith his greatest personal power. Besides calling upon the loyalty of his followers, Smith could enact a writ of habeas corpus on his own behalf. By doing so, Joseph essentially prohibited any civil authority from extraditing him to another courts's jurisdiction to face trial. The wanton abuse of his powers as a magistrate certainly contributed to Joseph Smith's premature demise.

Shortly after the founding of Nauvoo, Illinois, Joseph Smith was elected mayor of the fledgling city, a political position he would hold until his death. As mayor and magistrate, Joseph would never tire of calling upon his powers of habeas corpus when the need arose. By manipulating the legal system and enacting a writ whenever necessary, Joseph Smith successfully managed to remain a safe distance from the long arm of the law. No court was able to extradite him back to Missouri to face trial.

The White Horse Prophecy

Although officially denounced by the Mormon hierarchy, there is a long oral tradition within The Church of Jesus Christ of Latter-day Saints regarding the so-called White Horse Prophecy of Joseph Smith. Despite not being part of their "official doctrine" there is a strong undercurrent of support from within the active membership of the LDS Church. A vast majority of the Church's more than fifteen million members believe that this divine proclamation will one day be fulfilled as the leaders of the Mormon Church step forward to rescue America from the brink of disaster.

While none of the social, economic and political events described in the fabled "White Horse Prophecy" came close to being fulfilled during the life of Joseph Smith, the allure of Mormon Church leaders emerging from the crumbling debris of an American political system on the verge of collapse has always tantalized the hearts and minds of its active members. What faithful Latter-day Saint would not want the righteous men of God to take charge of a failing government? We should all be so lucky. Under the guise of government, the First Presidency of The Church of Jesus Christ of Latter-day Saints plans to create a group of dedicated, selfless individuals who taking orders and following the directions of the Church will lead American citizens into an era of prosperity. Most Mormons honestly believe the fabled land of milk and honey is their divine birthright.

Mormon historians since the time of Joseph Smith have cautiously held their breath when confronted with questions relating to the "White Horse Prophecy" for two reasons. First and foremost the prophecy in question has never been "officially" adopted as church doctrine and secondly the Prophet Joseph Smith never revealed the contents of this prophecy to his church as a matter of principle. What is known of this mysterious prediction is a by-product of second hand accounts and unconfirmed whispered hearsay. However much to their dismay, church historians and General Authorities are forced to repudiate written records of the Prophet's apocalyptic utterance.

There are several critical aspects of the "White Horse Prophecy" which cause real problems for The Church of Jesus Christ of Latter-day Saints, especially when viewed from the perspective of a registered American voter. Although church leaders have publicly denied involvement in the political process from the earliest days of the Church's founding, their actions would suggest a much different agenda is afoot.

Let us remember Joseph Smith advocated a separation of Church and State while simultaneously planning his bid for the office of U.S. President. We also cannot afford to overlook the multiple offices Joseph Smith held concurrently. First we have Prophet, Seer and Revelator of the Mormon Church, followed by his being elected Mayor of Nauvoo and culminating in the military power he held as Lieutenant General of the Nauvoo Legion. Although a substantial registry of power and control any man of the day would envy, this tiny list does not include the many business positions Joseph Smith also held throughout his Mormon Kingdom.

Before we continue let us consider why any religious organization would need or want to have so much power vested in the hands a single solitary person. Brutal dictators throughout history have held less power than Joseph Smith did prior to his death. I don't personally know of another instance in American history where the ultimate religious authority of a church had managed to effectively corral and wield far-sweeping political influence. Combine that with a sizeable military force of loyal soldiers ready to fight on the Prophet's command and you have a recipe for disaster. Let us not forget the Nauvoo Legion was the second largest military unit in America and it was loyal to Joseph Smith, Jr.

Instead of continuing with a would be long and drawn out clarification of exactly what the "White Horse Prophecy" represents, I believe the reader would be better served by studying the text and deciding for themselves what if any part of this prophecy is relevant to the current political establishment. While there does not exist any documentation of this prophecy during the lifetime of Joseph Smith, there is credible evidence to suggest the words were spoken as remembered by Edwin Rushton and Theodore Turley.

The following account of the White Horse Prophecy was recorded by the hand of Edwin Rushton almost ten years after the event in question occurred, but it was not until 1904, when Rushton lay on his death bed that he had the account notarized.

> *On or about the sixth day of May. 1843, a grand review of the Nauvoo Legion was held in Nauvoo (Illinois). The Prophet Joseph complimented them for their good discipline and evolutions performed. The weather being hot, he called for a glass of water. With the glass of water in his hand he said, "I drink to you a toast to the overthrow of the mobocrats."*
>
> *The next morning a man who had heard the Prophet give the toast returned to visit the Mansion of the Prophet, and so abused him with bad language, that the man was ordered out by the Prophet. It was while the two were out that my attention was attracted to them and hearing the man speaking in a loud tone of voice, I went toward them; the man finally leaving. There were present the Prophet Joseph Smith, Theodore Turley and myself. The Prophet began talking to us of the mobbings and drivings and persecutions we as a people have endured. But, said he, "We will have worse things to see; our persecutors will have all the mobbings they want. Don't wish them any harm. For when you see their sufferings you will shed bitter tears for them."*
>
> *While this conversation was going on we stood by his south wicket gate in a triangle. Turning to me he said: "I want to tell you*

something. I will speak a parable like unto John the Revelator. You will go to the Rocky Mountains. And you will be a great and mighty people, established there, which I will call the White Horse of Peace and Safety. When the Prophet said you will see it, I asked him, "Where will you be at that time?" He said, "I shall never go there. Your enemies will continue to follow you with persecutions and will make obnoxious laws against you in Congress to destroy the White Horse, but you will have a friend or two to defend you to throw out the worst part of the laws, so they will not hurt much. You must continue to petition Congress all the time, but they will treat you like strangers and aliens, and they will not give you your rights but will govern you with strangers and commissioners; you will see the Constitution of the United States almost destroyed; it will hang by a thread, as it were, as fine as the finest silk fiber."

At this point the Prophet's countenance became sad; he said, "I love the constitution. It was made by the inspiration of God, and it will be preserved and saved by the efforts of the White Horse and the Red Horse. Who will combine in its defense. The White Horse will raise an ensign on the tops of the mountains of peace and safety. The White Horse will find the mountains full of minerals and they will become very rich. You will see silver piled up in the streets. "You will see gold shoveled up like sand. Gold will be of little value even in a mercantile capacity, for the people of the world will have something else to do in seeking for salvation. "The time will come when the banks in every nation will fail and only two places will be safe where people can deposit their gold and treasures. These places will be the White Horse and England's vaults."

"A terrible revolution will take place in the land of America, such as has never been seen before; for the land will be literally left without a supreme government. And every species of wickedness

will run rampant. Father will be against son, and son against father, mother against daughter, and daughter against mother. The most terrible scenes of murder and bloodshed and rapine that have ever been looked upon will take place.

"Peace will be taken from the earth and there will be no peace only in the Rocky Mountains. This will cause many hundreds and thousands of the honest in heart to gather there; not because they would be Saints but for safety and because they would not take up the sword against their neighbor.

"You will be so numerous that you will be in danger of famine, but not for the want of seed time and harvest, but because of so many to be fed. Many will come with bundles under their arms to escape the calamities, and there will be no escape except by fleeing to Zion.

"Those that come to you will try to keep the laws and be one with you, for they will see your unity and the greatness of your organization. The Turkish Empire or the Crescent will be one of the first powers that will be disrupted, for freedom must be given for the Gospel to be preached in the Holy Land.

"The Lord took of the best blood of the nations and planted them on the small islands now called England and Great Britain, and gave them great power in the nations for a thousand years and their power will continue with them, that they may keep the balance of power and keep Russia from usurping her power over all the world. England and France are now bitter enemies, but they will be allied together and be united to keep Russia from conquering the world.

"The two Popes, Greek and Catholic, will come together and be united. The Protestant religions do not know how much they are indebted to Henry the VIII for throwing off the Pope's Bull and establishing the Protestant faith. He was the only monarch who could do so at the time, and he did it because this nation,

England, was at his back to sustain him. One of the peculiar features in England is the established red coat, a uniform making so remarkable a mark to shoot at, and yet they have conquered wherever they have gone. The reason for this will be known by them some day. The Lion and the Unicorn of Israel is their ensign, the wisdom and statesmanship of England comes from having so much of the blood of Israel in the nation.

"While the terrible revolution of which I have spoken has been going on. England will be neutral until it becomes so inhuman that she will interfere to stop the shedding of blood. England and France will unite together to make peace, not to subdue the nations; they will find the nations so broken up and so many claiming government, till there will be no responsible government. Then it will appear to the other nations or powers as though England had taken possession of the country. The Black Horse will flee to the invaders and will join with them. for they will have fear of becoming slaves again, knowing England did not believe in slavery, fleeing to them they believe would make them safe; armed with British bayonets. the doings of the Black Horse will he terrible." (Here the Prophet said he could not bear to look longer upon the scene as shown him in vision and asked the Lord to close the scene.)

Continuing, he said. "During this time the great White Horse will have gathered strength sending out Elders to gather the honest in heart among the Pale Horse, or people of the United States, to stand by the Constitution of the United States, as it was given by inspiration of God.

"In these days God will set up a kingdom never to be thrown down, for other kingdoms to come unto. And these kingdoms that will not let the Gospel be preached will be humbled until they will.

"England, Germany, Norway, Denmark, Sweden, Switzerland,

Holland, and Belgium, have a considerable amount of the blood of Israel among their people which must be gathered. These nations will submit to the kingdom of God. England will be the last of these kingdoms to surrender, but when she does, she will do it as a whole in comparison as she threw off the Catholic power. The nobility know that the Gospel is true but it has not enough pomp and grandeur and influence for them to embrace it. They are proud and will not acknowledge the kingdom of God, or come unto it, until they see the power which it will have. Peace and safety in the Rocky Mountains will be protected by a cordon band of the White Horse and the Red Horse.

"The coming of the Messiah among this people will be so natural, that only those who see Him will know that He has come, but He will come and give His laws unto Zion, and minister unto His people. This will not be His coming in the clouds of heaven to take vengeance on the wicked of the world.

"The Temple in Jackson County will be built in this generation. The Saints will think there will not be time to build it, but with all the help you will receive you can put up a great temple quickly. They will have all the gold, silver, and precious stones; for these things only will be used for the beautifying of the temple; all the skilled mechanics you want, and the Ten Tribes of Israel will help you build it. When you see this land bound with iron you may look toward Jackson County."

At this point he made a pause, and looking up as though the vision was still in view, he said. "There is a land beyond the Rocky Mountains that will be invaded by the heathen Chinese unless great care and protection are given." Speaking of the heathen nations he said, "Where there is no law there is no condemnation, and this will apply to them. Power will be given the White Horse to rebuke nations afar off, and they will be one with the White Horse, but when the law goes forth they will obey; for the law will go forth from Zion. The last great struggle Zion will have to contend with will be when the whole of the Americas will be made the Zion of our God. Those opposing will be called Gog and Magog (some of the world led by the Russian Czar) and their power will be great, but all opposition will be overcome and then this land will be the Zion of our God."

In spite of the fact almost every 20th century leader of the LDS Church has publicly denounced the substance of the "White Horse Prophecy" as having no merit in relation to the "official" teachings of The Church of Jesus Christ of Latter-day Saints, the central message still to this day remains a measurable component of an unofficial belief system a large majority of church members hope will one day be fulfilled. Regardless of how you may view Joseph Smith and his religious practices, he was without a doubt a master of rhetoric and he knew precisely what to say in order to excite his congregation of true believers.

Regardless of its official status within the Church, Joseph Smith, Jr. obviously believed in his own powers of prophecy as evidenced by his presidential campaign launched less than a year later. He intended to rise to the highest political office of our great nation, create the holy City of Zion and lead the Children of Israel into a millennial reign of righteousness.

Presidential Campaign

In the few short years following his two meetings with President Van Buren respectively in November of 1839, and again in February of 1840, Joseph Smith, head of The Church of Jesus Christ of Latter-day Saints, announced his campaign for the Presidency of the United States. While many Mormons would later claim Joseph's campaign centered on addressing and even correcting the perceived abuse and religious bigotry LDS communities had long suffered at the hands of intolerant people, his political platform would also encompass social issues such as slavery which only further pointed to the increasing moral decay many saw as rampant in American society. However it appears obvious to the unbiased reader, notwithstanding the moral issues of the day, Joseph Smith had political ambitions which clearly ran deep.

On January 29, 1844, in the Nauvoo, Illinois, mayor's office, Joseph Smith, Prophet of the Mormon Church, organized a meeting of the Quorum of the Twelve Apostles to discuss a third-party presidential campaign — to be run as an independent platform. A unanimous vote of support bolstered the charismatic Mormon Prophet in his bid for the highest office of the land. Next step? Gather the support of his faithful followers.

Six weeks later, with the Quorum of the Twelve Apostles in agreement, Joseph Smith convened for the first time in church history the Council of Fifty — a secret organization whose sole purpose was to manage the political affairs of the Kingdom of God. Hidden in obscurity, the Council of Fifty nonetheless played a crucial role in Joseph Smith's bid for U.S. President. Originally consisting of forty-six carefully selected men, the Council would swell to more than one hundred loyal followers of Joseph Smith, Jr. Unbeknownst to the general Latter-day Saint community, a secretive shadow government was being established within the Mormon hierarchy to plan, create and put into place a political theocracy that would one day supplant the governing body of the United States of America.

And so the story continues...

I do believe this was the first time in American history an ecclesiastical head of a religious organization openly campaigned for the office of President. Compounding his unorthodox behavior, Joseph Smith, Jr. despite being accused of and arrested for treason on multiple occasions sought to lead American citizens as the President of the United States. I can't remember a time in American history when a citizen of our great nation who had previously been charged with high treason campaigned to become Commander-in-Chief of our armed forces.

Barely two months had passed since the Quorum of the Twelve Apostles unanimously voted to support Joseph's Presidential campaign. It was on April 7, 1844 at a General Conference of the LDS Church when Brigham Young announced that elders of the Mormon Church would be called upon to serve as both missionaries and electioneers. More than three hundred "missionaries" eventually consented to serve as electioneers and preach the gospel of Joseph Smith's destiny to become the next U.S. President, but this did not happen without extreme pressure and cajoling being exerted by Brigham Young over the faithful flock of Latter-day Saints. It would appear there were a number of dissenting voices who opposed the idea of their Prophet being President of the United States.

This newly formed force of Mormon missionaries would be required to proclaim the righteousness of Joseph's political campaign in support of the Mormon Prophet while at the same time attempting to convert as many non-believers into faithful Mormons. From a simple perusal of the historical documents still in existence it remains unclear which activity was given a higher order of prominence, but missionaries left no stone unturned when it came to campaigning for Joseph Smith.

Tent revivals preaching the gospel of the Book of Mormon became intertwined with political meetings urging God fearing Christians to vote for the Mormon Prophet. One of the most bizarre realities of Joseph Smith's campaign for the United States Presidency was that church leaders thought the combination of missionary preaching and political campaigning was perfectly acceptable within the framework of Mormon theology.

In addition to sending out nearly three hundred Mormon missionaries to campaign for and politicize Smith's bid for the Office of United States President, a number of "missionaries" were sent to Russia, England, France, the Republic of Texas and Washington, D.C. in an effort to bring attention to the predicament facing many Mormons.

Does it seem peculiar a candidate would send ambassadors to foreign countries who clearly had no influence in American politics? Not if you consider Joseph Smith and the Council of Fifty were attempting to establish a New World Government.

Obviously the early leadership of the LDS Church saw no logical reason to separate church and state, not as long as the ruling body of the church could ultimately control the office of president from a safe and hidden distance. Case in point, Brigham Young as previously stated called for elders of the church to serve as electioneer missionaries and these men were sent to spread the word throughout the then 26 states as well as the Minnesota Territory. Of course this is in direct opposition to the publicly stated policy of the LDS Church of not directly influencing or interfering in matters of politics.

It stands to reason any active member of an organization be it religious or civic in nature will more than likely vote according to their own conscience when the occasion arises, but the issue at hand is whether or not a formal organized church is capable of influencing and shaping the voting patterns of its followers.

A Question of Treason

Despite efforts by General Authorities to whitewash Joseph's checkered past, more than a few well respected Mormon historians have reluctantly admitted Joseph Smith, Jr., Prophet, Seer and Revelator of the LDS Church, most assuredly committed the crime of high treason against the government of the United States on a number of occasions.

Whether or not you personally believe Joseph Smith actually committed the crime of treason against his native government is irrelevant. Any scholarly look at the life of Joseph Smith, Jr. would be seriously lacking in credibility if the subject was at the very least not considered.

We are attempting to ascertain, through documented and verifiable sources, if there is enough evidence to support a charge of treason against Joseph Smith, Jr. Although I am not a student of law, I believe the historical record contains enough *prima facie* evidence to warrant proceeding to trial.

Let us take a brief moment to pause and ponder the implications as we reflect upon a few key pieces of evidence. Any competent investigator would certainly let the historical record speak for itself. After seeing the evidence, it is my opinion that Joseph Smith certainly seemed to be following a specific pattern of behavior.

1. After three months of leading the Mormon militia in armed conflict against State troops, Joseph Smith and sixty other men were arrested on November 1, 1838, on charges of arson, larceny, murder and treason. Twenty-two men, women and children were confirmed casualties of the Missouri War of 1838. Many more died as a result of an injury or prolonged exposure.
2. On April 11, 1844, in a secret meeting of the Council of Fifty, Joseph Smith had himself crowned *King of Earth* after announcing his presidential campaign just one month earlier.
3. On June 18, 1844, Joseph Smith mobilizes the Nauvoo Legion and places the city of Nauvoo, Illinois, under martial law.

While this list may seem short, at least in regards to bona fide evidence against Joseph, his actions and attitude toward the "evil" and "corrupt" government of the United States speak volumes. Besides the few occurrences mentioned above, other sources have also documented the illicit behavior of the Mormon prophet and his treacherous behavior toward the United States of America.

If this case were being tried before a jury in a modern U.S. court of law, there appears to be ample evidence to secure an indictment from a Grand Jury.

Council of Fifty

Over the course of the next two decades immediately following his notorious First Vision, Joseph Smith's lust for power, glory and fame grew to become insatiable or at least to the curious onlooker that might very well appear to be the case. Capturing the imagination of friends, family and neighbors, Joseph continued to report strange visions and visitations from Angels while he grew to become an adult. All-in-all the young Prophet, tasked with the job of ushering in a new dispensation and restoring God's true church here on earth, would emphatically assert he had received a total of ten visions and visitations from heavenly beings between April of 1820, and June of 1829.

Who was this remarkable man of vision and why do we care?

According to LDS Church history, an uneducated farm boy barely fourteen years old secluded himself in the woods to implore of God answers to questions he had. Questions that troubled him to such a degree he felt could only be answered by seeking divine intervention. The story continues with the assertion, Joseph had scarcely begun his heartfelt prayer when he felt constrained by a thick darkness that threatened to destroy him.

Fighting the urge to abandon his life and succumb to the power of darkness, Joseph saw the heavens open and two beings descend into his midst. No sooner had Joseph gained control over of his power of speech than one of the beings spoke to him, calling him by name. The visitation continues, according to official Church history, with one heavenly personage acknowledging the other with this simple phrase, "This is My Beloved Son. Hear Him!"

B. H. Roberts, an Apostle of the LDS Church would years later relate the story of Joseph's First Vision in his book *History of the Church*. In his book, Elder Roberts compiled and edited a brief history of the Church purported to be written by the hand of Joseph Smith himself and thereby shares with the world the unique story of Mormonism's rise to power.

I find it however rather conspicuous the "official" version of Joseph's first vision, which can be found online at one of the many websites owned and operated by The Church of Jesus Christ of Latter-day Saints, is markedly different in both tone and substance than that which is recorded in the *History of the Church* published at the turn of the century by the LDS Church.

Both versions were ostensibly written by the Prophet Joseph Smith, yet there are subtle differences in the details which leads one to question the veracity of the claim.

> *After I had retired to the place where I had previously designed to go, having looked around me, and finding myself alone, I kneeled down and began to offer up the desires of my heart to God. I had scarcely done so, when immediately I was seized upon by some power which entirely overcame me, and had such an astonishing influence over me as to bind my tongue so that I could not speak. Thick darkness gathered around me, and it seemed to me for a time as if I were doomed to sudden destruction. But, exerting all my powers to call upon God to deliver me out of the power of this enemy which had seized upon me, and at the very moment*

when I was ready to sink into despair and abandon myself to destruction—not to an imaginary ruin, but to the power of some actual being from the unseen world, who had such marvelous power as I had never before felt in any being—just at this moment of great alarm, I saw a pillar of light exactly over my head, above the brightness of the sun, which descended gradually until it fell upon me.

Joseph Smith and B.H. Roberts, History of The Church of Jesus Christ of Latter-day Saints, Vol. I, Deseret News Press, 1902, page 5

I retired to a secret place in a grove, and began to call upon the Lord; while fervently engaged in supplication, my mind was taken away from the objects with which I was surrounded, and I was enwrapped in a heavenly vision, and saw two glorious personages, who exactly resembled each other in features and likeness, surrounded with brilliant light which eclipsed the sun at noon day.

History of the Church 4:535–536
Above quoted reference to Joseph Smith's First Vision can be found online at http://www.josephsmith.net.

Although Joseph's own journals of the visitation fail to indicate who the "two glorious personages" were, it is commonly accepted by members of The Church of Jesus Christ of Latter-day Saints that Joseph Smith, Jr. was visited by none other than God the Father and His Son Jesus Christ.

Joseph's historic First Vision in the Spring of 1820, was however just the beginning. For the next seven years, Joseph claimed to be privy to a rather astonishing series of heavenly visitations. A young Joseph Smith would emphatically declare to anyone who would listen, he and he alone had been called to establish God's one, true church upon the face of the earth.

Right about now you might be asking yourself, "What does any of this have to do with the political aims of the Mormon Church?"

To answer that question as succinctly as possible, I submit the following snippet taken right from the pages of Mormonism. By the way, this tidbit of information is taught to all members of the Church and is accepted as absolute historical truth within the greater context of Mormon theology.

At the tender age of fourteen, a young impoverished farm boy who would later rise to become the charismatic leader of the Mormon Church, claimed he had encountered God and His son Jesus Christ in a heavenly vision. Yet, the miracles did not stop there; that was just the beginning. During the decade immediately following his infamous first vision, Joseph recounted numerous visions of Angels, including being touched by resurrected beings such as John the Baptist. As a result of these spiritual experiences, Joseph Smith, Jr. believed he was called by divine appointment to start the one and only true church — as all other churches on the face of the earth were corrupt.

And now let me share with you the rest of the story which is not taught to new converts of the Church, nor is it openly discussed among members of the Church. There are but a handful of individual Latter-day Saints who are privy to the inner workings, secret councils and mandates handed down from ruling elite of The Church of Jesus Christ of Latter-day Saints. Speaking frankly, most members of the LDS Church, including families with long illustrious pedigrees, have no clue how many secret deals are conceived of and carried out behind closed doors.

So, once again let us return to the subject at hand...

Following God's command, Joseph ordered the members of the secret Council of Fifty to anoint him a Prophet of God in a coronation ceremony. During the ritual of this secret ceremony which vested the Lord's prophet with godly powers, Joseph Smith permitted his co-conspirators to cover him in a robe of office and place a crown upon his head as he was anointed with the everlasting title "King of the House of Israel." From that moment forward, Joseph Smith. Jr. believed he was no longer subject to any law made by man but only answerable to his creator, God Almighty.

The entire roster of spiritual visitations, heavenly manifestations and ecclesiastical powers that Joseph Smith, Jr. claimed he was privy to before he had yet reached the ripe old age of twenty-four is quite extraordinary. As Prophet, Seer and Revelator of a new dispensation, Joseph Smith, Jr. fully intended to rule the entire population of the earth as Commander of God's Army. He also would rule the earth as King and Vice-Regent to the Kingdom of God. Second in power only to Jesus Christ himself, Joseph Smith proclaimed he was the divinely appointed President of the Political Kingdom of God. Finally here is Joseph's ultimate coup d'état. As Prophet of The Church of Jesus Christ of Latter-day Saints, Smith would be the ultimate ecclesiastical authority on earth.

Throughout the course of my research I was constantly reminded about one curious little fact, a disturbing piece of information which continued to haunt me as I dug deeper into the tangled web of Mormon history. Trying to unravel the truth of my discovery I was forced to conclude, purely from the available evidence, Joseph Smith, Jr. the Prophet, Seer and Revelator of God's one true church was intentionally deceiving his congregation of followers. What differentiated the grand revelation of April 7, 1842, commanding the Prophet to establish The Kingdom of God and His Laws apart from all other revelations was that this particular revelation would be kept a strict secret.

You might think a revelation from the Lord calling his chosen people to establish a righteous form of government to lead his faithful would be cause for celebration, yet all but a few would ever know of it. Unlike all other previous revelations received in

Kirtland, Ohio, the one revelation which essentially called for the LDS Church leaders to establish the "Government of God" was never divulged to the Mormon community. That is never divulged, with the exception of a few handpicked select individuals who would later be called to serve as the elite ruling body.

Of course this revelation was kept secret from even those who would eventually become trusted advisors and regents of "God's Government" for the next two years. Not one word of this new revelation would be divulged to anyone within the community of Saints until the time was right.

Why did Joseph feel it was necessary to keep this secret even from his closest advisors? I can only surmise the emotional turmoil God's chosen prophet must have felt as he struggled to keep his secret plans under wraps and rightly so. It is not everyday a silent revolution springs to life to supplant our government.

Despite receiving a revelation on April 7, 1842, which unlike other previous revelations was never divulged to members of the Mormon community, to establish The Kingdom of God and His Laws, the Prophet Joseph Smith, Jr. did not actively begin to establish the physical structure of the "Government of God" for nearly two years. It was not until March 11, 1844, the Council of Fifty was formally convened as a ruling body when a group of Mormon converts, loyal to Joseph Smith, Jr., gathered to form the nucleus of a new world government.

As a ruling body the Council of Fifty existed sub rosa which in military terms denotes a covert organization. The rose as a symbol of secrecy dates back to Greek mythology. In the Middle Ages when a knight, or any other member of a council, entered a chamber and discovered a rose suspended from the ceiling it signified all who were present pledged to be bound by oaths of secrecy. Given the extreme confidentiality of these Council meetings, it is no surprise most people are unaware this group even existed.

Despite the extraordinary lengths Joseph Smith, Jr. went to in order to shield his political ruling body from being discovered, we learn from the diaries of John D. Lee some key elements about the nature of the Council of Fifty.

In addition to being a member of its elite inner circle, Lee fulfilled his duty to the Prophet by serving as the official scribe of this secretive group — he also just happened to be one of the culprits of the horrendous Mountain Meadows Massacre. In one of his many meticulously kept diaries, John D. Lee records an apt description of the function and intention of the Council.

> *...the Municipal department of the Kingdom of God set up on the Earth, from which all law eminates, for the rule, government & controle of all Nations Kingdoms & toungs and People under the whole Heavens but not to controle the Priesthood but to council, deliberate & plan for the general good & upbuilding of the Kingdom of God on earth.*
>
> *A Mormon Chronicle: The Diaries of John D. Lee, 1848-1876, Edited by Robert Glass Cleland and Juanita Brooks, Huntington Library Press, 1955*

The real purpose of the Council of Fifty often becomes mired in a tangled web of cross-reference simply because the Council, whose sole purpose was to establish a theocratic government, was known by so many different names throughout the history of the Church. From its inception Joseph's secret little council was known to its members by a list of names such as the "Living Constitution" or "Council of the Living Constitution," "The Kingdom of God," "Council of the Kingdom of God," "Legislative Council," "Municipal department of the Kingdom of God," "Council of Elders," "Council of the Presiding Authorities of the Church," "The Quorum of 50," "Special Council," General Council" and finally "Joseph Smith's Council," "President Young's Council," or "President Taylor's Council."

Why this exhaustive litany of names? Maybe the hidden agenda behind the list of names is a classic form of misdirection often used with shell games. Can you find the hidden ball?

Keep changing the name and soon the attention of anyone curious enough to peek inside the circus tent is diverted from discovering the purpose of the organization and onto an endless paper trail of references and cross-references. While this cleverly devised smoke and mirror parlor trick may have had nothing to do with the original purpose the council was formed in the first place, it has been exceptionally effective in its subtle deception and overall goal of misdirecting unwanted attention.

During a sacred ceremony held in the Endowment House at Nauvoo, Illinois, the Council of Fifty convened as Joseph Smith, Jr. was anointed, crowned and proclaimed, "King, Priest and Ruler over Israel on the Earth—over Zion & the Kingdom of Christ."

Although the coronation of Joseph Smith, Jr. as "King" could be seen as the natural culmination of his pursuit of power for more than two decades, apparently not everyone who attended the secret ceremony thought highly of this overt act of treason.

> *...I was also witness of the introduction (secretly) of a kingly form of government, in which Joseph suffered himself to be ordained a king, to reign over the house of Israel forever; which I could not conceive to be in accordance with the laws of the church, but I did not oppose this move, thinking it none of my business...*
>
> *William Marks, member of the Council of Fifty, Marks letter published in Zion's Harbinger and Baneemy's Organ, Volume 3, July 1853*

I am entirely satisfied the above remark answers my previous inquiry concerning secrecy regarding the formation and duties of the Council of Fifty. Exactly why Joseph Smith felt it was necessary to keep the Council of Fifty, whose task it was to establish the "Kingdom of God" here on earth, a secret from his church is not a difficult question to answer. The answer is simple. By establishing the Council of Fifty as a political organization, Joseph Smith, Jr. and other LDS Church leaders committed a blatant act of treason against the United States of America.

While the hubris of Joseph Smith was so great he not only allowed himself to be ordained a "King over Israel," he commanded his followers to perform this regal coronation ceremony. Why should we be concerned about the delusional actions of a megalomaniac that took place almost two hundred years ago? Because every single President of The Church of Jesus Christ of Latter-day Saints since the time of Joseph Smith has, without exception, been crowned a "King of Earth" in a similar coronation ceremony.

> *The anointing and ordination of John Taylor in 1885 as "King, Priest and Ruler over Israel on the Earth—over Zion & the Kingdom of Christ" is important as a verifying evidence. First, it corroborates the accuracy of earlier statements that Joseph Smith received the same ceremony at the hands of the Council of Fifty some forty years before. Second, it clarifies that Heber C. Kimball was alluding to Brigham Young's having received the same ordinance when Heber stated:*
>
> > *"The Church and kingdom to which we belong will become the kingdom of our God and his Christ, and brother Brigham Young will become President of the United States."*
>
> *The Council of Fifty and Its Members, 1844 to 1945*
> *by D. Michael Quinn, BYU Studies 20, No. 2, 1980*

And so the tradition of an unbroken kingly succession continues within the Mormon Church to this very day. George Washington, our beloved first President, rejected the idea of an American King and instead opted for a duly elected governing body. So, why in heavens name would any American citizen allow a scenario to play out where the shackles of slavery are a forgone conclusion?

Quite frankly I am amazed how so many modern day Mormons can easily slough off the notion their beloved Prophet was involved in a conspiracy to commit treason on a number of occasions. I grow tired of the pedantic posturing that is inevitable whenever this subject is approached. Despite the canned rhetoric Mormon apologists begin to instinctively spew when this particular theme becomes the topic of conversation, I am certain most American citizens would agree Joseph Smith's formation of the Council of Fifty and charging the body of men with the task of establishing the "Kingdom of God" here on earth is not the same as the founding Fathers gathering to sign the Declaration of Independence.

Members of the LDS Church chosen by Joseph Smith, Jr. to participate in the Council of Fifty believed they were God's representatives here on earth. I suppose in their heart they held the fervent belief their actions were ultimately serving a higher good. Whatever the members of the Council of Fifty may have thought or believed is only one piece of the puzzle.

Time is indeed a harsh mistress. Bear in mind more than one hundred seventy years has passed since these events transpired. Due to the significant gap of time and considering how radically the world has changed since the mid 1800's, we may never be able to truly understand the frame of mind the original Council members were working with, but we can examine the evidence left behind and look for clues. The personal diaries and journals of prominent members may offer a unique look into the thought process of those daring individuals who were an intimate part of this secretive subversive group.

Although some scholars would argue the real purpose of the Council of Fifty was intended to serve the temporal needs of the Latter-day Saint community, I find it particularly interesting the primary focus after 1845, seemed to revolve around nothing more than how the Mormon Church as a whole would vote in elections.

The early minutes of Council meetings contain hundreds of notes regarding the Prophet Joseph Smith's teachings about the U.S. Constitution, including his ideas about the all encompassing nature of the Kingdom of God and the function of the Council of Fifty in said "Government of God." Before his death, Joseph gave implicit instructions regarding the duties of the Council of Fifty which exist nowhere else in Mormon doctrine. Hence the political directives of the Prophet were clearly meant to only be discussed within a small select body of elite men who had earned the full trust and confidence of the Church leader.

In view of the fact that membership in the Council was restricted and kept a secret from members of the Church, what was discussed in meetings was not disseminated to the Mormon community in general. However we do know from personal journals and diaries kept during that time period a large volume of written material pertaining to the origins and purpose of the Council of Fifty was preserved after the death of Joseph Smith. Church historians have reported that nearly two hundred pages of notes, Council meeting minutes and other written material relating to the origins and organization of The Kingdom of God and His Laws were read to John Taylor on March 16, 1880. Apostles Joseph F. Smith and Franklin D. Richards were also in attendance at the meeting which took place a full seven months before John Taylor would officially assume the mantle of Prophet, Seer and Revelator.

Although Taylor had been effectively governing The Church of Jesus Christ of Latter-day Saints as President of the Quorum of the Twelve Apostles, he would not be officially sustained and recognized as the Prophet of the Church until October of 1880. This curious little fact brings us to yet another interesting historical anomaly in the timeline of the LDS Church. The standing chairman of the Council of Fifty was a position that had always been reserved for the President of the Church, yet the church for more than three years had no official President. Adding to the confusion, John Taylor was elected standing chairman of the Council of Fifty on April 10, 1880, six months prior to being ordained as the President of the LDS Church.

I mention this curious fact solely to shed light upon another commonly held belief among members of the LDS Church. The Church of Jesus Christ of Latter-day Saints teaches all church presidents are called by revelation, yet John Taylor was appointed standing chairman of the Council of Fifty six months before he was ordained as Church President — a position I might add that is reserved for the President of the Church. So it would seem Taylor's appointment might have been more political than prophetic. I also find it quite interesting that John Taylor was not an official member of the Council of Fifty before being elected standing chairman of the Council, yet John Taylor's son was however a very active member of the Council of Fifty.

What is clear is the Council of Fifty was a politically active group of elite church leaders, hidden from the Latter-day Saint community, who worked behind the scenes to silently guide the church toward the ultimate goal of its founding members — to establish The Kingdom of God and His Laws on earth. Joseph F. Smith, who would later become the 6th President of The Church of Jesus Christ of Latter-day Saints, wrote about the instructions given to the Council of Fifty by the Prophet Joseph Smith, Jr. by saying they were "Grand and Godlike."

The formation of the "Living Constitution" and the "Council of Fifty" has never been discussed openly outside of academic circles which causes some church historians to speculate on the real intent and purpose of the Council. Was it merely a symbolic organization filled with impotent men who did nothing but quibble among themselves or was there a master plan from the beginning? The Church most likely will never publicly reveal its true purpose.

Despite the stubborn determination of The Church of Jesus Christ of Latter-day Saints not to disclose the Council of Fifty's real purpose, we have more than enough evidence to make a compelling case. The following revelation which was received by John Taylor in Salt Lake City on June 27, 1882, forty years after the initial formation of the Council of Fifty, clearly summarizes the purpose, goals and ambitions of the Council:

> *Thus saith the Lord God who rules in the heavens above, and in the earth beneath: I have introduced My kingdom and My government, even the kingdom of God that My servants have heretofore prophesied of--*
>
> *And that I taught My disciples to pray for, saying, "Thy kingdom come, Thy will be done on earth as it is in heaven."*
>
> *For the establishment of My rule, for the introduction of My law, for the protecting of My church, and for the maintenance, promulgation, and protection of civil and religious liberty in this nation and throughout the world.*
>
> *And all men of every nation, color, and creed shall yet be protected and shielded thereby;*
>
> *And every nation, kindred, and people, and tongue shall yet bow the knee to Me, and acknowledge Me to be Ahman Christ, to the glory of God the Father.*
>
> *And My law, and My rule, and My dominion shall extend over the whole earth, and no one shall stay My hand, or question my authority;*
>
> *For I rule by right, in the heavens above and in the earth; and My right, and My rule and My dominion shall yet be known and extended to all people.*
>
> *A Revelation on the Kingdom of God in the Last Days given through President John Taylor at Salt Lake City on June 27, 1882, John Taylor Papers, LDS Archives, Utah*

The term or designation of the Council as a "Living Constitution" held a special significance for members of the Council. Its Mormon membership held the firm conviction the Council of Fifty were first and foremost administrators of God's Kingdom here on earth and secondly each and every member was subordinate to the LDS Church's First Presidency and the Quorum of the Twelve Apostles. There was never any doubt in their minds who they answered to.

Published in 1958 by the Utah Historical Quarterly, Mormon author James R. Clark plainly identifies the purpose of the Council of Fifty in his seventeen page article *The Kingdom of God.*

> *In territorial Utah the Council of Fifty, or General Council, was the policy-making body of the Kingdom of God. It was the body from which policies for the civil government of men on the earth were to emanate.*
>
> *The Kingdom of God: The Council of Fifty and the State of Deseret, Utah Historical Quarterly, Volume 26, April 1958, page 141*

There is nothing ambiguous or unclear about the above cited passage. The Council of Fifty was clearly political in nature. Can we as American citizens afford to stand idly by, watching as the Mormon political machine advances in its unrelenting bid to amass power, money and influence over the very system of government it professes to be in service to? To slough off this cleaver assault as nothing more than a fool's errand would be a grave mistake. There is more to the Mormon secret agenda than meets the eye, much more. For the faithful Latter-day Saint, this is no idle dream.

Before we move on to the extraordinary influence this secret Council of Fifty exerted over thousands of Mormon converts during the Mormon migration to Utah, I would like to share with you a tiny glimpse into the inner workings of the council and their ironclad parliamentary procedures. The following will demonstrate the extraordinary lengths the Council of Fifty was prepared to go to, including ejecting dissenting members in cases where a unanimous vote could not be achieved.

The Rules of the Kingdom

1. *The Council is convened and organized by the President of the Church subject to the rules of the Kingdom of God. He is elected standing chairman upon convening of the Council.*
2. *Members of the Council sit according to age, except the chairman.*
3. *According to the order of voting in the Council, a recorder and a clerk of the Kingdom are elected. The clerk takes the minutes of the meeting and the recorder enters the approved minutes into the official records of the Kingdom. They are voting members though they do not occupy a seat in the circle.*
4. *All motions are presented to the Council by or through the standing chairman. All motions must be submitted in writing.*
5. *To pass, a motion must be unanimous in the affirmative. Voting is done after the ancient order: each person voting in turn from the oldest to the youngest member of the Council, commencing with the standing chairman. If any member has any objections he is under covenant to fully and freely make them known to the Council. But if he cannot be convinced of the rightness of the course pursued by the Council he must either yield or withdraw membership in the Council. Thus a man will lose his place in the Council if he refuses to act in accordance with righteous principles in the deliberations of the Council. After action is taken and a motion accepted, no fault will be found or change sought for in regard to the motion.*
6. *Before a man can be accepted as a member of the Council his name must be presented to the members and voted upon unanimously in the affirmative. When invited into the Council he must covenant by uplifted hand to maintain all*

things of the Council inviolate agreeable to the order of the Council. Before he accepts his seat he must also agree to accept the name, constitution and rules of order and conduct of the Council.

7. *No member is to be absent from any meeting unless sick or on Council business. If this were not the case, rule five could be invoked to invalidate any action of the Council.*
8. *A member can be assigned to only one committee of the Council at a time.*
9. *Adjournment and specific date of reconvening the Council are determined by vote. The Council may be called together sooner at the discretion of the chairman. If the Council adjourns without a specific meeting date (sine die), it next meets only at the call of the standing chairman (or new President of the Church, if applicable).*

"It Seems Like Heaven Began on Earth": Joseph Smith and the Constitution of the Kingdom of God, BYU Studies 20, No. 3, 1980, pages 6-7

Imagine for a moment the mindset of any sane person who would willingly give away their own right to a system of democratic voting and become instead little more than a yes man for the autocratic whims of a self imposed tyrant. What type of person would behave in such a manner?

The so-called parliamentary rules enacted by Joseph Smith which set down an ironclad procedure and protocol for how the Council of Fifty would be governed, clearly wrested controlled from the group as a whole and placed all of the power squarely into the hands of one single person. How could any intelligent person be duped into following the commands of an apparent despot?

It is quite obvious members of the Council of Fifty were not only expected to go along with the so called party line as put forth by the Prophet, but complete and utter loyalty were demanded of council members if they hoped to keep their prestigious seat among the select few of God's elect. I suppose members of this elite ruling body did not mind conforming to the stringent dictates of the First Presidency, especially if it meant they would be afforded special privileges with the Mormon community.

Westward Migration

At the time the planned Mormon exodus from Nauvoo was revealed, the vast land that would eventually become the Utah Territory was the northern most part of Mexico. Brigham Young and the Council of Fifty intended to create a theocratic rule outside the borders of the United States.

Brigham Young envisioned a vast kingdom where he would be free to rule over his earthly domain and command his faithful followers as he saw fit.

> *I will say to you with regard to the kingdom of God on the earth—Here is The Church of Jesus Christ of Latter-day Saints, organized with its rules, regulations and degrees, with the quorums of the holy Priesthood, from the First Presidency to the teachers and deacons; here we are, an organization.... This is what we are in the habit of calling the kingdom of God. But there are further organizations. The Prophet gave a full and complete organization to this kingdom the Spring before he was killed. This kingdom is the kingdom that Daniel spoke of, which was to be set up in the last days; it is the kingdom that is not to be given to another people; it is the kingdom that is to be held by the servants of God, to rule the nations of the earth...*
>
> *Journal of Discourses by President Brigham Young, His Counselors, and the Twelve Apostles, Vol. 17, Published by Albert Carrington, Liverpool, 1875, page 156*

A large majority of LDS Church members fail to grasp just how critical the momentous journey from Nauvoo, Illinois, to the untamed Great Basin was for the continued success of The Church of Jesus Christ of Latter-day Saints. Immediately following Joseph Smith's death at Carthage jail, a crisis of succession griped his church. Floundering on the brink of extinction, the church and legacy Joseph dreamed of building came perilously close to having its flame extinguished forever. In the months following Joseph and Hyrum Smith's assassination, more than a few influential figures within the growing Latter-day Saint community stepped forward to assert their claim to power.

With Brigham Young, Sidney Rigdon, William Smith, William Marks, Lyman Wight, Alpheus Cutler and James Strang all vying for power and control of the ever expanding Latter-day Saint community, another question almost as important would rear its ugly head at this critical juncture. How would the church survive the death of its founder? This question was far more important in the historical timeline of the Mormon Church than most would ever care to believe.

With the image of their beloved Prophet etched into the hearts and minds of Mormon converts everywhere, the question of succession appeared to take precedence. Failing to name a legal successor, Joseph Smith left his church in a serious quandary.

In order for the Mormon community to continue as a unified cohesive unit and survive the death of their founding leader, a new successor must be named. This course of action seemed perfectly reasonably in the eyes of the Latter-day Saints who now, all of the sudden, had been left without a clearly defined successor to pick up the pieces. The process itself was fairly straightforward, but a serious question lingered in the back of everyone's mind. What direction would The Church of Jesus Christ of Latter-day Saints take in the absence of its Prophet?

Where the Church was heading, where it would focus its attention, what it would dedicate its precious few resources toward and lastly what the next few steps along this path would be, was a question that appeared to remain unanswered for a short period. For the time being, the question of leadership took center stage.

Who would lead the Saints forward? How the news of Joseph's death would impact his church was a far more important question than the succession squabbles of a few individuals hoping to seize the reigns of the LDS community. Would The Church of Jesus Christ of Latter-day Saints continue following Joseph Smith's original plans to establish the Kingdom of God and build a modern City of Zion outside of the legal jurisdiction of the United States government, or would the new leader take the remaining members in an entirely new direction? Only time would tell.

Rising from the ashes of chaos to ultimately claim leadership of the Church, Brigham Young would continue with the plans set in motion by the Council of Fifty and lead thousands of Mormon pioneers to the Great Basin to begin the process of building up the great state of Deseret. Nearly all Mormon converts are taught about the harsh trek to the Utah valley where faithful members hoped they would be able to enjoy the freedom to worship the glory of God free from prejudice and malice. Unbeknownst to most of the early pioneers trekking westward were the true objectives which lay behind the move.

As with any organization that is attempting to whitewash a distasteful and colorful history, the LDS Church relies on the ignorance of its own world-wide membership in order to perpetuate a more palatable history. Filled with faith promoting stories, the narration of suffering pioneers risking life and limb to settle in a land of milk and honey as promised by the Lord is a powerful tool when proselytizing to prospective converts. Whether or not these stories are historically accurate is another matter entirely.

Church members are either unaware, uninformed or both when it comes to the actual timeline of the Mormon exodus. Because of a lack of critical facts, most Mormons simply fail to recognize the historical significance of the westward migration on the Latter-day Saint community. I would bet less than one percent of all LDS Church members know the decision to move west, leaving the United States far behind was a plan of action put into place by Joseph's secret Council of Fifty in order to establish a theocracy and the Political Kingdom of God. I would further state a vast majority of Church members are equally ignorant of when these plans were first hatched.

Contrary to popular belief, the Mormon exodus was not a journey made out of necessity, but an event that had been planned for a number of years. The Latter-day Saints were not, as popular opinion would hold, fleeing persecution from a hostile nation, but rather they were fulfilling their ultimate destiny as planned by the Council of Fifty years earlier. Yes, it is true hostilities toward the followers of Joseph Smith, Jr. had reached an all-time high, but what is not known by the majority of Mormon converts is the Council of Fifty had for years held secret meetings with one purpose in mind. To create a city-state reminiscent of ancient capitols such as Greece, Mesopotamia and Babylon, where Joseph would rule his theocratic kingdom free from the "evil" influence of America and its heathen laws.

Joseph Smith, a self-proclaimed prophet of God, envisioned a grand and glorious city-state where he would rule over his followers while preparing for the return of Christ.

It may seem incomprehensible to most American citizens that a relatively small group of religious outcasts could muster enough support and political power to construct a city-state that would rival the governing body of the United States, yet that is exactly what the LDS Church did. Identifying, targeting and captivating the hearts and minds of those struggling to find a foothold in this chaotic world, in order to create a loyal body of believers is a skill the Mormon missionary program seems to have mastered.

Crime and Punishment

The City of Zion or New Jerusalem was originally envisioned by the Latter-day Saint Prophet Joseph Smith, Jr. as a prototype for his dream of a theocratic kingdom. Joseph's Mormon followers were told God had commanded them to build the mighty city in preparation for the Millennial reign of Christ here on earth. Under the guidance of his successor Brigham Young, the Council of Fifty became intimately involved in the daily activities of civil government. Select members of the Council were actively involved in the drafting of legislation, formation of ruling bodies and had their hand in recommending appropriate punishments for infractions of both U.S. laws and Church doctrine.

In an ironic twist despite the fact a vast majority of Church leaders sought to distance themselves from the long reach of the United States legal system, these same men, who had assumed the mantle of religious authority over the growing Mormon community, now claimed the right to impose and execute punishment on Mormon and non-Mormon settlers alike for crimes against the civil law of the land and also for anyone who dared violate church doctrine.

Although church leaders had intended for Latter-day Saints to cross U.S. borders and settle in free lands that were part of the Mexican territory, early Mormon pioneers found their trek had ended with the majority of LDS members settling in the Great Salt Lake Basin — an area recently acquired by the Government of the United States as part of the Mexican Cession. With their hopes of building a government that would be recognized by the United States dashed, Mormon leaders now rallied to draft a petition so they could formally apply for territorial status.

During the spring of 1849, Brigham Young, acting on behalf of the people of Utah as Prophet of the LDS Church, met with the Council of Fifty to draft a plan for the proposed State of Deseret. One of the most appalling aspects of the duties assigned and carried out by the Council of Fifty was their recommendations for the treatment and punishment of criminals. A unanimous vote cast on March 4, 1849, by the Council of Fifty declared that an imprisoned man "had forfeited his head." Their solution was to "dispose of him privately." Two weeks from that date Governor Young recommended two prisoners be decapitated for their crimes. Of course this was all in accord with the will of the Lord.

Although vehemently denied by the General Authorities of the LDS Church, blood atonement remains a significant tenet of Mormonism. Obviously a church with a world-wide global presence and one as well known as The Church of Jesus Christ of Latter-day Saints cannot afford to be linked to an act as barbaric as blood atonement, yet the ideal if not the actual practice still remains a key component in the theology of mainstream Mormonism. The Prophet Joseph Smith was the first church leader to advocate the use of execution methods which allowed the accused to shed their own blood thereby atoning for their sin, but it was Brigham Young who first publicly taught the principle of blood atonement.

Within mainstream Mormonism the memory of distasteful religious practices associated with early church leaders have lingered considerably longer than anyone would have expected. Blood oaths administered during the Mormon temple ritual is but another reminder of the Church's penchant for secrecy. Even to this day the pall of polygamy taints the message young Mormon missionaries preach world-wide.

Although modern Church leaders have managed to successfully side-step a variety of uncomfortable questions regarding the beliefs and practices associated with the early days of Mormonism, there are still a few questions which simply cannot be ignored or swept under the rug. Blood atonement is one such topic. The LDS concept of atoning for one's sin through the shedding of blood is not a mere relic of the distant past, but is very much a core component of modern Mormonism's theology.

In 1978, Bruce R. McConkie, an Apostle of The Church of Jesus Christ of Latter-day Saints and author of *Mormon Doctrine*, wrote a letter to Thomas B. McAffee of the Utah Law Review in response to Mr. McAffee's questions about the Mormon practice of blood atonement.

> *In order to understand what Brigham Young, Heber C. Kimball, Charles W. Penrose and others have said, we must mention that there are some sins for which the blood of Christ alone does not cleanse a person. These include blasphemy against the Holy Ghost (as defined by the Church) and that murder which is the unlawful killing of a human being with malice. However, and this cannot be stressed too strongly, this law has not been given to the Church at any time in this dispensation. It has no application whatever to anyone now living whether he is a member or a non-member of the Church.*
>
> *There simply is no such thing among us as a doctrine of blood atonement that grants a remission of sins or confers any other benefit upon a person because his own blood is shed for sins. Let me say categorically and unequivocally that this doctrine can only operate in a day when there is no separation of Church and State and when the power to take life is vested in the ruling theocracy as was the case in the day of Moses.*
>
> *Elder Bruce R. McConkie, Letter to Thomas B. McAffee of the Utah Law Review, Collage of Law, Utah University dated October 18, 1978*

Above quoted reference from the letter can be found online at http://www.shields-research.org/General/blood_atonemnt.htm

Despite his preemptive approach undertaken at the behest of Church President Spencer W. Kimball and the First Presidency, I consider Elder McConkie's attempt to dispel the notion blood atonement was ever an official doctrine of Mormonism a complete and utter failure. Although the letter clearly denies the practice of blood atonement in the modern era, it does not refute what earlier General Authorities have said on the subject.

Contrary to his original intent, Elder McConkie unwittingly makes a case for the use of blood atonement by further reiterating in his letter that the Church does in fact teach there are certain sins that are beyond the atoning power of the blood of Christ — he continues by stating that the practice of blood atonement is not possible except in a fully functioning theocracy.

Now we are coming to the crux of the matter. The number one goal of The Church of Jesus Christ of Latter-day Saints is the establishment of a world-wide theocratic government controlled by an elite ruling class of priesthood holders. The Political Kingdom of God, a theocratic Mormon government, envisioned by the Council of Fifty was nothing more than a carefully constructed ruse intended to maintain a stranglehold on the political power wielded by the Mormon Church. Of course this so-called government of God would be headed by none other than the Prophet of the Mormon Church.

And so we continue...

Using capital punishment as a deterrent was not a concept that was foreign to the early leaders of the Mormon Church. Evidence clearly points to the fact that church leaders welcomed the use of capital punishment as an effective disciplinary method. Many of the early Church leaders openly embraced the idea of atoning for grievous sin through the shedding of blood. A prime example of how easily members of the Mormon Church accepted this doctrine is evidenced in the laws of the Utah territory. Acting in his dual capacity as President of the Church and Governor of Utah, Brigham Young enacted several laws which allowed for a prisoner to be put to death either by firing squad or decapitation.

In 1856, Brigham Young proclaimed the time "is not too far distant" when the LDS Church would begin to enforce the law of blood atonement. In the spirit of fairness, I must point out Mormonism never officially canonized the Rite of Blood Atonement and it should also be noted that The Church of Jesus Christ of Latter-day Saints is not the only Christian sect to adopt similar attitudes toward capital punishment.

A large number of Christian denominations either openly or tacitly support the imposing of a capital sentence on individuals convicted of heinous crimes. What is unique to the theology of Latter-day Saints is a belief that the suffering of Jesus Christ and the blood he shed as an atonement for the sins of humanity is not a sufficient enough sacrifice to cover specific sins committed. Thus the sacrifice of Christ upon the cross is a moot point when viewed in light of the Mormon belief a man must shed his own blood as punishment for serious crimes.

Despite its Mormon heritage, the State of Utah officially banned the use of execution by firing squad on March 15, 2004. Idaho soon after followed suit. As America moves steadfastly forward into the Twenty-first century, we hopefully write the closing stanza of a century stained with blood.

To set the historical record straight, blood atonement was not introduced to the Latter-day Saint community by Brigham Young. It was first introduced as early as 1843, by the Mormon Prophet, Joseph Smith. In a recorded debate with George A. Smith, an Apostle of the LDS Church and a member of the First Presidency under Brigham Young, the Mormon prophet disagreed when his cousin opposed the killing of prisoners. Joseph and his cousin simply did not agree on the subject of blood atonement.

As a member of the Quorum of the Twelve Apostles, George A. Smith advocated the Church should institute a policy of imposing lengthy prison sentences instead of executing prisoners. Joseph Smith vehemently opposed incarceration of prisoners in cases where the law of blood atonement was believed to take precedence. Mormonism's first prophet, Joseph Smith, Jr. strongly favored the spilling of blood when dealing with condemned prisoners. Execution of criminals was to be carried out by either firing squad or decapitation. Joseph was certain only the spilling of blood would satisfy the requirements of God's law.

> *I replied, I was opposed to hanging, even if a man kills another, I will shoot him, or cut off his head, spill his blood on the ground, and let the smoke thereof ascend up to God; and if ever I have the privilege of making a law on that subject, I will have it so.*
>
> *Joseph Smith and B.H. Roberts, History of The Church of Jesus Christ of Latter-day Saints, Vol. 5, Deseret News Press, 1909, page 296*

Joseph Smith and Brigham Young were not alone in their barbaric beliefs behind the doctrine of blood atonement. A large number of Church Authorities were advocates of and taught the doctrine of shedding of blood in order to pay a spiritual debt. Not only did they advocate summary execution, many of the Church leaders thought it was their sacred duty to carry out such punishments.

> *I want their cursed heads to be cut off that they may atone for their sins, that mercy may have her claims upon them in the day of redemption.*
>
> *Brigham Young quote from diaries cited in The Mormon Hierarchy: Extensions of Power by D. Michael Quinn, Signature Books, 1997, page 247*

Further evidence of the wide spread belief in blood atonement among Latter-day Saints is found in an article published by *Desert*

News, a church owned newspaper. There are not many Mormons who would think to question the public declaration of a counselor to the First Presidency.

> *But if the Government of God on earth, and Eternal Priesthood, with the sanction of High Heaven, in the midst of all his people, has passed sentence on certain sins when they appear in a person, has not the people of God a right to carry out that part of his law as well as any other portion of it? It is their right to baptize a sinner to save him, and it is also their right to kill a sinner to save him, when he commits those crimes that can only be atoned for by shedding his blood. If the Lord God forgives sins by baptism, and... certain sins cannot be atoned for... but by the shedding of the blood of the sinner, query, whether the people of God be overreaching the mark, if they should execute the law... We would not kill a man, of course, unless we killed him to save him.*
>
> *Jedediah M. Grant, Counselor to the First Presidency, Deseret News, July 27, 1854*

> *There are sins that men commit for which they cannot receive forgiveness in this world, or in that which is to come, and if they had their eyes open to see their true condition, they would be perfectly willing to have their blood spilled upon the ground, that the smoke thereof might ascend to heaven as an offering for their sins; and the smoking incense would atone for their sins, whereas, if such were not the case, they would stick to them and remain upon them in the spirit world...*
>
> *Journal of Discourses by President Brigham Young, His Two Counselors, and the Twelve Apostles, Vol. 4, Published by S. W. Richards, Liverpool, 1857, page 53*

> *The man who commits murder, who imbrues his hands in the blood of innocence, cannot receive eternal life, because he cannot*

> *get forgiveness of that sin. What can he do? The only way to atone is to shed his blood.*
>
> *Elder Charles W. Penrose, Blood Atonement: As Taught by Leading Elders of the Church of Jesus Christ of Latter day Saints, Deseret News, 1916, page 21*

Of course as evidenced by this next quote, the psychological effect of deterring crime was a grand motivator for the Utah Territory adopting their laws regarding capital punishment.

> *The best way to sanctify ourselves, and please God our Heavenly Father in these days is to rid ourselves of every thief, and sanctify the people from every vile character. I believe it is right; it is the law of our neighboring state to put the same thing in execution upon men who violate the law, and trample upon the sacred rights of others. It would have a tendency to place a terror on those who leave these parts, that may prove their salvation when they see the heads of thieves taken off, or shot down before the public.*
>
> *Elder Orson Hyde from Journal of Discourses by Brigham Young, President of The Church of Jesus Christ of Latter-day Saints, His Two Counselors, the Twelve Apostles, and Others, Vol. 1, Published by F. D. and S. W. Richards, Liverpool, 1854, page 73*

Apparently the Mormon doctrine of blood atonement has a long and well documented history. Does it seem odd a Christian church would support the bloodshed of its own members in deference to an archaic religious practice? Let me add one final historical note on this subject. A poll published by the Salt Lake Tribune in December of 1973, showed eighty-seven percent of Mormon's favored the use of the death penalty as opposed to the July 1975, article published in the American Journal of Orthopsychiatry which noted that about fifty-five percent of American citizens approved of capital punishment.

Peering Behind the Veil of Secrecy

Despite strict oaths of secrecy required of its entire membership never to reveal or cause to be revealed any of the strategies discussed, a number of its most influential members would ultimately betray the confidence of their beloved Prophet by committing the secret plans of the Council of Fifty to paper. One can only assume the mindset involved in such an unintentional act, yet in their defence, the prophet himself had set a glaring precedent by ordering his scribe to keep detailed minutes of each meeting. Since The Church of Jesus Christ of Latter-day Saints refuses to allow historians access to the official minutes of Council meetings, the next most reliable and dependable source is undoubtedly the private diaries of confirmed Council members.

Obscured by the shadows of time and the willing subterfuge of its ultra secretive members, it would appear compiling a verifiable and well documented history of the Council of Fifty is a monumental task. A task that is difficult to prove conclusively, yet not altogether impossible. Of the myriad members who must have been sworn to secrecy, only one hundred twenty-six individuals are known with any certainty to have held active positions within this clandestine, elite political organization.

What we do know for certain is this. All of the Prophets and Presidents of The Church of Jesus Christ of Latter-day Saints since the time of Joseph Smith, Jr., have been appointed and ordained as Chairman of the Council, to sit at the head of the political Kingdom of God — reigning as sovereign regent in their self-serving role as "King" until Christ returns to earth.

Knowing all of this, we may state with certainty there are in fact a good many more members than can be properly documented through remaining historical documents. Lack of physical proof, whether it be diary entries or minutes kept by Council scribes, to back up claims of membership is not necessarily completely detrimental to this case.

The Council of Fifty and the political organization it represented was of course attempting to establish an elite group in secret — so membership would by definition be known only to a few key players. In the case of Prophets of The Church of Jesus Christ of Latter-day Saints we may however not only infer membership in the organization, but an actual leadership role in the Council. Every President of the Church, without exception, is appointed Chairman of the Council of Fifty and crowned King of All Living Inhabitants of Earth.

> *The authority of Jesus Christ sent down from heaven, conferred upon man by his holy angels, or by those that may have previously received Divine authority, is the true and only standard here upon the face of our earth; and to this standard all people, nations, and tongues must come, or be eventually taken from the earth; for this is the only standard which will endure, and this is the only authority which is everlasting and eternal, and which will endure in time and throughout all eternity.*
>
> *Elder Orson Pratt from Journal of Discourses Delivered by President Brigham Young, His Two Counselors, the Twelve Apostles, and Others, Vol. 7, Published by Amasa Lyman, Liverpool, 1860, page 372*

> *Every intelligent person under the heavens that does not, when informed, acknowledge that Joseph Smith, jun. is a Prophet of God, is in darkness, and is opposed to us and to Jesus and his kingdom on the earth. What do you suppose I think of them? They cannot conceive their own degradation. If they could, they would turn away from their wickedness.*
>
> *Journal of Discourses Delivered by President Brigham Young, His Two Counselors, the Twelve Apostles, and Others, Vol. 8, Published by George Q. Cannon, Liverpool, 1861, page 223*

As evidenced by the rousing words we have just read, both the Latter-day Saint Church President Brigham Young and one of his trusted advisors, Apostle Orson Pratt, firmly believe all nations must bow down to the leaders of the Mormon Church and acquiesce to the will of the Council of Fifty. As duly appointed ministers in the Kingdom of God it is perfectly clear the honest and moral men of the Council are only acting as stewards in His Holy Government, and of course they are acting on behalf of our best interest. At least this is the official stance the First Presidency of the Church presents to the world.

> *If Joseph had a right to dictate me in relation to salvation, in relation to a hereafter, he had a right to dictate me in relation to all my earthly affairs, in relation to the treasures of the earth, and in relation to the earth itself. He had a right to dictate in relation to the cities of the earth, to the natives of the earth, and in relation to everything on land and on sea. That is what he had a right to do, if he had any right at all. If he did not have that right, he did not have the Priesthood of God, he did not have the endless Priesthood that emanates from an eternal being. A Priesthood that is clipped, and lacks length, is not the Priesthood of God; if it lacks depth, it is not the Priesthood of God; for the Priesthood in ancient times extended over the wide world, and coped with the universe, and had a right to govern and control the inhabitants thereof, to regulate them, give them laws, and execute those laws. That power looked like the Priesthood of God. This same Priesthood has been given to Joseph Smith, and has been handed down to his successors.*
>
> *Elder Jedediah M. Grant from Journal of Discourses by Brigham Young, President of The Church of Jesus Christ of Latter-day Saints, His Two Counselors, the Twelve Apostles, and Others, Vol. 2, Published by F. D. Richards, Liverpool, 1855, pages 13-14*

Since the advent of Joseph Smith's first vision, adherents to the Mormon faith have consistently followed the dictates of their beloved prophets. Hanging on their every word members of The Church of Jesus Christ of Latter-day Saints exhibit what appears to be an over zealous, almost fanatical type of reverence for the teachings of Joseph Smith and his successors.

As the heir apparent to Smith, Brigham Young ruled the LDS Church much the same way his predecessor had. With the deification of Joseph well ensconced in Brother Young's mind, he would claim the same sovereign right to govern the Mormon community as the mouthpiece of the Lord Almighty — a prophet of God. Contained within the historical record itself there is a preponderance of evidence indicating exactly how Brigham Young felt about his role as spiritual leader of the Latter-day Saints. The second President of the LDS Church felt his first duty was to serve the community of Saints he was called to lead, even if that meant violating U.S. laws. Brigham Young was duty bound — answering to a higher authority.

Believing in his own prophetic powers, Brigham Young immediately assumed the mantle of authority — ruling the State of Deseret as a theocratic kingdom. As standing chairman of the Council of Fifty, Brigham Young not only wielded civic and political power over the residents of the Great Basin region, but he also held the highest ecclesiastical office in The Church of Jesus Christ of Latter-day Saints. Much like his predecessor, Brigham Young managed to consolidate all of the powers of civil and religious authority into a single office which he alone held. Vested with the offices of Governor of the State of Deseret, Prophet and President of the LDS Church, Brigham Young was virtually untouchable.

Presiding as Prophet of the Church, Brigham Young ruled his autocratic kingdom for nearly three years before the Utah Territory was created by an Act of Congress. As a political concession for settling Salt Lake City, Brigham Young would of course be appointed the first Governor of the newly formed Utah Territory in February of 1851. Despite being appointed to the office of Governor of the Utah Territory by U.S. President Millard Fillmore, Brigham Young continued to rule the Utah Territory and the rapidly growing number of Latter-day Saints as a theocracy — which was the ultimate goal of the Council of Fifty.

> *The Church of Jesus Christ will produce this government, and cause it to grow and spread, and it will be a shield round about the Church. And under the influence and power of the Kingdom of God, the Church of God will rest secure and dwell in safety, without taking the trouble of governing and controlling the whole earth. The Kingdom of God will do this, it will control the kingdoms of the world.*
>
> *When the day comes in which the Kingdom of God will bear rule, the flag of the United States will proudly flutter unsullied on the flag staff of liberty and equal rights, without a spot to sully its fair surface; the glorious flag our fathers have bequeathed to us will then be unfurled to the breeze by those who have power to hoist it aloft and defend its sanctity.*
>
> *Up to this time we have carried the world on our backs. Joseph did it in his day, besides carrying this whole people, and now all this is upon my back, with my family to provide for at the same time, and we will carry it all, and bear off the Kingdom of God. And you may pile on state after state, and kingdom after kingdom, and all hell on top, and we will roll on the Kingdom of our God, gather out the seed of Abraham, build the cities and temples of Zion, and establish the Kingdom of God to bear rule over all the earth, and let the oppressed of all nations go free.*
>
> *Journal of Discourses by Brigham Young, President of The Church of Jesus Christ of Latter-day Saints, His Two Counselors, the Twelve Apostles, and Others, Vol. 2, Published by F. D. Richards, Liverpool, 1855, page 317*

Although Brigham Young was appointed Governor of the Utah Territory, a group of Mormon Elders continued to hold secret "General Assembly" meetings under the leadership of President Young as part of a shadow government of the State of Deseret. Nearly twenty-two years would pass before The Church of Jesus Christ of Latter-day Saints would give up their attempts to establish a theocratic government and state based on LDS theology. Much to the chagrin of Latter-day Saints, the LDS Church would never realize the creation of a "Mormon State."

Let us return once again to the concept of secrecy. We have already asked why Joseph Smith, Jr. felt it was necessary to keep the magnificent news that he was now called to establish a New World Order of Government from the world and even from his own followers. The following quote from John Taylor, the third Prophet and President of The Church of Jesus Christ of Latter-day Saints, reveals the real reason LDS Church authorities wanted to keep this radical course of action from public scrutiny.

> *We have got this kingdom to build up; and it is not a phantom, but a reality. We have to do it, God expects it at our hands. We have got to have—now do not tell any body for it is a great secret; we have got to have political power. What, will not that be treason? Perhaps so, but no matter; we have got to go on and progress in these things. We have got to establish a government upon the principle of righteousness, justice, truth and equality and not according to the many false notions that exist among men. And then the day is not far distant when this nation will be shaken from centre to circumference.*
>
> *Journal of Discourses by President John Taylor, His Counselors, the Twelve Apostles and Others, Vol. 21, Published by Albert Carrington, Liverpool, 1881, page 8*

The question of treason is explicitly asked and answered in the affirmative by none other than the President of the LDS Church.

For those church leaders who are quietly and carefully devising a sinister plan to covertly usurp our nation's government, it would appear that secrecy is valued above all else. Prying eyes and ears have always been the bane of those who choose to lurk in the shadows. Any conspirator worth their salt knows the intrinsic value in waiting for the most favorable moment to arrive. Only a complete and utter fool would think about launching a strike against a foe before the time was ripe. To be successful, you must strike when the iron is hot.

With all of the evidence put forth so far, there still remains a nagging question. Why wait to launch your political campaign against the government? Did not the LDS Church already have a considerable number of faithful followers who had previously demonstrated a willingness to die for the ideals of their Prophet? That question can be answered quite simply. Until you have had enough time to prime the pump, the water will never flow. Timing is everything. You must have the unquestionable loyalty of thousands upon thousands of people willing to fight and die for you, if you are to effectively overthrow a government. It has already been demonstrated Joseph did have the loyalty of thousands of Saints, but apparently has was not quite ready to take that final leap of faith, just yet.

We may never know with absolute certainty the answer to those questions. We do know the Prophet obviously did not think it was wise to lead his Nauvoo Legion in an armed revolt against U.S. troops. Could the utter defeat and eventual surrender of the Mormon militia at Far West, Missouri, years earlier have played a role in his decision? The prospect of incarceration for life and or the possibility of death for the crime of treason could very well have influenced Joseph's decisions.

The truth may be even simpler than that. Let us suppose, just for a moment, Joseph Smith, Jr. was not endowed with the spiritual gift of prophecy as the LDS Church would have us believe and he simply did not know his days would be short lived. Without the aid of his miraculous prophetic visions, Joseph would have been unable to ascertain the magnitude of danger he faced personally. Moreover his chief concern at this point in history could have been the destruction of evidence.

According to D. Michael Quinn, author and Church historian, Joseph Smith not only ordered the burning of his controversial 1843 revelation concerning the practice of plural marriage, but also commanded his secretary and scribe burn or otherwise destroy the copious notes which had recorded the topics of discussion during the Council of Fifty meetings. Heber C. Kimball, a valued member of the Council of Fifty and one of Joseph's original Twelve Apostles of the Church, noted in his diary the Prophet sent word to all priesthood holders in the east to destroy their Endowment Garments received in Nauvoo.

Was Joseph Smith trying to eliminate evidence which might be used against him in a criminal trial? We can only surmise what his internal motivations might have been. What we do know with a credible amount of certainty, is Joseph was a master of the unspoken lie. Secrecy seemed to be his best friend.

Secrecy seems to be an integral part of Mormonism as evidenced in the following quotes by one of the Church's leading Apostles. Secrecy was not only a common denominator in the early church, but has been used effectively throughout the entire history of the Latter-day Saint community right up to the present day.

> *There is a temptation for the writer or the teacher of Church history to want to tell everything, whether it is worthy or faith promoting or not. Some things that are true are not very useful.*
>
> *Elder Boyd K. Packer, The Mantle Is Far, Far Greater Than the Intellect, BYU Studies 21, No. 3, 1981, page 263*

I think it is fair to point out Apostle Boyd K. Packer is currently serving as the ruling President of the Quorum of the Twelve Apostles and has held the position of General Authority within the Mormon Church for more than fifty years. He further continues his speech by saying:

> *The writer or teacher who has an exaggerated loyalty to the theory that everything must be told is laying a foundation for his own judgment.*
>
> *Elder Boyd K. Packer, The Mantle Is Far, Far Greater Than the Intellect, BYU Studies 21, No. 3, 1981, page 264*

And finally Apostle Packer gets right to the point.

> *The scriptures teach emphatically that we must give milk before meat. The Lord made it very clear that some things are to be taught selectively and some things are to be given only to those who are worthy.*
>
> *Elder Boyd K. Packer, The Mantle Is Far, Far Greater Than the Intellect, BYU Studies 21, No. 3, 1981, page 265*

As citizens of the United States of America we are blessed with freedom of religion and our government has also granted us the right to say and publish just about anything, without interference from others who may not subscribe to our point of view. Quite ironically, it is this same right which we cling to so dearly that gives a few people with truly dangerous agendas a national, if not global stage, and grants them protection under our legal system.

Unfortunately there is no Freedom of Information Act that would force a church or any other private organization to reveal their concealed documents. Regrettably the notes and minutes from secret meetings held by the Council of Fifty most likely will never see the light of day. Which brings up the following question.

Was the inherent secrecy of early Latter-day Saint leaders a fluke or is deception a common practice among all Mormon leaders?

The answer is glaringly obvious. As far as the historical record is concerned, cleverly crafted subterfuge appears to be the norm when the subject of Mormonism is raised. For all of the curious individuals who have eyes to see and ears to hear, there is a staggering amount of evidence to support this claim.

The simple fact of the matter is this. Faithful church members who hold prominent positions within the hierarchical structure of The Church of Jesus Christ of Latter-day Saints, continue to follow the example set by early church leaders. Even today, as we navigate the ever growing information super-highway of the twenty-first century, Church authorities remain as tight-lipped today about many of its secret practices as the infamous leaders of the past.

Consider now for a moment how young Mormon missionaries are encouraged to engage prospective converts in round-about discussions that do not require them to give direct answers to questions asked. This so-called "Lying for the Lord" is a practice taught by Church authorities to all missionaries in training.

Missionaries are taught to avoid uncomfortable and specifically challenging questions. Questions which might lead a prospective convert to question the validity of Mormonism and its teachings are avoided like the plague. By engaging in such practices, Mormon missionaries never fully divulge the real teachings of the Mormon faith to spiritual seekers. Which accomplishes the number one goal of Mormonism, conversion and indoctrination of new members.

Maintaining a steady stream of converts to the Mormon faith, even if it requires tacit omission of fundamental principles inherent to Mormonism and its theology is apparently not only acceptable to current Church leaders, but is taught to young missionaries as its preferred *modus operandi*.

Does the end justify the means?

Decades of Violence

Born from the seeds of rebellion, the United States of America is certainly no stranger to bloodshed. Old habits are sometimes hard to set aside and true to form the same can be said of America. Whether or not it is inextricably linked to the birth of a nation remains to be seen. What is clearly evident is that the rise of our great nation — a fledgling country that did indeed experience its own birth pangs on the battlefield — would continue to be involved in conflict and bloodshed for much of its formative years. Ironically while ushering in a new era of utopian ideals which included political reform, personal freedoms and religious tolerance, this unfortunate pattern of armed conflict would persist for much of the 19th century.

Once Pandora's Box has been opened, it is much more difficult to close than we could have ever imagined. Time and time again, it has proven to be virtually impossible to cage the beast once it has been set free. Our obsession with war, and of course the profits of war, would ultimately spill over into the 20th and 21st century. One da,y we as a collective society may conclude the ultimate cost of war is a burden that is too heavy for any society to bear.

Regardless of your own personal feelings about the inevitability of war, one fact remains absolutely certain. Armed conflict has changes the lives of millions of people forever. Our history books are stained red as an indelible reminder of humanities past indiscretions. Whether or not our apparent preoccupation with violence would be justified by the end result is a subject which lay far beyond the scope of this book. Did the Revolutionary War ultimately defeat a long standing history of British tyranny and did it not pave the way for a free and democratic society? I think we can all answer with a resounding yes, but one can hardly ignore the fact early American history was certainly turbulent and not without its own inherent cost.

Tumultuous times also lay ahead for Latter-day Saints in search of religious freedom. Woven into the fabric of a time not that far removed, a series of armed conflicts between followers of the LDS faith and its leaders — namely Joseph Smith, Jr. and Brigham Young — would stain the memory of our great country. In no less than seven separate confrontations arising from between 1834, on through until the end of 1858, as many as three hundred sixty-eight men, women and children would lose their lives in what would later come to be known as the Mormon Wars. A few of these battles would be viewed as little more than skirmishes, but that does not diminish their overall effect upon the American populace. Unfortunately these figures do not account for an untold number of Native American's whose lives were cut short by Mormon hostilities toward indigenous people.

Cooler heads may have prevailed where men of ill temper simply were not well suited for the delicate task that lay ahead. History would eventually condemn all involved as neither side could claim to be completely innocent. A violent conflict loomed on the horizon. As opposing forces continued adding fuel to the fire, a clash between armed men seemed inevitable. In a bizarre twist of fate, defenders who once ran for their lives quickly turned the tables and became the aggressor — seeking retribution with a vengeance. Unfortunately the end result was a terrible loss of life with a number of atrocities being committed by all parties.

Which leads us to another question on our quest for truth. Why would members of a supposedly peaceful Christian faith readily resort to taking up arms against their neighbors? Certainly there must have been other options to consider. What were the mitigating circumstances that warranted the use of such violent tactics by Latter-day Saints? To answer these questions, let us once again step back for a moment and pause while we consider some of the lesser known facts.

Although frequent episodes of unbridled violence were a predominant theme in early Mormon history, there is not a single occurrence of hostility where sole blame for an incident can be laid at the feet of an unprovoked aggressor. In fact quite the opposite is true. If all the facts are presented and the truth be told, an unbiased observer might find a good deal of evidence to support why the supposed aggressor felt inclined toward taking action in a certain way. History loves to paint the picture of a sinister villain, yet the real truth is hardly ever so black and white. Regardless of which side you might choose to empathize with in any given conflict, what is patently clear is that in the aftermath — once the dust had settled — neither side, Mormon and non-Mormon alike, could be viewed as completely blameless.

Which leads us full force into a particularly sticky situation. Within the sheltered confines of the LDS Church, faithful converts are rarely exposed to the brutal truth. Most, if not all, Latter-day Saint converts are spoon-fed a whitewashed, sanitized version of actual historical events. Very few Mormons understand just how culpable early church leaders were for the decades of violence they willingly or unwillingly subjected their members to.

I think it is time for The Church of Jesus Christ of Latter-day Saints to come clean about its unsavory history. It is time to put aside the revisionist's pen and let the chips fall where they may.

The age-old adage "The truth will set you free" easily comes to mind. There is no time better than the present for leaders of the LDS Church to embrace this motto. In my opinion Church leaders would do well to reveal their long held dark secrets of ages past and move forward into the future with a clean conscience.

Yes, it is true a substantial number of Latter-day Saints were driven from their homes and deprived of property under threat of violence as church members, unaware of the political machinations taking place behind the scenes, attempted to settle in one city after the next. Many innocent victims were forced to flee leaving practically everything behind in those unsettling early years, but what is all too often glossed over by church historians and apologists are the unsavory actions committed by Joseph Smith and his followers which caused surrounding neighbors to react so violently and expel the Latter-day Saints from their community.

Let us start at the beginning...

City of Zion

Several mitigating factors set the stage which would unfortunately latter erupt into physical violence between Mormon settlers and the early inhabitants of Missouri. First and foremost were the revelations of LDS Prophet Joseph Smith. These were extremely unsettling for the mostly non-religious citizens of Independence, Missouri. The question of unnatural devotion most assuredly entered the minds of the local towns folk. Why would a group of seemingly intelligent people blindly follow the directives of a man who claimed to speak with God? The residents of Jackson county Missouri simply did not understand the invisible influence Church leaders held over their Mormon congregation. Secondly there was a growing resentment among non-Mormons, as the followers of Joseph Smith limited virtually all business transactions to their own community. Of course banks and lending institutions were the apparent exception. Latter-day Saints borrowed heavily from non-Mormon banks to further their endeavors. Joseph's band of Mormons were extremely reluctant to share any possible wealth with those outside of their faith, choosing instead to only purchase goods and services from their own brethren. Finally, the last point of contention was possibly the most salient. The largely agrarian and rural populace greatly feared the combined political power of the Latter-day Saint community.

As early as June of 1831, barely one year from the official founding of the Church of Christ by Joseph Smith, Jr., tensions between early settlers of the Western States and adherents to the rapidly growing Mormon faith began to mount. The primary cause of the latest apprehension between Mormon's and non-Mormon's was because of a revelation given on June 7, 1831, in Kirtland, Ohio. In this new revelation, the Prophet Joseph Smith, Jr. proclaimed the Lord would deliver the land of Missouri into the hands of his followers.

> *And thus, even as I have said, if ye are faithful ye shall assemble yourselves together to rejoice upon the land of Missouri, which is the land of your inheritance, which is now the land of your enemies.*
>
> *Doctrine & Covenants 52:42*

Throw a large enough spark onto a powder keg and a sure bet would be to expect a massive explosion. At a time when the citizens of Jackson county were primed and ready to explode, along comes Joseph striking his flint and steel. Through yet another divine revelation, the Lord had confided in his one true Prophet the land of Independence, Missouri, was to be given to the members of the Latter-day Saint community as an inheritance for their righteous behavior. Furthermore the Lord commanded Joseph and his followers to build upon the land a New Jerusalem. God had revealed to Joseph Smith that Independence, Missouri, would be ground zero for establishing the City of Zion. The grand and glorious City of Zion, built by God's chosen people, was to be the blessed city where Christ would return — in flesh — and inaugurate his thousand year millennial reign of Earth.

The Lord had spoken, Joseph his humble servant was duty bound to follow God's will, or so the story goes. What we do know with certainty is Joseph Smith, Jr. claimed to receive a revelation indicating the city of Independence in the county of Jackson, Missouri, was declared sacred and the Mormon Saints were commanded to erect a Temple to God where the lost children of Israel would gather in the final days.

On July 20, 1831, in this new City of Zion, Joseph was given explicit instructions directing the Saints to buy every tract of land throughout Independence, Missouri, and every tract lying westward. It seems clearly evident the Lord was certain his Temple and the City of Zion were to be erected in the land of Missouri.

The gathering place of the Saints had been appointed by the Lord and revealed to his prophet. It appears as if no other place on earth was suitable to the task at hand.

> *Hearken, O ye elders of my church, saith the Lord your God, who have assembled yourselves together, according to my commandments, in this land, which is the land of Missouri, which is the land which I have appointed and consecrated for the gathering of the Saints.*
>
> *Wherefore, this is the land of promise, and the place for the city of Zion.*
>
> *And thus saith the Lord your God, if you will receive wisdom here is wisdom. Behold, the place which is now called Independence is*

the center place; and a spot for the temple is lying westward, upon a lot which is not far from the courthouse.

Wherefore, it is wisdom that the land should be purchased by the Saints, and also every tract lying westward, even unto the line running directly between Jew and Gentile;

And also every tract bordering by the prairies, inasmuch as my disciples are enabled to buy lands. Behold, this is wisdom, that they may obtain it for an everlasting inheritance.

Doctrine & Covenants 57:1-5

God had answered the Saints prayers. The earthly plot where the righteous City of Zion was to be built prior to Christ's return had been identified. The Saints were overwhelmingly confident, they had a final destination and prepared to fulfill their heavenly purpose. God had revealed to his Prophet the glorious City of Zion was to be built in Independence, Missouri. In less than a year, thousands of Latter-day Saints had flooded into Jackson county hoping to claim a piece of their promised land.

The Lord had spoken and proclaimed His will. Joseph Smith, God's one true Prophet and humble servant, could not help but be overjoyed. The quest for the promised land was nearing completion, at least that is what the Joseph and his followers believed.

Conflict in Missouri

Official Church history as conveyed by The Church of Jesus Christ of Latter-day Saints is quick to remind adherents of the Mormon faith of the overwhelming persecution suffered by early Latter-day Saints at the hands of their enemies, yet they often forget to mention much of the blame can be laid at the feet of overzealous LDS leaders. As with any conflict that is objectively evaluated solely from a purely unbiased perspective, neither side can be held completely harmless. Battle lines often become blurred while embroiled in the heat of the moment. Many of the contributing factors often overlooked by church historians were the direct result of poor decisions made by early Church leaders. Of course this is not totally unheard of, especially by those who choose to be seen as helpless victims.

It is not for me to lay blame solely on the LDS Church. I do not intend to point an accusing finger at anyone, but to simply report historical facts so that you the reader may come to an informed decision. My hope is that you will weigh the facts and take into consideration the many varied and numerous events which unfolded over time, before determining what the true catalyst of conflict was between the Mormon Church and the citizenry of the United States. In order to gain a real perspective of these historical events, we must examine both real and imaginary injuries and insults perpetuated by all involved.

> *Although Mormon military action was generally initiated in response to reports of violence, the Mormons tended to overreact and in some instances retaliated against innocent citizens. Their perception of themselves as the chosen people, their absolute confidence in their leaders, and their determination not to be driven out led Mormon soldiers to commit numerous crimes. The Mormons had many friends among the Missourians, but their military operations undercut their support in the non-Mormon community.*
>
> *Stephen C. LeSueur, The 1838 Mormon War in Missouri, University of Missouri Press, 1987, page 4*

Sorry, but once again I am putting the cart before the horse. Before we continue our forward march, let us pause for a brief moment and take a step backward in time to the winter of 1830.

The Church of Jesus Christ of Latter-day Saints was still very much in its infancy and working to establish itself as a new religion. It had existed for less than one year old when Joseph Smith, the churches Prophet, Seer and Revelator, received a revelation from God to move his base of operations nearly three hundred miles away from Palmyra, New York, in the dead of winter.

Joseph would claim God had told him to uproot his entire family and settle in Ohio. At a church conference held on January 2, 1831, Joseph revealed his plan to relocate the headquarters of the Church to Kirtland, Ohio. Arriving in Kirtland on February 1, 1831, Joseph and his wife Emma prepared for the eventual influx of Latter-day Saints.

Within months of relocating the Church to Kirtland, Ohio, Joseph directed Latter-day Saints to also settle the land in and around Independence, Missouri. Jackson County was the first place the Prophet attempted to establish his United Order, a communal system of living among Latter-day Saints that failed to gain a foothold. Sadly for most Mormons, the Prophet's dream of collectivism never become fully established as Joseph Smith had envisioned it for his church. The United Order or Christian communalism as the residents of Missouri called it was but one of the major sources of contention between Mormons and non-Mormons who lived in the area. Jackson County, Missouri, and the surrounding counties was ground-zero for many of the early challenges faced by the inexperienced community of Saints.

One fatal flaw in their plan was the determination to remain a separate group, refusing to interact with the existing residents in matters of commerce. Imagine a group of about one thousand or so foreigners, with odd religious beliefs, move into a fairly unsophisticated, rough frontier town and keep to themselves. You are certainly not going to win over many friends acting that way. The residents of Jackson County simply did not trust the newcomers. Adding fuel to the fire, Rev. Finis Ewing publicly opposed Joseph Smith and his band of Mormons, referring to them as "the common enemy of the mankind."

You would think an assemblage of faithful God fearing people, who claimed to be lead by a prophet who spoke with the Lord, would do more to endear themselves to their new neighbors. Apparently not. Not only did the LDS community fail to ingratiate themselves to non-Mormons, but they continued publicly preaching the land of Missouri was given to the followers of Joseph Smith by God. Despite revelations claiming Missouri to be the new promised land for God's faithful, Joseph made no efforts to relocate the Church headquarters to Independence, Missouri. Instead he chose to keep his church headquartered in Kirtland, Ohio. As the bitterness grew between the two factions, the original settlers of Jackson County began forming mobs to deal with what they called the Mormon menace. It did not take too long before their conflict of interests broke out into full scale mob violence against the Latter-day Saints.

During this season of social unrest the work of the Lord would not be stopped. On August 3, 1831, Joseph Smith and a small group of priesthood holders, ignoring the obvious social tension lay the cornerstone for a new temple in Independence, Missouri and consecrate the plot of land to the Lord. Turning a blind eye toward the growing resentment, faithful Latter-day Saints remain hopeful amid a climate of animosity. Joseph and other leaders of the LDS Church are certain the sanctuary they plan to build on Temple Lot will be the center for their soon to be established New Jerusalem. Did the Latter-day Saint Church leaders really expect the citizens of Jackson County to openly embrace a new political and religious paradigm so easily?

Tensions continued to escalate until the citizens of Jackson County held a town council on July 20, 1833, where more than five hundred men voted to throw the Mormons out. The die was cast. One way or another the Mormons were going to leave, they simply were no longer welcome. As a result of the town meeting the Latter-day Saint community would be forced from their homes.

An edict emanating from the ensuing vote to remove the Mormons was crystal clear as the voters proclaimed, "peaceable if we can...forcibly if we must!" Steadfastly remaining in their homes even in the face of growing hostility, the community of Latter-day Saints would no doubt have to be physically removed. In late fall of 1833, the towns people of Jackson County illegally evicted all of the Mormons from their homes.

Fearing a rise in mob violence, Mormons took flight across the Missouri River and settled in Clay County, Missouri. The next couple of years were just as rocky and unsettling for Joseph and his Mormon cohorts.

After suffering a humiliating defeat at the hands of your enemies, you might start thinking about ways to appease those individuals who remained hostile towards your way of life. Did church leaders who literally held the lives of the Saints in their hands do this? No and not only is the answer no, but a big hell no. The elite Mormon rulers would have none of that. Joseph Smith continued to openly proclaim Latter-day Saints were entitled to the land of Missouri because God had ordained his church as the chosen people and Missouri was the promised land.

So that you can fully understand the magnitude of the strife that was growing between Mormons and non-Mormons, I will give you a quick peek into the mind of Joseph and his followers, but in order to do that we must consider three things. First, Joseph Smith revealed to his fellow brethren that God had commanded the Latter-day Saints to move to Jackson County, Missouri. Secondly, the Saints were to claim the land of their inheritance. The third and final piece to this puzzle, members of the LDS Church were explicitly told it was their duty to establish the City of Zion in Missouri. Now to rub a little salt into the wound. Mormons referred to anyone who was not a member of their faith as Gentiles. A practice by the way, they continue to this day.

Let us also remember the word gentile comes to us from the Bible? In the New Testament the term "gentile" is used to denote non-Israelite's, but not always. In the case of Matthew, the term is used as a pejorative. It is clear from the context in which Matthew is using the word, Jesus is warning the righteous to avoid pagan culture. In other words, do not associate with the unrighteous heathen. In fact, the King James version of the Bible actually translates the Greek word used to signify a person of non-Hebrew lineage as heathen instead of gentile. It is used in this manner more than one hundred twenty times.

> *These twelve Jesus sent forth, and commanded them, saying, Go not into the way of the Gentiles, and into any city of the Samaritans enter ye not: But go rather to the lost sheep of the house of Israel.*
>
> *Matthew 10:5-6*

Just something to think about when you consider how members of the LDS Church use the word gentile and precisely what it means to the leaders of the Church.

The established dogma of the LDS Church would have you believe all members of the Mormon faith are remnants of the lost tribes of Israel and that it is their sacred responsibility to gather all of the lost sheep together before the coming of the Lord. As if converting to Mormonism instantly transforms you into a Semite and guarantees you a seat in the House of Israel. Of course that is exactly what The Church of Jesus Christ of Latter-day Saints teaches its members. All Mormons who have been baptized and accepted as full members of the church, are also adopted into one of the original twelve tribes of Israel. Basically the idea is by virtue of your conversion to Mormonism you magically become a literal descendant of the ancient Hebrew people.

Right about now you might be asking yourself this question.

Why is this such an important topic for Mormons? It really is very simple. In order to be counted among God's chosen people, members of the LDS Church have to somehow identify themselves with God's original chosen people. The many blessings promised by Mormon theology literally depend upon members of their church being adopted into the House of Israel as children of the One, True God. To accomplish their goal, they simply usurped the ancestral lineage of an ancient people and now claim to be spiritual descendants of Abraham, Isaac and Jacob.

I must apologize for going off on that tangent, but I thought it was necessary for the reader to be fully aware of Mormonism's bizarre preoccupation with the ancient bloodline of the Hebrew prophets and other biblical personalities.

Let us continue with the story at hand.

Mormon ideology essentially segregated many Latter-day Saints from would be neighbors, which only created an air of mistrust among those considered to be outsiders. Their self imposed isolation, coupled with what looks like an almost pathological craving to be special in the eyes of everyone else certainly did not win them any popularity contests. Bear in mind, the Mormon horde, as large numbers of Missourians saw them, were little more than northerners encroaching on southern land.

Although members of the Mormon community were chased out of their homes they refused to leave the state of Missouri altogether. After fleeing across the Missouri River in October of 1833, members of the Mormon Church immediately took refuge in Clay County near Liberty, Missouri. Months after the dust settled, the vast majority of Latter-day Saints were allowed to return to Jackson County and the city of Independence to dispose of their property at fair market price. Once again the self proclaimed Saints were free to dust themselves off, pick up the pieces and live under the rule of Joseph Smith.

Zion's Camp

In the midst of the chaotic storm that was raging against his church, Joseph used every means available to him to shore up the unity of the Missouri brethren while providing much needed solace, comfort and peace of mind to dejected church members. The next two months were most assuredly a period of uncertainty for the self appointed prophet of God.

Unwilling to relinquish his plans to build the City of Zion in Jackson County, Joseph Smith receives yet another revelation over the course of two days beginning on December 16, 1833, calling for the redemption of Zion.

> *Therefore, let your hearts be comforted concerning Zion; for all flesh is in mine hands; be still and know that I am God.*
>
> *Zion shall not be moved out of her place, notwithstanding her children are scattered.*
>
> *They that remain, and are pure in heart, shall return, and come to their inheritances, they and their children, with songs of everlasting joy, to build up the waste places of Zion—*
>
> *And all these things that the prophets might be fulfilled.*
>
> *And, behold, there is none other place appointed than that which I have appointed; neither shall there be any other place appointed than that which I have appointed, for the work of the gathering of my Saints—*
>
> *Until the day cometh when there is found no more room for them; and then I have other places which I will appoint unto them, and they shall be called stakes, for the curtains or the strength of Zion.*
>
> *Behold, it is my will, that all they who call on my name, and worship me according to mine everlasting gospel, should gather together, and stand in holy places;*
>
> *Doctrine & Covenants 101:16-22*

Wary of the Missouri militia, Joseph reminded the demoralized Latter-day Saints of a previous revelation received four months earlier on August 6, 1833, in which God forbade the community of Saints from seeking retribution against those who had earlier displaced them from their homes. Instead he directed his followers to seek political favor through their appointed representatives and to further request restoration of lost property by appealing to the courts. In an interesting side note, the same revelation that spoke of forgiveness also proclaimed God would issue a call to arms when the time was right and further that the Lord would fight their battles, until the Saints had avenged themselves on all their enemies to the fourth generation.

Latter-day Saints did not have to wait too long before receiving word, God was now ready to march with them under the banner of war. I find it interesting how the tides of war flow rather quickly. Let us pause again just for a moment and recap the series of events that unfolded over the past nine months. In August of 1833, God commanded his servants to forgive their enemies, but also encouraged those willing to be faithful to His commands by letting them know, He would lead the battle charge when the time was right. A few months later in December of 1833, the Lord again revealed through His appointed prophet that God's faithful servants would have their inheritance restored to them once again. Finally in late February of 1834, God commanded the place where Zion was to be built must be taken with force.

> *But verily I say unto you, I have decreed that your brethren which have been scattered shall return to the lands of their inheritances, and shall build up the waste places of Zion.*
>
> *For after much tribulation, as I have said unto you in a former commandment, cometh the blessing.*
>
> *Behold, this is the blessing which I have promised after your tribulations, and the tribulations of your brethren—your*

redemption, and the redemption of your brethren, even their restoration to the land of Zion, to be established, no more to be thrown down.

Nevertheless, if they pollute their inheritances they shall be thrown down; for I will not spare them if they pollute their inheritances.

Behold, I say unto you, the redemption of Zion must needs come by power;

Therefore, I will raise up unto my people a man, who shall lead them like as Moses led the children of Israel.

For ye are the children of Israel, and of the seed of Abraham, and ye must needs be bled out of bondage by power, and with a stretched-out arm.

And as your fathers were led at the first, even so shall the redemption of Zion be.

Therefore, let not your hearts faint, for I say not unto you as I said unto your fathers: Mine angel shall go up before you, but not my presence.

But I say unto you: Mine angels shall go up before you, and also my presence, and in time ye shall possess the goodly land.

Verily, verily I say unto you, that my servant Joseph Smith, Jun., is the man to whom I likened the servant to whom the Lord of the vineyard spake in the parable which I have given unto you.

Therefore let my servant Joseph Smith, Jun., say unto the strength of my house, my young men and the middle aged—Gather yourselves together unto the land of Zion, upon the land which I have bought with money that has been consecrated unto me.

And let all the churches send up wise men with their moneys, and purchase lands even as I have commanded them.

And inasmuch as mine enemies come against you to drive you from my goodly land, which I have consecrated to be the land of Zion, even from your own lands after these testimonies, which ye

have brought before me against them, ye shall curse them;
And whomsoever ye curse, I will curse, and ye shall avenge me of mine enemies.
And my presence shall be with you even in avenging me of mine enemies, unto the third and fourth generation of them that hate me.
Let no man be afraid to lay down his life for my sake; for whoso layeth down his life for my sake shall find it again.
And whoso is not willing to lay down his life for my sake is not my disciple.

Doctrine & Covenants 103:11-28

With the Lord squarely in their corner, Joseph Smith prepared to lead his flock into battle. God commanded Joseph to raise up a company of five hundred men to march into the land of Zion to reclaim their inheritance. In a strange turn of events Joseph also coincidentally professed that God knowing the folly of man had allowed his command of five hundred strong to be reduced down to three hundred and finally to a manageable figure of one hundred in strength.

As dawn approached an advanced party of no more than twenty men left Kirtland, Ohio, on May 1, 1834, to prepare their first camp for the arrival of more troops. Within a week's time, reinforcements arrived in New Portage, Ohio, with a third company making its way to Missouri. By the time all three regiments rendezvoused at the home of James Allred, more than two hundred men, women and children had joined the expedition.

Armed to the teeth with muskets, pistols, swords and knives, the Saints marched forth. The overall willingness of the inexperienced Latter-day Saints to rush headlong into battle demonstrated the strength of their faith and commitment towards their leaders, nevertheless the Saints were severely lacking in military skill of any kind. Despite God's promise to fight their battles for them, fate was not kind to the Mormon expedition.

In early June of 1834, a cholera epidemic broke out among the assembled militia. More than sixty-eight of Zion's Camp were stricken ill. Before the end of June, a total of fourteen had succumbed to the blight of cholera. Upon learning the "old settlers" of Missouri had formed a militia which far exceeded the number Joseph commanded, the Lords' prophet issued another revelation claiming God had punished the Latter-day Saints for failing to unconditionally support the effort of Zion's Camp.

> *Verily I say unto you who have assembled yourselves together that you may learn my will concerning the redemption of mine afflicted people—*
>
> *Behold, I say unto you, were it not for the transgressions of my people, speaking concerning the church and not individuals, they might have been redeemed even now.*
>
> *But behold, they have not learned to be obedient to the things which I required at their hands, but are full of all manner of evil, and do not impart of their substance, as becometh Saints, to the poor and afflicted among them;*
>
> *And are not united according to the union required by the law of the celestial kingdom;*
>
> *And Zion cannot be built up unless it is by the principles of the law of the celestial kingdom; otherwise I cannot receive her unto myself.*
>
> *And my people must needs be chastened until they learn obedience, if it must needs be, by the things which they suffer.*
>
> *I speak not concerning those who are appointed to lead my people, who are the first elders of my church, for they are not all under this condemnation;*
>
> *But I speak concerning my churches abroad—there are many who*

will say: Where is their God? Behold, he will deliver them in time of trouble, otherwise we will not go up unto Zion, and will keep our moneys.

Therefore, in consequence of the transgressions of my people, it is expedient in me that mine elders should wait for a little season for the redemption of Zion—

That they themselves may be prepared, and that my people may be taught more perfectly, and have experience, and know more perfectly concerning their duty, and the things which I require at their hands.

And this cannot be brought to pass until mine elders are endowed with power from on high.

For behold, I have prepared a great endowment and blessing to be poured out upon them, inasmuch as they are faithful and continue in humility before me.

Therefore it is expedient in me that mine elders should wait for a little season, for the redemption of Zion.

For behold, I do not require at their hands to fight the battles of Zion; for, as I said in a former commandment, even so will I fulfil—I will fight your battles.

Doctrine & Covenants 105:1-14

A dejected Joseph Smith abandoned his plans to reclaim the land of Zion by force and returned home defeated, but with the firm conviction there would come a day when the Lord God Almighty would gather His Saints under His wing and lead them to a glorious victory. And so without firing a single musket ball, the ill-fated mission to reclaim Mormon property suffered the loss of fourteen souls. Although the aftermath of leading a failed expedition had a disastrous effect on Joseph Smith's reputation as a prophet of God, the entire Zion's Camp debacle became little more than a historical footnote.

Troubles in Missouri Continue

Mormon refugees fleeing from mob hostility between October and November of 1833, were initially welcomed by the residents of Clay County for almost the exact same reason Latter-day Saints were evicted from Jackson County. A larger population in Clay County would help to tip the scales of political and economic power in favor of the smaller county. At first a peaceful alliance was maintained between Mormons and their new northern neighbors, but as more and more church members migrated to Clay County, the once unassuming residents who had opened their hearts to the plight of the refugees began to second guess their initial hospitality.

A palatable cloud of apprehension hung in the air as Mormons and the people of Clay County engaged in peaceful, but tense talks in June of 1836. Clay County residents were quick to remind the Mormon refuges of their pledge to leave the county when they were no longer welcome. It appeared as if the people of Clay County, who early on had been nothing but supportive and hospitable, were ready for the Saints to move-on. They certainly did not entertain the notion of allowing the Mormon refuges to stay as permanent neighbors, nor did they relish the idea of more Latter-day Saints pouring into their county.

Tensions began to mount as the people of Jackson County attempted to persuade the residents of Clay and other surrounding counties, the growing Mormon menace was little more than an infestation of unwanted vermin. Adding to their troubles, Latter-day Saints simply could not keep their mouths shut about their intent to posses all of the land in and around Jackson County. Mormons obviously lacked even the smallest amount of tact. Peace just did not seem to be in the cards dealt to the Saints. Within eighteen months of their arrival in Clay County, the old sentiments of animosity started to resurface as the Mormon presence grew.

With the continued invasion of Latter-day Saints, the ever expanding Mormon population loomed large on the horizon. Much to their chagrin, the citizens of Clay County were growing impatient with the continued presence of Latter-day Saints among them. In fact, the Mormon presence throughout the entire state of Missouri was quickly becoming a problem that just would not go away. Gradually the residents of Ray County came to dislike the Mormon community as much as the citizens of Jackson County. Concerned members of the Missouri legislature sought to relieve the mounting pressure by creating a new county specifically for the purpose of housing a permanent Mormon settlement.

In December of 1836, the Missouri legislature created two new counties by taking portions of the much larger Ray County. Caldwell and Daviess County sprung into existence days before the new year. Missouri residents were happy to isolate the growing Mormon problem in the newly created county of Caldwell. Latter-day Saints were now in possession of land they could call their own. They also had the right to be represented in the state legislature and to establish their own militia. What more could church members ask for?

Despite the highly unorthodox law pushed through the Missouri legislature by Alexander Doniphin which created the county of Caldwell exclusively for Mormon settlement, the growing influx of Latter-day Saints spread into the surrounding counties of Ray and Daviess. Soon after founding the town of Far West in Caldwell County, the followers of Joseph Smith grew restless and began testing the boundaries imposed upon them by establishing settlements in Adam-ondi-Ahman and DeWitt.

Much of the need for new Mormon settlements to be established was a direct result of the banking disaster in Kirtland, Ohio. As Saints fled Ohio, they poured into Missouri by the hundreds. Of course residents of Clay, Daviess and Ray Counties felt this was a direct violation of the 1836 compromise. Once again residents felt overwhelmed by the increasing Mormon presence and feared the inevitable political and economic fallout.

At a time when members of this new American religion needed spiritual guidance the most, their once tight-knit leadership was beginning to unravel. In the midst of everything that was going on, some rather serious allegations of embezzlement were levied against W. W. Phelps and John Whitmer. The entire fiasco involved the purchase of land near Far West, Missouri, using funds raised by the Church for aiding poverty stricken members. The good brethren of Missouri were so busy fighting among themselves they had little time to pay attention to the increasing hostilities which seemed to be surrounding them on all sides. Tempers were flaring, Mormon Saints were in grave peril and it looked as if the once strong foundation of the LDS Church in the state of Missouri was on the verge of collapse. One wrong step and the whole house of cards would come tumbling down.

The attractive facade so many devotees had pinned their hopes to was in the process of crumbling to pieces — leaving little more than a heap of dust where once faith had stood as a towering monument to the indelible nature of humanity.

Life during this period was very bleak for the Mormons of Missouri. While it seemed as if the fabric of life was disintegrating right before their very eyes, not only did Oliver Cowdery sell off church land in Jackson County that had been reserved for the City of Zion, but he openly questioned Joseph's ability to lead the struggling community of Saints. Apparently selling off assets and cashing in so the Church might be in a better financial position to weather the storm, was a much higher priority than following God's dictate of building the City of Zion.

Maybe Cowdery and a few other elite Mormon authorities knew something the rest of Joseph's flock was not privy to. Whatever the case was, a public challenge to Joseph Smith's authority could not go unanswered. As the impending storm seemed to rage on endlessly, Cowdery and nine other prominent Mormons were summarily dismissed from their Church callings, including Bishops and Stake Presidents. The faithful followers of Joseph Smith living in Missouri were sorely vexed. Latter-day Saints had to defend themselves from the almost constant verbal attacks from their once peaceful neighbors and to top it all off, several high ranking leaders of the Mormon community were publicly disgraced and excommunicated from the Church.

Running from the law on charges of illegal banking, Joseph Smith relocates his Church headquarters to Far West, Missouri, in March of 1838. With the Latter-day Saints again on the move, this time from Ohio, the population of Caldwell County soon exceeded five thousand. A plentiful harvest in Daviess County provided a welcome relief for thousands of impoverished Mormons escaping the mayhem in Ohio.

Despite the 1836 compromise in which Mormon settlers agreed to reside only within the boundaries appointed by the Missouri legislature, Joseph Smith reneged on his promise and urged his faithful followers to move from Caldwell County where Oliver Cowdery, David Whitmer, John Whitmer, Hiram Page and W. W. Phelps owned considerable land holdings.

There is no doubt Joseph knew with absolute certainty the severe ramifications that lay in store for Latter-day Saints should they venture beyond the agreed upon boundaries and attempt to establish other settlements in the state of Missouri. Knowing full well the consequences they faced, Joseph encouraged his community of loyal supporters to launch new outposts beyond the borders of Caldwell County.

In the end, additional Mormon settlements were established in the border counties of Carroll, Clinton, Daviess and Ray. This was a direct violation of the peace accord that established a safe haven for Latter-day Saints just over a year prior. Joseph apparently had little regard for the law of the land, especially when circumventing the law meant he could create a spark that would cultivate further growth among his people.

At this point, I would propose the Mormon Prophet was feeling very much like a cornered animal. There were not many options left on the table. Facing both an external and now an internal enemy, Joseph Smith, Prophet of God, foolishly formed a secret society known as the Danites to silence the impending threat.

Rise of the Danites

Sensing a need to protect the Latter-day Saint community, Joseph Smith unwisely deputized a band of no more than one hundred armed men and charged them with the task of shielding church members from the onslaught of ill will being thrust in their direction, yet their "true" purpose lay concealed beneath the surface. Purposefully obscured from the unsuspecting casual observer, members of the Danite crew were initiated by Joseph Smith, Jr. to function as a group of vigilantes. Much in the same fashion as the ancient priests of Mithras were gathered together into a fraternal organization, so were the Danites under the direct leadership of Joseph Smith.

There is absolutely no doubt whatsoever that Joseph Smith clandestinely formed a band of vigilantes to serve as his own secret police, but the actual date of June 1838, is questioned by some historians. Another plausible date for the creation of the Danite band is May 4, 1834, when Joseph organized a militia known as the "Armies of Israel" to lead the failed Zion's Camp march. Despite being a secret fraternal organization, the Danites played a central role in the Mormon War of 1838, and remained an important icon and subset of Mormonism until the much publicized Mountain Meadows Massacre of September 11, 1857.

In response to the increasing ill-will being projected upon the Saints of Missouri, a secret solution was conceived of and implemented in short order. Make no mistake, the highest ranking member of the Mormon Church was the father and architect of this sinister plan.

From their shadowy beginning the Danites were formed to silence the voice of internal dissent, such as Oliver Cowdery and W. W. Phelps, but they soon found the task of protecting the good name of the Mormon Church much larger than anyone had expected. Not only was the Church being attacked from within, but the external assault on Mormonism had escalated. Within months Joseph refocused the main force of his vigilante body to protecting Latter-day Saints in Missouri from non-Mormon harassment. By the summer of 1838, tensions between Mormons and the citizens of Missouri had reached an all-time battle pitch.

> *The citizens of Daviess, Coroll, and some other normal counties have raised mob after mob for the last two months for the purpose of driving a group of fanatics, (called mormons) from those counties and from the State. These things have at length goaded the mormons into a state of desperation that has now made them the aggressors instead of acting on the defensive.*
>
> *Stephen C. LeSueur, The 1838 Mormon War in Missouri, University of Missouri Press, 1987*

Thomas B. Marsh a former President of the Quorum of the Twelve Apostles who left the Mormon Church over the mishandling of church finances reported being at a secret meeting where a conclave of Danites swore an oath "to support the heads of the church in all things that they say or do, whether right or wrong." Fanatical support of Church authority was an unwritten rule expected of all the men who secretly joined the Order of Danites. Although initially it seemed as if Joseph Smith was uncertain how to handle the question of dissension from within his church, a few of the more merciless members among their ranks suggested killing all of the dissenters so they would not have an opportunity to besmirch the reputation of the Church.

Although eliminating any and all dissidents would have been an effective tool for dealing with the question of betrayal, it appears not all of the men assigned to the Danite companies were entirely comfortable with the concept of blanket killings for dissenters, nor did they believe it was a part of their religious duty ordained by God. Once the problem of internal dissent had been dealt with to Joseph's satisfaction, the group of men commonly known as Danites were assigned three primary roles.

1. Enforcement of the Law of Consecration.
2. Carrying our political activities under the direction of the First Presidency.
3. Engaging in military activities under the direction of the First Presidency.

What was never discussed within earshot of any possible bystanders, but was implicitly understood as one of their appointed tasks, was that members of the Danite band — as a function of their office — would enforce the highly controversial and barbaric concept of blood atonement. If further evidence is needed to convince you of the bloodthirsty deeds perpetrated by members of the Danite organization, there is page after page of evidence recorded in *Senate Document 189*.

I have provided a few of the entries from the document which is subtitled, *"The Testimony Given Before the Judge of the Fifth Judicial District of the State of Missouri, on the Trial of Joseph Smith, Jr., and others, for High Treason and Other Crimes Against that State."*

State of Missouri County of Carroll.}

I, John N. Sapp, do solemnly swear that I resided in Daviess county, State aforesaid, for about the space of five months, and was a member of the church of the people styled Mormons, and that I left them about the 15th day of August last by stealth. When I left them they (said people styled Mormons) were building block houses, and calculated this fall to build fortifications for the protection of themselves and families in time of war, for which they were making every arrangement, and the understanding is, that each man has to cultivate one acre of land, and if the produce raised on said acre is not sufficient for their maintainance, and that of their families, they are to take the balance from the Missourians, (thereby meaning the people of other denominations;) and I do further say there are betwixt eight and ten hundred men, well armed and equipped, who have taken an oath to support Joseph Smith and Lyman Wight, in opposition to the laws of the State of Missouri, or otherwise, which said men are called Danites; and I was a member of said body of Danites, and have taken the above oath; and I do further say, I have heard Sidney Rigdon and Lyman Wight say, they had twelve men of their church among the Indian and that their object was to induce the Indians to join them (the said Mormons,) in making war upon the Missourians, and they expected to be fully prepared to commence war this fall, or next spring at furthest. And I also say, the Danites aforesaid, are sworn to cowhide any person or persons, who may say aught against Joseph Smith and Lyman Wight, and if that will not prevent them from speaking about said Smith and Wight, then they are to assassinate them.
JOHN N. SAPP. X his mark

Senate Document 189, 26th Congress,
2nd Session, February 15, 1841

John Corril, a witness produced, sworn, and examined in behalf of the State, deposeth and saith: That about last June I was invited to a private meeting, in which an effort was made to adopt some plan to get rid of the dissenters. There were some things I did not like, and opposed it with others, and failed. After that, I met President Rigdon, and he told me I ought not to have any thing to do with it; that they would do as they pleased. I took his advice. I learned afterwards that they had secret meetings; but I was never invited. None of the first presidency was present at the meeting above referred to. We have a rule in the church, authorizing any member to consecrate or give volustarily his surplus property to the church, for charitable purposes. President Rigdon last summer preached a sermon, commonly called the Salt sermon, which seemed to have for its object to produce a feeling among the people to get rid of the dissenters, for crimes alleged, and because they disagreed with them. In a few days there seemed considerable excitement among the people, and the dissenters left, as I advised them they were in danger. I was afterwards invited to one of these meetings, where an oath, in substence the same as testified to by Dr. Avard, was administered. The society was ultimately organized into companies, and captains of tens and fifties were appointed. I took exceptions only to the teachings as to the duties of that society, wherein it was said, if one brother got into, any kind of a difficulty, it was the duty of the rest to help him out, right or wrong. At the second, or at least the last meeting I attended, the presidency, (to-wit: Joseph Smith, jr., Hiram Smith and Sidney Rigdon,) and also George W. Robinson, was there. There was at this meeting a ceremony of introducing the officers of the society to the presidency, who pronounced blessings on each of them, as introduced, exhorting, to faithfulness in their calling, and they should have blessings.

Excerpt from Senate Document 189

A few days before the 4th day of July last, I heard D. W. Patten, (known by the fictitious name of Captain Fearnaught) say that Rigdon was writing a declaration, to declare the church independent. I remarked to him, I thought such a thing treasonable -- to set up a government within a government. He answered, it would not be treasonable if they would maintain it, or fight till they died.

Excerpt of W. W. Phelps testimony from Senate Document 189

Elk Horn, Oct. 23, 1838.

Gen. Atchison.
DEAR SIR:—The Mormons have burnt Gallatin and Mill Port, and have ravaged Daviess county, driven out the citizens, burnt the post office, taken all kinds of properly from the citizens; have gone into Livingston county, and taken the cannon from the citizens there; they have threatened to burn Buncombe and Elk Horn, and have been seen near, and on the line between Ray and Caldwell. In consequence of which I have ordered out, my company to prevent, if possible, any outrage on the county of Ray, and to range the line between Caldwell and Ray, and await your order and further assistance. I will camp at Field's, 12 miles north of this, to night, I learn that the people of Ray are going to take the law into their own hands, and put an end to the Mormon war.

In haste, your obd't serv't,
SAMUEL BOGART,

P. S. Please be explicit in your express to me as to my course.
S. B.

Richmond, Mo., Oct. 23, 1838.

His Excellency the Governor of Missouri.

Dear Sir:- The Mormon difficulties are arising and have arisen here to an alarming height. It is said (and I believe truly) that they have recently robbed and burned the store-house of Mr. J. Stollings in Gallatin, Daviess County, and that they have burned several dwelling houses of the citizens of Daviess, taken their arms from them, and have taken some provisions. Mormon dissenters are daily flying to this county for refuge from the ferocity of the prophet Jo Smith, who they say threatens the lives of all Mormons who refuse to take up arms at his bidding, or to do his commands. Those dissenters (and they are numerous) all confirm the reports concerning the Danite band of which you have doubtless heard much, and say that Jo infuses into the minds of his followers a spirit of insubordination to the laws of the land, telling them that the Kingdom of the Lord is come which is superior to the institutions of the earth, and encourages them to fight and promises them the spoils of the battles.

A respectable gentleman of my acquaintance from Livingston is here now who informs me that the Mormons are robbing the citizens of Livingston, on the borders of Caldwell, of their corn and whatever else they want; that they have taken a cannon from Livingston County and are prowling about the country, a regularly formed banditti.

That the prophet Jo Smith has persuaded his church that they are not, and ought not to be, amenable to the laws of the land, and is still doing it I have no doubt. The Danite band as I am informed by numbers of the most respectable of the Mormons (who are now dissenters) binds them to support the high council of the Mormon church, and one another in all things whether right or wrong, and that even by false swearing. I have taken much pains to be informed correctly about this Danite band, and am well satisfied that my information as above stated is correct. I have no doubt but that Jo Smith is as lawless and consumate a scoundrel as ever was the veiled prophet of Chorassin. I believe the criminal law in Caldwell County cannot be enforced upon a Mormon. Grand Juries there will not indict. Jo declares in his public addresses that he can revolutionize the U.S. and that if provoked, he will do it. This declaration has been heard by Col. Williams of this place, and other gentlemen of equal veracity. I have hoped that the civil authorities would prove sufficient for the exigency of the case, but I am now convinced that it is not, so long as indictments have to be found by the jury of the county in which the offense may be committed.

I do not pretend to have wisdom enough to make a suggestion as to what Your Excellency should do. The evil is alarming beyond all doubt. I suggest the foregoing facts for your consideration.

I am very respectfully,
Your ob't serv't,

Thos. C. Burch

I could continue with a few hundred more pieces of evidence, but I think we all get the point. Ninety-seven pages of testimony, as well as letters from military officers and correspondences from local citizens were admitted as evidence against Joseph Smith and his co-conspirators at the Richmond Court of Inquiry. Although the aforementioned document itself is filled with the type of legalize jargon one might expect to find in a court document, it is clearly evident the men who belonged to the secret Danite organization were ready and willing to follow any command, directive or order issued by their Mormon leaders.

Now that we have a clear picture of the historical landscape and ascertained the nature as well as the mindset of those men who served as members of the Danite band of vigilantes, let us return to the course of events that intensified the many problems existing between Mormons and non-Mormons.

The weeks and days leading up to the first real outbreak of violence between local Missourians and Mormons was an intense period of uncertainty for all involved. Neither side seemed to display the slightest interest in maintaining a peaceful coexistence or amicably resolving their differences.

If we took the time to list all of the precursors which contributed to the Mormon War of 1838, the Salt Sermon given by Sidney Rigdon on Sunday, June 17, 1838, would certainly appear near the top of that list. Although the target of his famous "Salt Sermon" were a handful of Mormon dissenters, Brother Rigdon was particularly skilled in the art of oration and could easily whip a gathered crowd into a frenzy.

A particularly stirring oration given by Sidney Rigdon at the Independence Day celebration held on the fourth of July in Far West, Missouri, would contribute greatly to the perceived problem of persecution among Mormon converts. This unfortunate and ill conceived speech by Church leader, official spokesperson, personal scribe to Joseph Smith and member of the First Presidency of the Church would later serve as a catalyst for igniting tempers on both sides of the early Mormon conflict in Missouri.

> *We take God and all the holy angels to witness this day, that we warn all men in the name of Jesus Christ, to come on us no more forever, for from this hour, we will bear it no more, our rights shall no more be trampled on with impunity. The man or the set of men, who attempts it, does it at the expense of their lives. And that mob that comes on us to disturb us, it shall be between us and them a war of extermination; for we will follow them until the last drop of their blood is spilled; or else they will have*

to exterminate us, for we will carry the seat of war to their own houses and their own families, and one party or the other shall be utterly destroyed...

Speech given by Sidney Rigdon,
First Counselor to Joseph Smith, Jr.
Far West Missouri, July 4, 1838

Barely one month later, tempers once again flared as both sides came to blows in what historians have called the Gallatin Day Battle. Local Missourians were just plain sick and tired of the constant proselytizing of Mormon elders. Moreover they were quickly becoming agitated with the LDS Church which seemed to take childish delight in openly flaunting the strength of their political power. Both sides were near their breaking point.

Besides their duties as enforcers of "Mormon Law," the Danites were also involved in political activities. Some of their activities included distributing tickets with the names of candidates the First Presidency approved of just prior to the August 6th election. With less than twenty votes cast for the opposing party, the Mormon candidate won a seat in the Missouri House of Representatives in a near unanimous vote. The ensuing landslide resulted in many people believing the Latter-day Saints had exercised an unfair advantage in the polling process.

With roughly one thousand men swelling the ranks of the Danite enforcement squads, nearly one out of every ten church members held some place within the ruthless band of vigilantes. Although a number of Mormon apologists have claimed the primary directive of the Danites was one keeping the peace and protecting Mormon settlers from hostile forces, there were far too many deaths laid at the feet of Smith's secret police for there not to have been another agenda. By the end of the Mormon War in Utah, members of the Danites were found complicit in multiple deaths which included civilian and military personal.

Notwithstanding the seemingly endless number of times The Church of Jesus Christ of Latter-day Saints has publicly denounced the vigilante group commonly known by the name Danites as having no official connection to the ruling authority of the Church, Ann Eliza Young, one of Brigham Young's wives, published an account of Danite activity shortly after testifying before a Congressional committee. In her autobiographical book entitled *Wife No. 19*, published late in 1875, Ann alleges a band of Danites were very active in the Utah territory after the death of Joseph Smith and that their primary task was to discretely murder and dispose of any Mormon dissenter or non-Mormon who posed a public threat to the power and authority of Brigham Young.

As a result of her testimony, sworn under oath before members of the U. S. Congress, a slew of Latter-day Saints were removed from their judicial positions in Utah under the Poland Act, thus facilitating the successful prosecution of polygamy within the Utah Territory. Of course this act of betrayal earned her a permanent spot on God's black list. How dare she defy a prophet of God and speak the truth. Despite the fact that members of Congress found Ann Young to be a credible witness, Mormon apologists are quick to point out there are no surviving historical documents, such as court records verifying the actual murder and disposal of bodies by members of the Danites.

Evidence gets lost, misplaced and destroyed all of the time. Lack of an existing body of evidence in the form of "real" and tangible historical documents does not prove innocence. Well there you have it. Without any "real" evidence against the Mormon Church, they are free to create an alternate revisionist history. Apparently you can whitewash just about any despicable act, as long as you are able to get rid of any evidence which supports an alternate reality. And the moral of the story is, if you do not get caught burying the body it must have never happened.

Mormon War

Beginning with the Gallatin Day Battle and ending in the Mormon militias surrender at Far West, Missouri, the first of the so-called Mormon Wars took place between August of 1838, and November of the same year. Fearful the solidarity of a Mormon vote could drastically affect the overall results of any given election, ruthless politicians often spoke disparagingly about the growing Latter-day Saint population. Spurred on by wide-spread rumors the Mormon community as a whole had a habit of selling their vote to the highest bidder, the gullible citizens of Daviess County were certainly wary of Mormon voters at the polling booth.

In a desperate attempt to excite the fears of local residents, William Peniston, a savvy politician who just happened to be a candidate for the state legislature, sought to prevent Mormons from voting in the Gallatin election by appealing to mob mentality. Whether out of fear the Latter-day Saints might block him from obtaining political office or out of sheer spite, Peniston whipped the gathered crowd into a frenzy by speaking against the growing electoral power held within the ever widening Mormon community. William Peniston was not taking any chances when it came to the Mormon vote. Not in this election. He sought to eliminate the perceived threat entirely.

Did Mormons have the political power to sway a vote in favor of a candidate of their choosing?

That certainly was one possible outcome. Mormon's were known to vote in blocs. Peniston's fear that an organized community of Latter-day Saints could drastically alter voting results may very well have been warranted under the circumstances, but that does not, in any way, excuse his reckless and blatantly malicious behavior. Despite whatever conclusions the historical facts may support, I am somewhat disturbed by how easily otherwise rational and sensible people are manipulated simply by rhetoric. Can we not think for ourselves? In my opinion it is a sad commentary on our political system, but we must face the hard fact that decent citizens are consistently being manipulated by ambitious individuals.

A group of about two hundred non-Mormons had gathered on August 6, 1838, the day of the Gallatin election, with the firm intent of prohibiting any Latter-day Saint from casting a vote. Vocal anti-Mormon sentiment at the polls on election day only exacerbated an already untenable situation. Instead of quelling the budding storm, the presence of ruffians who hoped to suppress the Mormon vote by intimidation had the exact opposite effect. By interfering in the democratic process, those who sought to control the voting outcome only succeeded in throwing more fuel on a fire that was already raging out of control.

Despite being warned not to attempt to vote, more than thirty Mormon men approached the polling place. Mormons insisted the callus remarks of William Peniston in which he claimed LDS leaders were "horse thieves, liars and counterfeiters" were utterly false and declared their intent to vote. This confrontation triggered a fight. In the ensuing brawl, Mormons we able to withstand their attackers. Missourians who by now had no love for the Mormons left the pools to gather arms, swearing they would either drive the Mormon horde from Daviess County or kill them all. And so a few ignorant men who could not master their emotions, sparked the beginning of the Mormon War of 1838.

Let us step back for a moment and take a look at what prompted the Gallatin Day Battle in the first place. Several factors that are quite often glossed over by historians trying to sway an audience to their point of view, turn out to be crucial elements of the story. I have uncovered numerous references to the Mormon War of 1838, but all fail to mention one simple fact. Under statutes governing the rights of Missouri voters, which existed at the time the election battle took place, only legal residents of any county in question could cast a ballot in the election. Assuming that was in fact the case, the following points would have all been true.

1. Per a compromise agreed upon in 1836, the county of Caldwell was created by the state legislature exclusively for Mormon settlement.
2. Any Mormon living beyond the borders of Caldwell County would have been in violation of the compromise agreement.
3. Gallatin was the county seat of Daviess County.
4. All elections at the time were held in Gallatin.
5. Anyone not a legal resident of Daviess County would be barred from voting at the county seat in Gallatin.

On the August 6th ballot was a referendum on whether or not Mormons would be allowed to settle in Daviess County.

As you can see from the points above, the fight that broke out on election day was just the tip of the iceberg. I am certain the citizens of Daviess County were simply protecting their rights to vote as granted by the Missouri State legislature, but before you make up your mind and decide who was right, let us consider the Mormon point-of-view. On the other hand Mormon settlers believed they had a constitutional right to vote in each and every election. Granted, the legality of the Mormon vote in Gallatin on August 6, 1838, is at best a very gray area. Which leads us to another question. Did the Mormons who showed up to vote know their votes may not have been legal? That is a question I will leave for law professors to determine at a future date.

This whole fiasco brings to mind the devious machinations currently taking place in the American political system. Is it ever a good idea to attempt to strip a citizen of their right to vote? I hope this comparison gives you pause as you contemplate the incredible lack of wisdom being exhibited by individuals within our own society who obviously believe voter suppression is advantageous to their cause. Once again I have managed to stray off point. We now return to our story.

Word of the skirmish spread quickly and rumors there were casualties surfaced as well, but were soon put to rest. Less than forty-eight hours had elapsed since the unfortunate brawl in Gallatin had taken place when the Prophet Joseph leading a faction of one hundred men surrounded the home of Judge Adam Black. After hearing a rumor Judge Black may be supporting vigilance committees, the armed men visited his home to ascertain whether or not he was involved with the anti-Mormon mobs. Initially refusing to comply, Judge Adam Black eventually conceded, under duress, to sign an affidavit affirming he was in no way connected to any group of vigilantes.

You can hardly blame the Mormons for being overly cautious. With all that had already transpired it is no wonder they were predisposed to believe the citizens of Missouri were out to "get" them. No matter what their rational may have been, Joseph and his band of men made a series of rash decisions that, in the end, turned out badly for everyone involved. Mormon mobs also visited the homes of Sheriff William Morgan and several other prominent citizens of Daviess County, forcing them to sign statements they did not support nor endorse the activities of vigilance groups and to further disavow any association with such groups in general.

With no end in sight, both sides resorted to violent tactics. As the threat of violence escalated Joseph Smith shrewdly retained the legal services of attorneys David R. Atchison and Alexander W. Doniphan just days before being summoned by Judge Austin A. King to appear at a preliminary hearing in Daviess County. Besides being attorneys of record for Joseph Smith and other prominent Mormons, both men served as soldiers in the Missouri State Guard with the ranks of major general and brigadier general respectively. There is no doubt Joseph knew his attorneys were soldiers and as such would be called upon to serve as militia officers, should the clash between Mormons and non-Mormon escalate to the point of warranting military intervention. This strategic move proved to be highly advantageous for the captured prophet during the Mormon surrender at Far West, Missouri. Why had Joseph specifically hired those two men? Did Joseph believe his attorneys would intercede on behalf of the Mormons during the Missouri conflict?

Three days after Joseph Smith and Lyman Wight posted bail, Judge Austin A. King orders General Atchison to raise four hundred troops to disband groups of Mormon and non-Mormon vigilantes alike. By mid September the arguments between Mormon and non-Mormon settlers became such a widespread problem that Governor Boggs felt he had to address the issue. Ordering two thousand troops to march on Daviess County, Lilburn W. Boggs prepares to lead the militia march in order to suppress rioting or other lawless behavior. Upon reaching his destination, General Atchison, armed with a cadre of four hundred men, easily disperses local mobs in Daviess County.

Under the direction of Governor Boggs, troops en route are dismissed less than a week later when the governor receives a dispatch from General Atchison attesting to the fact that vigilante forces have successfully been dissolved with all parties returning home. Atchison orders General Parks and a force of one hundred men to remain in Daviess County to maintain the peace.

Latter-day Saints are warned not to remain in DeWitt the same day vigilantes return from Daviess County. Despite the presence of peacekeepers only miles away, when rumors spread state militia troops have turned away and are no longer marching to Daviess County an emboldened vigilante group rides to the town of DeWitt in Carroll County and burns the barn of Smith Humphrey. Later that day DeWitt is surrounded by armed men mostly from Carroll County. Sealed off from supplies or outside support, a five day siege of the town commences.

Powerless and without any visible sign of aid or support, frightened Mormons appeal to Governor Boggs for help. Days later General Parks arrives in Carroll County on October 6, 1838, with his detachment of one hundred soldiers. Although General Parks was in command of a sizable militia force, the dissenting mob ignored orders to disperse and continued their harassment of Mormon settlers. Parks had to concede defeat and leave the battlefield when his own troops, who hated the Mormons as much as anyone else, threatened to join the mob and help drive the Mormons out. Falling back to a secure position in Ray County, General Parks dispatches a letter to his immediate superior. Hoping the Governor would come to recognize the severity of what is quickly becoming an untenable situation, General Parks appears eager to avoid bloodshed and further loss of property.

In his correspondence to General Atchison a beleaguered Parks writes, "a word from his Excellency would have more power to quell this affair than a regiment." Finally receiving word regarding their plea to the Governor for help, Mormons are disheartened to hear Governor Boggs is unwilling to intercede on their behalf. All but dismissing the Mormon cry for help, Boggs pays little attention to their plight. The trivializing tone of his response advises the besieged community of Latter-day Saints to seek protection from local authorities. Fearing for their lives, Mormon leaders abandon DeWitt and seek shelter in nearby Caldwell County. Bolstered by their recent success and hearing of Governor Lilburn W. Boggs' reluctance to intervene in the fight, vigilantes from Carroll County pledge to help rid Daviess County of the Mormon scourge.

On the heels of such a callous response from Governor Boggs, Joseph Smith and Sidney Rigdon decided to take matters into their own hands. Within days Smith and Rigdon had put out the call for Mormon soldiers and rode ahead of a force of four hundred troops toward Adam-ondi-Ahman.

Determined to protect Latter-day Saints from the abuse suffered at the hands of lawless Missourians, Alexander Doniphan reported to Joseph Smith a small group of non-Mormons from Clinton, Missouri, had begun burning outlying homes and harassing Mormons in Daviess County. Against the advice of General Doniphan, one of Joseph's attorneys, plans were made to cross the northern boundary into Daviess County. Although he was sympathetic to the Mormon plight, Doniphan again renewed his objection stating emphatically Caldwell militia could not legally enter into Daviess County. Acting under orders from General Doniphan, a small company of state militia commanded by Colonel William A. Dunn of Clay County were sent to Adam-ondi-Ahman. Ignoring the advice of legal counsel, a Mormon judge residing in Caldwell County authorized Colonel George M. Hinkle to lead the Caldwell militia north into Daviess County.

Numerous reports of Mormon aggression were widely circulated among the towns people over the next couple of weeks. Quite a few of the stories made their way into newspapers, shocking local residents. Mormons and non-Mormons alike were troubled by the escalating violence. Dismayed citizens were outraged by the reported actions blamed on Danite gangs. Clearly the situation had reached a breaking point.

> *Richmond, October 14, 1838.*
>
> *DEAR SIR. — As Mr. Williams will be to see you in reference to our Mormon difficulties, I will be able to say all to you perhaps that can be said. I deem it a duty notwithstanding to give you such information as I have sought and obtained, & is such I assure you may be relied on. Our relations with the Mormons are such*

that I am perfectly satisfied that the arm of the civil authority is too weak to give peace to the country. Until lately I thought the Mormons were disposed to act on the defensive: but their recent conduct shows that they are the aggressors, and that they intend to take the law into their hands. Of their recent outrages in Daviess, you have probably heard much already. I will give you the general facts, however. On Sunday before they marched to Daviess, Jo Smith made known his views to the people, and declared the time had come when they would avenge their own wrongs, and that all who were not for them, and taken up arms with them, should be considered as against them, that their property should be confiscated, and their lives also forfeited.

With this declaration and much else said by Smith, calculated to excite the people present -- the next day was set to see who was for them and who against them; and under such severe penalties, that there was some, I learn, who did not turn out; and about 3 or 400 men, with Smith at their head, marched to Daviess. This was on Tuesday; the next day was the snow storm, and on Thursday they commenced their ravages upon the citizens, driving them from their homes and taking their property. Between 80 and 100 men went to Gallatin, pillaged houses and the store of Mr. Stollings and the post-office, and then burnt the houses. They carried off the spoils on horseback and in wagons, and now have them, I understand, in a store house, near their camp. Houses have been robbed of their contents, — beds, clothing, furniture, &c. and all deposited, as they term it, "a consecration to the Lord." At this time, there is not a citizen in Daviess, except Mormons. Many have been driven without warning, others have been allowed a few hours to start. This stock of citizens have been seized upon, killed and salted by hundreds; from 50 to 100 wagons are now employed in hauling in the corn from the surrounding country. They look for a force against them, and are consequently preparing for a seige — building block houses, &c. They have lately organized themselves into a band of what they call "Danites," and sworn to support their leading men in all they say or do, right or wrong — and further, to put to instant death those who will betray them. There is another band of twelve, called the "Destructives," whose duty it is to watch the movements of men and of communities, and to avenge themselves for supposed wrongful movements against them, by privately burning houses and property, and even laying in ashes towns, &c. I find I am running out my letter too much in detail. I do not deem it necessary to give you a minute detail of all the facts of which I am possessed, but I give you the above in order that you may form some idea of the disposition of these people. The Mormons expect to settle the affair at the point of the sword, and I am well warranted in saying to you that the people in this quarter of the state look to you for that protection which they believe you will afford when you have learned the facts. I do not pretend to advise your course, nor make any suggestions other than what I have stated, that it is utterly useless for the civil authorities to pretend to intercede. The country is in great commotion and I can assure you that either with or without authority, something will shortly have to be done.

I hope you will let me hear from you by the return of Mr. Williams, and if you should come up the country shortly, it will give me pleasure to take the trouble to see you.

I am very respectfully,
AUSTIN A KING.

Within the archives of the State of Missouri there still exists dozens of letters written by state militia officers as well as ordinary citizens attesting to the rampant violence and overall lack of officers available to deal with the expanding Mormon problem.

By October 18, 1838, the tables had turned. Mormon militia's had quickly degenerated into little more than a marauding mass of vigilantes bent on vindictive destruction. Splitting their numbers into three groups, Latter-day Saints attacked the settlements of Gallatin, Millport and Grindstone Fork. Driving all non-Mormon residents from their homes, Mormon men plundered everything they could get their hands on and burnt or destroyed the rest. Leaving nothing but destruction in their wake, Mormon vigilantes vented their anger on every living soul. Not even those who had always been friendly and kind to Latter-day Saints were spared.

A perfect example is the unfortunate case of Jacob Stollings, a Gallatin merchant who had befriended the Mormon settlers by allowing them to purchase goods and supplies from his mercantile on liberal credit terms. In return the good Mormon settlers looted and burned Mr. Stollings' store to the ground.

John Corrill, a prominent Mormon leader who had been elected to the Missouri State Legislature only a few months earlier, is reported as saying, "the love of pillage grew upon them very fast, for they plundered every kind of property they could get a hold of." Apparently the so-called "Saints" of Mormonism were not the helpless victims of religious persecution The Church of Jesus Christ of Latter-day Saints would have us believe.

In the days that followed Mormon vigilantes, under the direction of Lyman Wight, sacked smaller settlements — plundering and burning as they went. According to an eyewitness account, house fires lit the night sky for nearly two weeks. When their lust for destruction seemed to wane, the Mormon troops had succeeded in laying waste to the entire county. Nearly every house in Daviess County had been put to the torch.

Not wanting to risk any further looting, destruction of property or the intrusion of Mormon forces into Ray County, General Atchison dispatches orders for Captain Bogart and his men to patrol a strip of land just south of the Caldwell border. In theory this was a sound military strategy, but in retrospect the entire affair achieved nothing and the cost was a price that was just too high to pay.

General Atchison's choice to appoint Captain Samuel Bogart to police the border between Caldwell and Ray County was a colossal failure. Captain Bogart's prior association with anti-Mormon vigilante groups may have clouded his judgment and should have automatically disqualified him as a commanding officer in this particular military campaign, but such was the life of a militia officer in mid 19th century America.

Sometimes referred to as a less than genteel man, Captain Bogart — in his zeal to perform his duties — overstepped the bounds of his assignment. Where subtlety should have been the order of the day, Samuel Bogart and his men took an entirely different approach. Instead of policing the assigned territory and arresting any encroachers, Captain Bogart visited the homes of Mormons living in the area, confiscated their arms and ordered them to leave Ray County immediately. Technically any Mormon living outside of Caldwell County was in violation of the 1836 accord, but once again tact and a little finesse would have gone a long way to improving the situation.

Aside from straying a little too far north of the hypothetical line when following orders, Captain Bogart actually crossed the line by ordering his men into Caldwell County where they similarly harassed Mormon settlers. Whether or not this was an unintentional mistake made in the "heat of battle" is an argument best left for the historians to decide. What we do know is upon returning to Ray County, Bogart's company captured three Mormon men.

Rumors that a hostile mob had taken Mormons with the intent to kill them quickly made their way to the Church headquarters in Far West. Camping along the banks of the Crooked River, Captain

Bogart and his men prepared to settle in for the night. Embarking just after midnight, a contingency of Caldwell militia travelled throughout the night to retrieve their captured brethren. Unaware of any rumors and certainly not expecting any opposition, the small company of men under Samuel Bogart's command was unprepared for an early morning rescue party. At daybreak on October 25, 1838, an unknown number of assailants encountered the forward sentries guarding Captain Bogart's encampment of militia.

History remains mute on who fired the first shot, but in the ensuing blaze of muskets, one of the sentries had been mortally wounded by a member of the approaching Mormon group.

Continuing their approach to the camp, the Mormon force divided into three groups to mount an offensive. A firefight commenced between the opposing forces, but the militia under Bogart's command held the strategically stronger position. Taking charge of the Mormon force, David Patten throwing caution to the wind charges the Missouri militia yelling, "God and Liberty!" Bogart's men having fired their guns and having no swords or sidearm's to defend themselves, broke rank and scrambled across the river. As the militia retreated Mormon aggressors continued firing into the fleeing soldiers, thus Moses Rowland the only casualty of the Missouri militia was shot in the back and killed.

Although Mormon forces suffered three times as many casualties, including David Patten who had lead the charge across river, the men mustered under the banner of Mormonism claimed the day and took the spoils of war. Making quick work of the equipment left behind at the abandoned camp, Mormon militia gathered their dead and made their way back to Far West.

Despite the fact the Battle of Crooked River was a relatively miniscule fight, the Mormon men who survived were filled with pride as they marched back homeward. Much to the dismay of Mormons world-wide, the bravado displayed after their short lived victory made its way to the ears of Governor Lilburn W. Boggs. Not wanting to be directly involved for fear of political reprisal, Governor Boggs, who had up until now taken a hands off, backseat approach to the messy affair, was now ready to step in with a state sponsored solution.

In the end exaggerated reports of Mormon violence was the straw that broke the camel's back. Reports of the Caldwell militia's ferocious attack on Captain Bogart's men, how they overran his camp, decimated his forces and spared none who stood against them, was just the type of boisterous tale that ultimately sealed the fate of the Mormons settlements in Missouri.

Within forty-eight hours of highly exaggerated reports concerning the Battle of Crooked River reaching his office, Boggs made the biggest blunder of his entire political career. Instead of coming to the aid of the Mormon community and protecting their rights as citizens of Missouri, Governor Boggs issued *Missouri Executive Order Number 44* on the morning of October 27, 1838. Backed into a corner and feeling his back pressed firmly against the wall, Lilburn W. Boggs was finally ready to take decisive action.

Calling upon more than eighteen hundred men, Governor Boggs mobilized a sufficient number of militia to suppress the Mormon revolt once and for all. Fearing a war of rebellion had begun, Executive Order Number 44 authorized General John B. Clark to use whatever force was deemed necessary to quell the uprising and restore peace.

Refusing to take part in the forced removal of Mormon settlers from the state he loved, General David R. Atchison fervently opposed Boggs' Executive Order. The very next day on Sunday — October 28, 1838, Latter-day Saints at Haun's Mill became worried about the increasing number of militia and voted to form a defensive unit of twenty-eight men to ward off any future attacks. Later that night a representative from the militia camp negotiated a truce. Nearly two days would pass without incident. Unfortunately on the afternoon of October 30, 1838, it appears the truce was broken as Colonel Jennings — commanding more than two hundred men — rode into the settlement.

Catching the Mormon settlement of Haun's Mill ill-equipped to defend themselves, the attacking militia approached from all sides. With nowhere to run except south into the woods, women and children tried to flee across the dam to safety while the men sought cover in the blacksmith's shop. Although the men of the settlement had previously resolved to use the shop as defensive cover, if and when a battle looked imminent, that decision turned out to be a fatal mistake. Trapped in a confined space that offered little protection from bullets and invading troops, the bloodiest conflict of the Mormon War was about to become a massacre

By the end of the attack, eighteen including one non-Mormon were dead and thirteen seriously wounded. The militia who led the assault emerged relatively unscathed, only three soldiers out of two hundred forty engaged in the battle were wounded. Upon arriving in Far West, survivors of the massacre shared details of the horrific scene which took place at Haun's Mill.

October 31, 1838, All Hallows Eve, found the town of Far West, Missouri — headquarters of The Church of Jesus Christ of Latter-day Saints — under siege by Major General Samuel D. Lucas. Demoralized by the savagery of the recent massacre, Joseph Smith sent Colonel Hinkle, head of the Mormon militia, out to seek terms with General Lucas. Fearing for his own safety, Joseph beseeched Colonel Hinkle to "beg like a dog for peace." The terms of surrender were harsh.

1. Mormons must give up their leaders for trial.
2. Mormons must surrender all of their arms.
3. Mormons who had taken up arms against the state of

Missouri was to deed over their property to pay for damages and the cost to muster state militia.
4. Mormons who had taken part in any armed conflict were to leave the state.

Negotiations between Latter-day Saints and General Lucas were fruitless. Realizing Samuel Lucas was unwilling to accept anything less than full compliance of his stated terms, Joseph agrees to the conditions of surrender. Lamenting their lost cause, Joseph Smith, Jr. sends word at 8:00 am on the morning of November 1, 1838, for Mormon troops to surrender.

Thus with no more than twenty-two fatalities, the Mormon War of 1838, ended just eighty-eight days after it had began.

As a result of his forced surrender, Joseph Smith, Jr. faced the real possibility of losing control over his church. In an attempt to salvage his reputation as a prophet of God and further subjugate his followers, he would later callously write about the unfortunate events at Haun's Mill in a disparaging way. "Up to this day God had given me wisdom to save the people who took counsel. None had ever been killed who abode by my counsel."

I do not how any sane person could ever consider being killed in a massacre as part of a faith promoting experience, but current Church leaders still play upon the memory of past ghosts to emphasize just how important it is to always, without question, head the counsel of God's representative.

Escaping Justice

With one of Joseph's lawyers refusing to take part in the final solution authorized by Governor Lilburn W. Boggs and the other one refusing direct orders from General Lucas to execute prisoners following a court martial, Joseph Smith Jr. and his treasonous associates appear to have narrowly escaped the clutches of death.

On the eve of the Mormon surrender at Far West, Missouri, General Doniphan was ordered by General Lucas to take the Mormon prisoners to the center of town square and summarily execute them for treason.

> *You will take Joseph Smith and the other prisoners into the public square of Far West and shoot them at 9 o'clock tomorrow morning.*

Refusing on the grounds that Joseph and members of his Mormon militia were in fact not military officers, but private citizens, General Alexander William Doniphan replied:

> *It is cold-blooded murder. I will not obey your order. My brigade shall march for Liberty to-morrow morning, at 8 o'clock, and if you execute those men, I will hold you responsible before an earthly tribunal, so help me God!*

Disobeying a direct order from a superior officer could have had serious consequences for a solider regardless of his rank, but Alexander Doniphan was confident his course of action was the only moral choice he had. The next morning General Doniphan marched Joseph and approximately sixty other men to Richmond, where they were turned over to Judge Austin A. King to stand trial for their crimes.

A court of civil inquiry was convened on November 12, 1838. After seventeen days of reviewing the evidence and hearing testimony from a score of witnesses, all but six of the defendants were released for lack of sufficient evidence.

Concluding there was ample evidence to hold the prisoners for trial, Judge King remands Joseph Smith, Sidney Rigdon, Lyman Wight, Caleb Baldwin, Hyrum Smith and Alexander McRae to the jail in Liberty, Missouri, on November 29, 1838. Joseph was eventually indicted for his crimes in Daviess County on April 11, 1839. Generals Doniphan and Atchison once again came to his rescue by successfully petitioning the court for a change of venue.

En route to Boone County where the trial was scheduled to take place, Joseph and four other Mormons were allowed to escape custody on April 16, 1839.

As fate would have it, the arrest of Joseph Smith, Jr. on the charges of treason was quickly becoming a political nightmare for Governor Boggs. With all that was happening in the State of Missouri at that time, the escape of several key prisoners may very well have been the easiest way out of a very sticky situation. After all the civil unrest that had taken place leading up to the surrender at Far West and the subsequent arrest of militia officers, there is ample evidence to presume Governor Boggs was complicit in the escape of Joseph Smith. Historians may very well never uncover a direct chain of evidence linking Lilburn W. Boggs to any type of executive order which allowed the Prophet to escape custody, but he most likely looked the other way in a desperate attempt to put the entire mess behind him.

Facing expulsion from Missouri, Latter-day Saints reluctantly leave their homes behind to begin life anew. Assuming a guilty verdict would have been rendered in his trial, Joseph and his conspirators would most likely have served lengthy prison sentences, if not faced execution, for their acts of treason. And so another chapter of Mormon history comes to a close with Joseph Smith and his co-conspirators escaping prison and rejoining the remaining Saints who had already fled to Quincy, Illinois.

Fleeing in the face of danger yet again, it looked as if the promised land of Missouri could no longer offer safe harbor for the bewildered community of Latter-day Saints. Which undoubtedly left an unanswered question on the minds of Mormons everywhere. What was to become of their beloved Zion?

With more than one hundred forty active Temples dotting the globe and thirteen currently under construction with an additional sixteen more in the planning stages for a grand total of one hundred seventy, The Church of Jesus Christ of Latter-day Saints has yet to accomplish their original goal of building even a single temple in Independence or Far West, Missouri.

Only time will tell, but the immediate future does not look very promising for the Church or its millions of followers. Maybe one day Jesus Christ will return to embrace his chosen people as prophesied by Joseph Smith. In the meantime, Mormons worldwide wait for the appointed hour of Christ's triumphant return. Which brings up a further question.

How much longer will faithful Latter-day Saints willingly suffer the false prophecies of their beloved prophet?

Once again we are getting off track, so let us return to our story.

Mormon War of Illinois

Fleeing a tide of evil "persecution," a claim that was championed by the vast majority of Mormons who were forced to leave their homes and property in Missouri following the surrender of Church leaders at Far West, Missouri, droves of Latter-day Saints crossed over the Mississippi River into Illinois. Evicted from their homes by state militia, Mormons were once again on the move. Agreeing to leave the state as soon as weather permitted, a large portion of Latter-day Saints found temporary refuge in Quincy, Illinois.

Released from prison months before Joseph Smith and the remaining Mormon captives could maneuver their escape, Sidney Rigdon sought to procure a suitable parcel of land for Latter-day Saint refugees. Upon managing his escape, Joseph Smith fled to Commerce, Illinois, to rejoin his scattered flock. Reclaiming his mantle as Prophet, Seer and Revelator of the Latter-day Saints, Joseph Smith renamed the town "Nauvoo." Proclaiming the name meant "to be beautiful," Joseph set about organizing the city according to the "plat of Zion" he had created years earlier.

John C. Bennett, Quarter Master General of the Illinois State Militia, converted to Mormonism in the spring of 1840, and quickly became a close confidant of Joseph's. Using his considerable influence with the Illinois state legislature, Bennett would be instrumental in securing a charter for the city of Nauvoo. For his service John Bennett was rewarded by being elected the city's first mayor, named chancellor of the University of Nauvoo and was ordained as a member of the Church's First Presidency.

The City of Joseph was off to a roaring start. Within two years of Joseph's return to the helm, the city of Nauvoo had established a militia, a High Council, a University, several newspapers and had laid the cornerstone of the glorious Nauvoo Temple. This era marked an all-time high for the Mormon Church, but Latter-day Saints were not out of the woods just yet. As the population of Saints grew in Illinois, an underlying wave of mistrust also began to rise among non-Mormons. Wait just a minute! It seems like we have been here before. Oh, it must be déjà vu.

Once again non-Mormons in adjacent towns felt Joseph Smith held too much power and just as before, the old custom of Mormon bloc-voting was infuriating. Coincidentally the accusations levied against the Mormon community appeared to be justified and of course the resentments of settlers outside of the Mormon faith were not entirely without foundation. On numerous occasions Missouri courts attempted to extradite Joseph on a list of charges stemming from the Mormon War of 1838. Each time an arrest was made, Joseph compelled the Nauvoo Municipal Court to issue a writ of habeas corpus.

As long as Joseph Smith, Jr. wielded the power to force his release, justice would never be served. Of course his followers did not see it in quite the same way. They believed it was the hand of God sparing their beloved Prophet through divine intervention. Joseph was not the only Latter-day Saint to benefit from such blatant legal maneuvers. Essentially all of Joseph Smith followers were exempt from prosecution, unless a Mormon tribunal found a church member at fault. It was only with the approval of the Prophet that a Mormon living under his protection would be arrested by a non-Mormon court.

> *In the winter of 1843-4, the common council passed some further ordinances to protect their leaders from arrest, on demand from Missouri. They enacted that no writ issued from any other place than Nauvoo, for the arrest of any person in it, should be executed in the city, without an approval endorsed thereon by the mayor; that if any public officer, by virtue of any foreign writ, should attempt to make an arrest in the city, without such approval of his process, he should be subject to imprisonment for life, and that the governor of the State should not have the power of pardoning the offender without the consent of the mayor. When these ordinances were published, they created general astonishment. Many people began to believe in good earnest that the Mormons were about to set up a separate government for themselves in defiance of the laws of the State.*
>
> *Gov. Thomas Ford, History of Illinois from Its Commencement as a State in 1818 to 1847, S. C. Griggs & Co., 1854, page 320*

Clearly Joseph Smith and his High Council had taken their liberal use of political power way too far. For a mayor to presume to dictate the limits of power a sitting governor can exercise, is not only unconscionably arrogant, but borderline psychotic. Although Governor Ford did uphold the Nauvoo court's decisions to deny extradition as legal, the Mormon abuse of power did not go unnoticed. As non-Mormons began to clamor about this serious subversion of judiciary power by Nauvoo courts, internal dissent crept into the Church's highest office.

William Law, Second Counselor in the First Presidency, was summarily dismissed from his position within the Church because his wife Jane Law had refused the sexual advances of Joseph Smith. Jane claimed the Prophet had "asked her to give him half her love; she was at liberty to keep the other half for her husband." Remaining faithful to Mormonism for the remainder of his life, William knew from that moment forward Joseph was at best a fallen prophet and at worst a servant of Satan.

Seeking to expose Joseph's deceit to his faithful followers, William Law and a small group of Latter-day Saints published the first and only issue of the *Nauvoo Expositor* on June 7, 1844. The newspaper criticized Joseph Smith on three points:

1. Smith had once been a true prophet, but had fallen because of his introduction of plural marriage, exaltation and other controversial ideas to Mormon doctrine.
2. As church president and Nauvoo mayor, Smith held too much power and desired to create a theocracy.
3. Smith was corrupting young women by forcing or coercing them into the practice of plural marriage.

Within days Joseph Smith voted with the Nauvoo City Council to destroy the printing press on the grounds Law and his group were spreading libelous slander. At 8:00 pm on June 10, 1844, the city marshal carried out Joseph Smith's illegal order. By violating a simple process such as freedom of the press, a sovereign right guaranteed by the Illinois State Constitution, the out-of-control autocrat signed his own death warrant.

For the next few days, Nauvoo courts had a field day fending off warrants issued for Joseph's arrest. Writs of habeas corpus were used to protect Smith from prosecution, until Joseph declared martial law on June 18, 1844. Calling up the Nauvoo Legion, Joseph commanded a force of five thousand men to protect him.

Governor Ford, who had previously sided with the Nauvoo courts, proposed the Prophet surrender himself for trial by a non-Mormon jury to be held at the county seat of Carthage. Governor Thomas Ford personally guaranteed the safety and well-being of Joseph Smith, Hyrum Smith and the fifteen other city council members who had been charged with inciting a riot.

Planning to flee Nauvoo, Illinois, to avoid arrest, Joseph Smith reluctantly changed his mind after receiving word his followers were beginning to criticize him for once again attempting to outrun prosecution. On June 25, 1844, a disheartened Joseph surrendered to constable William Bettisworth on the lesser charge of inciting a riot. Immediately upon their arrival at Carthage, Illinois, Joseph and his brother Hyrum Smith were charged with the crime of treason for declaring martial law.

Pending trial the fifteen city council members were each released on $500 bond, but the judge had other plans for the Mormon Prophet and his brother. Joseph and Hyrum were to be held in jail until they could be tried for the capital offense of treason.

Playing a dangerous game of cat and mouse, Joseph believed he would be free within days of his surrender. Otherwise the Mormon Prophet would never have given up so easily. On the day of his death one of Joseph's jailers expressed concern about an approaching mob. Smith causally calmed him saying, "Don't trouble yourself... they've come to rescue me."

Unfortunately for Joseph Smith, that was not the case.

Late in the afternoon of June 27, 1844, Joseph Smith and his brother Hyrum lay dead from bullet wounds, yet the battle was not so one sided. Joseph had shot and wounded three of his assailants with a small pistol he had concealed in his vest. Hyrum was shot in the face and died in his jail cell. After emptying his pistol Joseph attempted to escape by jumping from the jailhouse window, but his luck had finally run out.

American Prophet, Polygamist and Presidential Candidate, Joseph Smith, Jr. was shot twice in the back and once in the chest as he fell to the ground below. The death of their beloved Prophet was just the tip of the iceberg. Reeling from a devastating loss, the Saints would once again be put to the test.

Throughout the state of Illinois, Latter-day Saints were reviled. Once more there was talk of casting the religious sect out of the state. Opposition to a continued Mormon presence grew, especially in the towns of Warsaw and Carthage. The resulting conflict soon escalated into the Mormon War of Illinois.

Mainly instigated by the Carthage Greys, a militia unit blamed for the murder of slain Mormon leaders, more than one hundred twenty-five homes were put to the flame. Several hundred armed Mormon men searched the county for those responsible, but they found not a single soul to arrest or do battle with.

It appears lawlessness was the flavor of the month.

Governor Ford finally authorized General Hardin to raise a force of three hundred fifty men and ordered him to suppress the fighting. The ravages of Mormons were put in check and the fugitive anti-Mormon mobs were sent scurrying. Still, all was not well in the state of Illinois. At least one man was killed with absolutely no provocation. Franklin Worrell, the person in charge of Carthage Jail the day Joseph and Hyrum Smith were killed, was assassinated by some coward hiding in a wooded thicket.

Late in September of 1844, Governor Ford ordered military commanders in the town of Quincy to march toward Hancock County. Ford had received word the people of Hancock were assembling for a fall "wolf hunt." With his suspicion aroused, Governor Ford felt the term wolf hunt was a coded message with a much more sinister meaning. Fearing an attack on Mormons, he saw the necessity of ordering out troops. Under Governor Ford's authority the Quincy Riflemen marched for Hancock County.

When the Illinois state legislature met next in December of 1844, there was an overwhelming call to repeal the charter for the city of Nauvoo which had been granted only a few years earlier. Conceding the Mormons had severely abused their chartered power, Governor Ford still urged the state legislature to amend the original document and not dissolve it completely. He feared they could not survive without some form of legal protection.

In a landslide decision, the State of Illinois landed a devastating blow to the Mormon community. Passing the House and Senate with a majority vote in favor of repeal, the city of Nauvoo officially had their charter revoked on January 29, 1844.

By the winter of 1845, it was quite evident it was not possible to achieve a peaceful accord with the antagonist locals. Accepting there would be no end to the constant fighting, Church leaders negotiated a truce with their opponents. This short lull in the fighting gave Latter-day Saints the much needed time to prepare for their departure. Abandoning the city of Nauvoo, Illinois, to the wolves, Brigham Young and an advanced vanguard company headed toward their final destination in February of 1846.

Mormon Battalion

In a strategic move to gain much needed supplies and money, Brigham Young offered the services of nearly five hundred sixty church members to fight in the Mexican-American war. The impetus for his decision was a simple matter of necessity, the Saints were in desperate need of money to purchase supplies for their exodus from Illinois. Brigham Young allowed one hand to wash the other as he called upon political connections to achieve his goals. With the aid of political allies, secret negations were entered into as Church President Brigham Young bartered with U.S. President James Polk to create an all Mormon military unit.

Although the mutually beneficial alliance entered into by James Polk and Brigham Young solved an immediate financial need, the long-term political capital gained cannot be overlooked. Both were equally important to the survival of the Church. In a self-serving letter to Latter-day Saints, Brigham Young called for volunteers to serve the needs of the Church.

> *The United States wants our friendship, the President wants to do us good and secure our confidence. The outfit of this five hundred men costs us nothing, and their pay will be sufficient to take their families over the mountains. There is war between Mexico and the United States, to whom California must fall a prey, and if we are the first settlers the old citizens cannot have a Hancock or Missouri pretext to mob the Saints. The thing is from above for our own good.*
>
> *B. H. Roberts, The Mormon Battalion: Its History and Achievements, Desert News, 1919, page 18*

The Mormon Battalion, as they later came to be known, volunteered one full year of service from July 1846, until July 1847, in exchange for roughly $24,000 which was given over to the LDS Church's general fund. Technically the money was paid to each enlisted man as a uniform allowance — paid in advance, however President James Polk allowed the Mormon Battalion to wear civilian clothes during their military service. Hence the money was allocated to Brigham Young and used to fund the westward migration of Latter-day Saints into what would eventually become the Utah Territory.

In addition to the uniform allowance, each volunteer was paid an annual salary as well as being supplied with a musket and four rifles, which each man was allowed to keep at the end of their service. The strategy of Brigham Young appeared to be a financial windfall for the struggling Latter-day Saints. Not only had the

Church collected a very tidy bounty, courtesy of the U.S. Treasury, to cover expenses for the impending move west, but the salaries of the Mormon Battalion fetched nearly another $30,000 over the next year in hard currency. Funding which was sorely needed for the LDS exodus from Illinois.

Finally The Church of Jesus Christ of Latter-day Saints, through shrewd negotiations, had garnered some positive public relations and had succeeded in arming more than five hundred Mormon men with the latest military weapons available.

Utah War

A mere four years prior to the bloodshed of the American Civil War where Union and Confederate armies clashed in armed conflict — a war fought between brothers and neighbors which pitted the Northern states against the political and economic ideologies of the Southern states, there occurred in the newly formed Utah Territory a clash between U.S. military forces and members of the Nauvoo Legion.

After years of struggle, yet another armed offensive arose involving Mormon militia. This time U.S. troops were rallied in a call to arms. The Utah War, also known as the Mormon Rebellion and Buchannan's Blunder, was an armed conflict between Mormon settler's under the command of Brigham Young and nearly one third of the entire U.S. Army. Lasting from May 1857, on through July of 1858. While no official battles were recorded their were several raids and even a couple of cold-blooded massacres.

Mormon strategy for engaging the enemy was a classic approach, ripped straight from the pages of "Guerrilla Warfare: 101." John Taylor, next in line for the Mormon Presidency, was instructed to harass the enemy with surprise attacks at night, so they could not sleep or rest comfortably. Another tactic used by Taylor and his band of guerrillas was to set the grasslands ablaze when U.S. troops were caught with the wind against them, in hopes the fire would engulf their forces. Livestock in the camps were purposefully stampeded and wagons set on fire in the ensuing confusion. By and large the Latter-day Saint combatants were fairly successful in hindering U.S. troops from receiving supplies while remaining hidden from their enemy.

Mormons certainly were familiar with armed resistance and warfare against their would be oppressors. Surely there must be more to the story than meets the eye. What pieces of the puzzle are we missing? Latter-day Saint historians would have you believe minions of Satan have stalked and tried to eradicate God's faithful servants since the time of Joseph Smith's first vision. Their revisionist history suggests every action taken by Mormon Saints was either at God's direction or a necessary step to avoid their total destruction by the forces of "evil." Not once has The Church of Jesus Christ of Latter-day Saints admitted culpability for years of destruction and bloodshed.

By now I am sure you are asking the same questions I did. Why another war and why now? And of course, I am sure you want to know how it all started. Let us continue on with the story as we peruse the final chapter in the 19th century Mormon War.

Years earlier U.S. President Millard Fillmore had appointed the Mormon Prophet Brigham Young as the governor of the Utah Territory, yet it did not take long before Young and his associates were at odds with federal appointees not of their choosing. Having anyone other than Church authorities govern the people of Utah was an affront to their concept of a theocratic rule. The Church of Jesus Christ of Latter-day Saints fully intended to establish the Political Kingdom of God and rule by their own authority.

A common belief held by many American citizens living in the Eastern United States was the Mormon settlers of Utah were ruled by a religious tyrant who used the power of the Danites to enforce his will and subjugate his followers. This view was particularly popular on Capitol Hill and as a matter of fact the notion was not without some merit.

High ranking members of the Latter-day Saint community, which were essentially the small body of ruling elite who ran the Church, supported Brigham Young in his defiance of U.S. policy. Young and his cohorts had for years maintained a separate regime and a functioning government in a land Mormons called Zion. God's second prophet of the Mormon Church was quite happy to masquerade as lord of his own little fiefdom, Brother Young had no intention of surrendering his political kingdom.

So now we come to the crux of the matter. Two key issues that came to the forefront of the 1856 Presidential Elections were polygamy and popular sovereignty. Democratic candidate James Buchanan campaigned heavily against polygamy and like many other east-coast politicians, was appalled at the idea a theocratic government could exist within the borders of a U.S. territory.

All of the stories and rumors coming out of the American West eventually came to a boiling point when supreme court justice William Drummond, assigned to the Utah Territory, tendered his letter of resignation on March 30, 1857. Justice Drummond asserted the Mormon Church, ruled by their Prophet, had negated and set aside the constitutional law of the land in favor of their own interpretation of God's will. He went on to further state there was nary a male soul who acknowledged any authority except that of the LDS priesthood.

Justice William Drummond levied a number of substantial charges against the Mormon Church including murder, destruction of federal court records and harassment of federal officials. Drummond concluded his letter with an appeal for newly sworn in President Buchanan to appoint a Governor who was not a member of the Mormon Church to oversee the Utah Territory. His final request was for the President also to send a detachment of military troops to enforce the transition of power.

By mid April military troops were gathered together for use in the upcoming Utah Expedition. Although assembled and ready for marching orders, the first wave of soldiers did not depart from Fort Leavenworth, Kansas, until June of 1857. Rumors that Brigham Young had been replaced as governor spread quickly among the community of Saints, but no official word had reached Salt Lake City. Adding to their growing apprehension of a military intervention, Brigham Young himself announced to a gathering of Latter-day Saints an army was approaching Utah.

Continued exaggerated reports and widespread rumors fueled a number of President Buchanan's faulty decisions, including declaring Utah was in an active state of rebellion against the government of the United States. Lack of communication on both sides greatly hampered any possibility of a peaceful resolution. As a result of reports from forward scouts, Brigham Young ordered all able bodied men between the ages of fifteen and sixty to fulfill their duty and enlist as part of the Nauvoo Legion.

While vacillating between all out war or a calculated retreat, Young ordered Daniel Wells, commanding officer of the Mormon militia, to engage in delaying tactics as long as possible. By harassing soldiers Brigham Young hoped to hamper the movement of federal troops long enough to enter into negotiations with key members of Buchanan's administration.

Apostle Heber C. Kimball remarks what a blessing it would be for the people of Utah if the wagons and cattle arrived in the territory alone and without troops. On August 2, 1857, Brigham Young openly discusses with Latter-day Saints the possibility of their Mormon theocracy seceding from the United States in order to establish an independent kingdom. Brigham Young, President of The Church of Jesus Christ of Latter-day Saints, declares martial law on August 5, 1857. Disregarding all manner of civility and throwing caution to the wind, Apostle Heber C. Kimball jumps right smack into the center of the fray by issuing a curse against President James Buchanan and openly calls for his death.

While en route to Salt Lake City to deliver a letter to the Mormon Prophet Brigham Young, ordering him to prepare accommodations and to provide supplies for the troops when they arrive, Army Captain Stewart Van Vliet receives word his small escort of men are in danger from Mormon raiders. Deciding discretion is the greater part of valor, Van Vliet arrives in Salt Lake City alone and without escort on the eve of September 8, 1857.

Although Captain Stewart Van Vliet was known among the Latter-day saints as a man of his word, Brigham Young fearing a similar fate as former Mormon Prophet Joseph Smith, Jr. rejected the premise that the Army's only mission was to maintain peace during the transition of power. Captain Van Vliet quickly realized the requested supplies would not be made available as the resentful Mormon leader could not be convinced of the Army's peaceful intentions. Before taking his leave, Captain Van Vliet promised Brigham Young he would stop the Utah Expedition on his own authority. Upon rejoining the Army, Captain Stewart Van Vliet reported the Mormon resolve was so strong they were prepared to burn their homes and crops before letting any soldier or officer benefit from their hard work

All the while declaring Mormons had no desire for war, Brigham Young proclaimed he would not allow a new governor nor federal officers to enter Utah. The day following Van Vliet's departure from Salt Lake City, the Mormon Prophet again declares martial law on September 15, 1857. Why declare martial law twice? To better understand Young's motives, we need to back track just a few days to September 11, 1857.

Just prior to the horror of September 11th, Brigham Young discusses the need for the Mormon Kingdom of God to secede from the United States. While addressing a crowd he announces:

> *I shall not go in for anything half-way. We must have the kingdom of God, or nothing. We are not to be overthrown.*
>
> *Journal of Discourses Delivered by President Brigham Young, His Two Counselors, the Twelve Apostles and Others, Vol. 5, Published by Asa Calkin, Liverpool, 1858, page 168*

Playing upon the frayed emotions of his followers, Brigham Young excites Latter-day Saints to an all-time fevered pitch. Less than two weeks later, the greatest atrocity of the Utah War was committed by a band of Mormons disguised as Paiute Indians.

A wagon train of relatively wealthy individuals were on their way to California when they stopped near Salt Lake City to restock their supplies during the month of August. Most wagon trains of the time would stopover in Salt Lake City to resupply and graze cattle as they headed west. Members of the Baker-Fancher wagon train continued south past the Mormon settlements of Parowan and Cedar City. Although they were peacefully passing through the territory and were hundreds of miles from Salt Lake City, officers in the Mormon militia held several meetings to decide how they would enforce Brigham Young's declaration of martial law. During a weekly High Council meeting following church services on Sunday, September 6, 1857, a plan to create a Native American type of massacre was announced. Not all in attendance voiced their support.

Following the High Council meeting, Stake President Isaac C. Haight sent a message to John D. Lee. The contents of that message will forever remain a mystery, but it does not take a genius to follow a chain of events. The next day the Baker-Fancher party was ambushed at Mountain Meadows by men disguised as Paiute Indians. Fighting back members of the Baker-Fancher party chained their wagons together and dug trenches to withstand the attack. A siege lasting four days ensued. Seven people were killed in the initial attack with several others wounded.

Under the guise of friendship two militia members rode into the besieged camp displaying a white flag on September 11, 1857. John D. Lee accompanied the two men into the camp and explained he was a Native American agent. He went on to tell the Baker-Fancher party, a truce had been negotiated with the Paiute tribe and Mormon militia would protect them as all members of the party were escorted to safety. Following an agreement to be guarded, each of the men in the wagon party were separated and paired with an armed militia escort.

Unbeknownst to the helpless members of the Baker-Fancher party, they had been duped by the Mormons and instead of being lead to safety were marching straight to their death. Playing the role of protector, the armed militia escort waited until a predetermined signal was given when then turned and mercilessly killed all the male members of the Baker-Fancher party.

The remaining women and children were quickly ambushed by militia men hiding in nearby ravines. One hundred twenty innocent souls lost their lives on that awful day. Of the murdered victims, only seventeen children all too young to tell of the horror they had just witnessed were spared. Oaths of silence were taken by all of the men who planned and participated in the bloody massacre. Sadly justice was never served upon those cowardly, despicable men who committed this ghastly atrocity.

Quickly following the horrific events of the September 11th Mountain Meadows Massacre, Mormon militia once again were the protagonist with the so-called Aiken Massacre occurring in October of 1857.

Barely one month had passed since the unprovoked attack upon the Baker-Fancher wagon train left a trail of blood and one hundred twenty men, women and children lying lifeless. Perpetrating another ruse upon innocent travelers, not unlike the tactic used on the Baker-Fancher party, six Californians travelling through the Utah territory were arrested as spies for the U.S. Army. Lulled into a false sense of safety by their release, the unsuspecting travelers are quickly hunted down and murdered in cold-blood.

If you are searching for a reason to explain these heinous crimes, look no farther than pure profit as a motive. What do both massacres have in common? Just like the Mountain Meadows Massacre, those poor souls slain in the Aiken Massacre had all of their possessions stolen. I do not find it a coincidence at all that livestock were taken by Mormons and a large amount of personal property ended up at the Bishop's storehouse in Cedar City where it was auctioned off to local Mormons.

With blood stained hands the Nauvoo Legion proved to be equally ruthless. Using guerrilla-style maneuvers, Lot Smith of the Nauvoo Legion leads his men in an attack as they descend upon U.S. Army supply wagons. Fifty-two wagons and supplies belonging to civilian outfitters were torched. No compensation was every made for the loss.

Tensions appeared to be cooling down as winter set in, but by March of 1858, Brigham Young again implements a scorched earth policy. Saints were ordered to move to Provo, Utah, and prepare to burn their homes.

President Buchanan grants a general amnesty to all who will abide by the authority of the government. With the arrival of the Army in Salt Lake City, Brigham Young finally surrenders the title of governor to Alfred Cumming.

And so the Mormon Wars come to an end.

Bending to Political Pressure

Signed into law by Abraham Lincoln, 16th President of the United States, on July 8, 1862, the Morrill Anti-Bigamy Act specifically targeted the objectionable Mormon practice of plural marriage. Not only did it target individual adherents of polygamy, but it also targeted the real estate property holdings of the Church by limiting church and non-profit ownership in any territory of the United States to $50,000.

Later amended and strengthened by the Edmonds Act of 1882, and again reinforced in 1887, by the Edmonds-Tucker Act, the Morrill Anti-Bigamy Act was the first strike against the Church's long standing religious practice of polygamy. While it would appear the party was over, it was not quite that simple.

With enhanced legislative powers, in hand, to legally suppress and prosecute polygamous practices throughout the United States, President Lincoln made a bold political move. Entirely unprecedented and unheard of at that time, Lincoln agreed not to enforce the Morrill Anti-Bigamy Act if Brigham Young and the growing Mormon militia, including all male members of the Church would not become involved in the escalating Civil War.

Federal forces stationed at Fort Douglas, Utah, under the command of General Patrick Edward Connor, were given explicit orders not to confront the Mormon Saints over this or any other issue. With a nod and a wink, a savvy political agreement essentially prolonged the Latter-day Saint practice of plural marriage for another few decades — but Mormon polygamists were not out of the woods just yet. The Civil War would end, a new President would be elected and Congress would once again renew its moral objection to the practice of plural marriage.

With the Edmonds Act of 1882, which made polygamy within the U.S. and its territories a felony, bolstered and strengthened by the passing of the Edmonds-Tucker Act of 1887, the LDS Church was in peril of losing a considerable amount of wealth. Beginning with the indictment of George Reynolds on October 23, 1874, more than one thousand three hundred Latter-day Saints were arrested, convicted and sentenced to imprisonment in Utah's penitentiary for polygamy and or unlawful cohabitation. Any man convicted of plural marriage would lose their right to vote and hold political office. Women were typically not prosecuted.

Under pressure from U.S. law makers, Latter-day Saints began pleading with Church President Wilford Woodruff to make concessions in regards to the principle of celestial marriage. Prior to his death in 1844, Joseph Smith, Jr. warned the membership of his church further trials and tribulations would appear and to hold fast — to prove faithful to God's commands — lest He find others to carry on His work. Despite the forewarning by their beloved prophet, the intense mounting pressure seemed almost too much for some of the faithful to bear. Some members of the LDS Church, in order to remain safe from impending prison sentences, were signing oaths stating they had no belief in, would not support and did not practice plural marriage. An estimated nine hundred priesthood holders signed such oaths.

Regardless of the amount or intensity of the pressure exerted on Latter-day Saints to abandon the contemptible practice of polygamy, a few steadfast members risked their freedom and property in support of the principle of celestial marriage. Lorenzo Snow, a member of the Quorum of the Twelve Apostles — the ruling body of The Church of Jesus Christ of Latter-day Saints — was indicted, convicted and sentenced under the Edmonds Act. Sentenced on January 16, 1886 to eighteen months imprisonment and fined nine hundred dollars, Lorenzo Snow was the highest-ranking member of the Church to be convicted of ploygamy.

Appearing in the First District Court of Ogden, Utah, on behalf of the United States, assistant U.S. district attorney Victor Beirbower declared, "The defendant Mr. Snow was the most scholarly and brightest light of the Apostles." Mr. Bierbower further predicted, "a new revelation would soon follow changing the Divine law of celestial marriage."

> *Whatever fame Mr. Bierbower may have secured as a lawyer, he certainly will fail as a prophet. The severest prosecutions have never been followed by revelations changing a divine law, obedience to which brought imprisonment or martyrdom. Though I go to prison, God will not change His law of Celestial Marriage. But the man, the people, the nation, that oppose and fight against this doctrine and the Church of God, will be overthrown.*
>
> *The Millennial Star 48:111*

Yet, as we all know, eventually The Church of Jesus Christ of Latter-day Saints did indeed cave to political pressure and certainly did abolish their long standing practice of polygamy. Even though we know where this is leading, let's not jump too far ahead in our commentary. So once again, the story continues...

Wielding the Edmonds-Tucker Act of 1887, as their primary weapon in the fight against the LDS Church, congress began to use the court system to punishment those who continued practicing polygamy. Attorneys for the United States argued their second case related to the Mormon practice of polygamy before the Supreme Court of the United States on January 16, 1889.

In the end, a trial which lasted two days concluded with The Church of Jesus Christ of Latter-day Saints being officially disincorporated. Stripped of their corporate status and any protection associated with legal incorporation, the fate of the Mormon Church appeared tenuous at best. As a result of the Supreme Court's decision, a great deal of the Church's wealth and property was in jeopardy of being confiscated. The estimated seizure of real property would have amounted to more than three million dollars. The Church of Jesus Christ of Latter-day Saints was now facing a very real crisis.

By the end of August of 1889, Church President Wilford Woodruff received verification the U.S. Government did in fact intend to seize and confiscate Mormon temples as authorized by the Edmonds-Tucker Act. Further legislation would have targeted the personal property of Church members as well as all of the tangible assets held in trust by the Church. The Church's financial interests quickly became the primary focus with matters of faith taking a back-seat.

On May 19, 1890, the Supreme Court upheld the Edmonds-Tucker Act and the prior decision to dissolve the incorporation of the LDS Church. Although the ruling clearly authorized the courts to confiscate its property, the U.S Attorney for the Territory of Utah reportedly only seized $381,812 in assets — leaving most, if not all, of the real property including Temples, in the Mormon Church's possession. Within months of the high court's ruling, Wilford Woodruff, President of The Church of Jesus Christ of Latter-day Saints, issued the 1890 Manifesto banning the future practice of polygamy.

To Whom It May Concern:

Press dispatches having been sent for political purposes, from Salt Lake City, which have been widely published, to the effect that the Utah Commission, in their recent report to the Secretary of the Interior, allege that plural marriages are still being solemnized and that forty or more such marriages have been contracted in Utah since last June or during the past year, also that in public discourses the leaders of the Church have taught, encouraged and urged the continuance of the practice of polygamy—

I, therefore, as President of The Church of Jesus Christ of Latter-day Saints, do hereby, in the most solemn manner, declare that these charges are false. We are not teaching polygamy or plural marriage, nor permitting any person to enter into its practice, and I deny that either forty or any other number of plural marriages have during that period been solemnized in our Temples or in any other place in the Territory.

One case has been reported, in which the parties allege that the marriage was performed in the Endowment House, in Salt Lake City, in the Spring of 1889, but I have not been able to learn who performed the ceremony; whatever was done in this matter was without my knowledge. In consequence of this alleged occurrence the Endowment House was, by my instructions, taken down without delay.

Inasmuch as laws have been enacted by Congress forbidding plural marriages, which laws have been pronounced constitutional by the court of last resort, I hereby declare my intention to submit to those laws, and to use my influence with the members of the Church over which I preside to have them do likewise.

There is nothing in my teachings to the Church or in those of my associates, during the time specified, which can be reasonably

> *construed to inculcate or encourage polygamy; and when any Elder of the Church has used language which appeared to convey any such teaching, he has been promptly reproved. And I now publicly declare that my advice to the Latter-day Saints is to refrain from contracting any marriage forbidden by the law of the land.*
>
> *Wilford Woodruff*
> *President of The Church of Jesus Christ of Latter-day Saints.*

Despite the inevitable action taken by the Mormon Prophet, to safeguard church property from being confiscated by the U.S. Government, Wilford Woodruff unfalteringly professed until the day he died, that he did in fact receive a vision in which the Lord placed before him two choices.

1. Stand for the law and let the Gentiles and government confiscate both Church and individual property, and leave the battle for the Lord to fight.
2. Issue the Manifesto, hold on to the property, but open the way for whoredom and destruction among the people, the result of rejecting the perfect law of social conduct.

Whether the Latter-day Saint prophet lacked the faith of his own convictions or simply knew the Mormon teaching of celestial marriage was wrong, the world may never know. What we do know is President Woodruff did not "leave the battle for the Lord to fight," but instead chose to protect the property of the church. With that decision the divinely inspired law of celestial marriage as practiced by members of the Mormon Church was doomed. Based on Wilford Woodruff's decision, the world can clearly bear witness to exactly what the leaders of The Church of Jesus Christ of Latter-day Saints valued and held sacred.

In the end it seems as if financial security won the day.

> *I have arrived at a point in the history of my life as the President of The Church of Jesus Christ of Latter-day Saints where I am under the necessity of acting for the temporal salvation of the Church. The United States Government has taken a stand and passed laws to destroy the Latter-day Saints on the subject of polygamy, or patriarchal order of marriage, and after praying to the Lord and FEELING INSPIRED, I have issued the following proclamation which is sustained by my counselors and the Twelve Apostles.*
>
> *Journal Entry, Sept. 25, 1890*
> *Scott G. Kenney, Editor, Wilford Woodruff's Journal 1833 - 1898: Typescript, Volume 9, Signature Books, 1985*

Published by Wilford Woodruff in the church owned newspaper, the Deseret Weekly, the Manifesto which called for an end to polygamy was made public in its entirety prior to being voted on by Church members. Although there was no doubt the Manifesto was issued by LDS Church President, Wilford Woodruff a voice of dissent still seemed to linger in the air.

> *Whatever is done by the Church, or its leaders, or its members, should always be done in this spirit. Be sure you are right, then go ahead. Never mind what the world may say or do. Never think to gain their favor by yielding to their requirements. When a thing is right, do it. When it is wrong, or unwise, refrain from it. Let the wicked rage. Let the heathen imagine vain things. But be not swerved to the right or the left by what they may howl, nor think for a moment that they will ever be satisfied.*
>
> *Deseret News, Oct. 4, 1890*

Despite all of the controversy surrounding the publication of his proclamation, Wilford Woodruff's 1890 Manifesto calling for the end of plural marriage was formally accepted by unanimous vote and sustained by the presiding General Authorities and the church membership as a whole on October 6, 1890 during the 60th General Conference of the Church held in Salt Lake City.

The Church's relationship with the U.S. Government continually improved from that point forward. Raids on Mormon settlements ceased and polygamy as well as the act of cohabitation was severely restricted, especially in the Utah territory, but the practice would continue into the 20th century. Church property was returned in 1893, the Utah Territory was allowed to continue its pursuit of statehood and the Mormon Church's People's Party was disbanded, with the anticipation of bringing Utah politics into alignment with those of the already established national political system.

A further benefit to and for members of the LDS Church was President Grover Cleveland issued a general pardon in 1894, to all Mormon men not actively engaged in the practice of polygamy.

Identifying consistent patterns is a useful tool that is often employed when a researcher is attempting to decipher fact from fiction. Writers are often confronted with urban mythology, which makes our job all the more difficult. To be objective, a good writer must separate the chaff from the wheat before they can discover the kernel of truth.

One of the most intriguing patterns to be found in early LDS teachings revolved around the often repudiated practice, or as faithful Mormons would contend the non-practice, of polygamy. Consider this for a moment. Polygamy as a practice was encouraged among the elite of the Church — its de facto "inner circle" of powerful men. If the divine law of celestial marriage was a key element of salvation and a requirement for entry into the Celestial Kingdom, then why was it not practiced openly by the majority of Latter-day Saints instead of being reserved for the elite?

Also let us consider, when Church President Wilford Woodruff issued the 1890 Manifesto he did not end polygamy, but merely wanted to give the appearance The Church of Jesus Christ of Latter-day Saints was abandoning the practice. This was done for two primary reasons:

1. To gain political favor with the U.S. Congress.
2. The Church of Jesus Christ of Latter-day Saints never officially renounced polygamy.

Now before everyone gets bent out of shape and starts calling me all kinds of nasty, vile names, give me an opportunity to explain my previous statement.

As we have already discovered, the only reason President Woodruff issued the Manifesto of 1890, was to save the Mormon Church's considerable wealth and property. By giving into the demands of congress, the LDS Church had in fact gained some very valuable political capital it hoped to spend in the very near future. Let us not forget, leading authorities of the Church never intended to eradicate the principle of celestial marriage from their theological beliefs, but it was no longer prudent to flaunt it in open defiance of U.S. Law. So polygamy had to go underground until it could be safely reintroduced, at a not too distant time, when Saints would be allowed to freely practice the law of celestial marriage without legal repercussions.

You see, the cold hard fact is Mormonism still to this day teaches polygamy is a sacred contract not only condoned, but ordained by God. One of the basic doctrines of their faith is, and will continue to be, the plurality of marriage. Faithful members of the Church eagerly await the day and time they can reclaim this blessed covenant. All members of the LDS Church who have received their endowment in a Mormon temple believe with their heart and soul they will one day be blessed to practice the principle of celestial marriage — if not in this life, then surely when they enter the heavenly Kingdom of God.

Compromise and Concession

Despite Brigham Young's relentless efforts to achieve statehood, his beloved Utah Territory was never admitted into the Union during his lifetime. With Congress breathing down their neck on the issue of polygamy, the LDS Church was quickly losing ground on Capitol Hill. Surrendering the sacred ordinance of celestial marriage was just the first in a series of political concessions that would be demanded of The Church of Jesus Christ of Latter-day Saints before the Territory of Utah would eventually be allowed to enter the Union as the 45th State.

With the First Presidency of the Church caving under the enormous pressure being exerted upon them by governmental agencies, a great many of the hopes and dreams of loyal and faithful Latter-day Saints were in danger of being obliterated. Would God continue to bless his chosen people if they would not stand their ground and fight for their beliefs? As long as Latter-day Saints cowered before the shadows cast by the long arm of the law, they had no hope of establishing the great City of Zion. Giving up even a portion of their religious rites was by far the greatest compromise Latter-day Saints were forced to endure.

President Wilford Woodruff's willingness to concede to political pressure by calling for the end of plural marriage as a religious sacrament signaled the beginning of the second great crisis of the Mormon faith. What new indignities would their "evil" tormenters next force upon God's faithful servants?

The apparent willingness of the Church to abandon their flock in this great time of need was very unsettling for a number of members. By caving in to political pressure, the General Authorities essentially placed members of their faith directly under the yoke of their "ungodly" oppressors. Latter-day Saints who felt betrayed broke away from those who did not have the stomach to obey

God's commandments, which resulted in the second largest schism in the history of the The Church of Jesus Christ of Latter-day Saints. Why had divinely appointed church leaders forsaken the eternal salvation of its valiant members?

In an effort to safeguard its coffers and stave off further loss of wealth and property The Church of Jesus Christ of Latter-day Saints gave up the practice of polygamy and for no other reason. Of course that was not the only hurdle Church leaders would encounter in their race to achieve statehood. Between October of 1890, and March of 1895, no less than seven major obstacles had to be dealt with before Congress would even consider passing the Enabling Act of 1894, which allowed Utah to join the Union as the 45th State. Church authorities had finally ceded power over the Utah Territory. All that remained was for the people of Utah to vote on delegates for a Constitutional Convention and to draft a new State Constitution.

Believing old wounds were finally healing, U. S. President Grover Cleveland made a colossal blunder when he pardoned all Mormon men who had earlier been disqualified to vote because of their practice of polygamy. The vote for constitutional delegates heavily favored Mormons over those not of the faith. No less than four Latter-day Saint Apostles were elected to the body of one hundred seven men, while only twenty-eight elected delegates were non-members. Republicans heavily outnumbered Democrats, but at least the process was underway.

Three of the seven existing roadblocks to statehood had previously been addressed. The Church had publicly repudiated the practice of polygamy, although we know they continued practicing plural marriage secretly, they also had disbanded the Church run political party a few years earlier and free public schools were no longer an issue. Despite Brigham Young's rally against establishing a system of free education for the children of

Utah a decade earlier, the Edmonds-Tucker Act of 1887, wrested control of secular education from the clutches of the Mormon Church's hierarchy in July of 1890.

> *Many of you may have heard what certain journalists have had to say about Brigham Young being opposed to free schools. I am opposed to free education as much as I am opposed to taking away property from one man and giving it to another who knows not how to take care of it.*
>
> *...Would I encourage free schools by taxation? No! That is not in keeping with the nature of our work;*
>
> *Journal of Discourses by President Brigham Young, His Counselors, and the Twelve Apostles, Vol. 18, Published by Joseph F. Smith, Liverpool, 1877, page 357*

Despite the Mormon hierarchy's enthusiastic objection to the Federal Government's insistence public schools be free of religious indoctrination, the issue of education was at this juncture in time a moot point. All of the remaining issues that once made up the bulk of the original hurtles, could easily be overcome if delegates of the Constitutional Convention would agree to incorporate the following items into the new State Constitution:

- Reinstate women's right to vote
- Grant women the right to hold political office
- Give up any claim to Indian lands
- Agree public funds are not to be used to aid religious schools

Convening on March 4, 1895, elected delegates would wrestle with various issues such as eminent domain, female suffrage, plural marriage, right to work and separation of church and state for two months until a final draft was approved on May 7, 1895.

Although it may appear as if the LDS Church gave up a considerable amount of power in order for Utah to become a State, they also gained a foothold into the political process on a much larger scale. Once the Territory of Utah was admitted as a State, the people of Utah would be electing and sending representatives to Washington to pursue their own agenda in Congress.

The elite upper echelon of the Mormon Church would now have a golden opportunity to use the political process to garner support and sway public policy in their favor. Which brings up another question. Did leaders of the LDS Church consider their ultimate endgame when making concessions? I also think two more important questions need to be asked at this point.

1. Do the General Authorities of The Church of Jesus Christ of Latter-day Saints plan to reinstate the law of celestial marriage upon their successful establishment of the Kingdom of God?
2. Why surrender to the laws of man when such a burning testimony for the laws of God remained etched in their hearts and minds?

A case can be made that by making such a sacrifice and allowing the good and faithful Saints to part with a small portion of their everlasting covenant with God, leaders of the LDS Church merely acquiesced to the folly of man in an effort to lull them into a false sense of victory. The real truth of the matter is leaders of the The Church of Jesus Christ of Latter-day Saints never intended to completely abandon the law of celestial marriage, but simply put its practice on hold until the time when the principles of God are the only rule of law adhered to. And so we wait.

If the above scenario holds true, then every American citizen should think long and hard before casting votes in the next election. Why? You may ask yourself. Let me explain.

Assuming a great many of the political concessions agreed to by the ruling hierarchy of the Mormon Church were only done to bide time until humanity lived according to the rule of God's righteous laws, then only one plausible scenario would be evident. The Church of Jesus Christ of Latter-day Saints believes it will one day be in a position to control the governing body of the United States to such a degree as to easily and effortlessly change laws which affect their own religious practices.

God forbid we ever live long enough to see that day of sorrow.

Finally as we bring this chapter to a close, I want to leave you with this thought. If what I am reporting to you is the truth, then I am not a crazy, deluded, whacked out, nut job, constantly spouting an implausible conspiracy theory. Of course that will not stop the people lurking in the shadows, who want to hide the truth from the world, of accusing me or you of being slightly off kilter or even outright insane for believing what is patently obvious.

Church Involvement

From the very onset of the Latter-day Saint movement, church leaders where both involved in and concerned with the politics of the day. Despite publicly decrying involvement in local, state and national policies, the LDS Church has in years past been very active in politics and continues to exert considerable influence in the current political arena.

Throughout much of the 19th century the "Mormon" agenda was quietly pushed to the forefront — a policy which continued for all of the 20th century and still continues today.

The religious beliefs and practices associated with The Church of Jesus Christ of Latter-day Saints were, from their inception, viewed by outsiders as politically controversial. Early on in the presidential election of 1856, the subject of Mormonism and the practices of its followers became a national issue when members of the Republican Party condemned polygamy and southern slavery as social and moral evils. Almost overnight Mormon theology was thrust onto the political stage for all to see. Lumping both slavery and polygamy together, these practices were vilified by the Republican platform as the "twin relics of barbarism."

Political involvement by high ranking members of the Mormon Church continued to be par for the course in the Utah Territory, where there was little distinction between the political community and the dominant religion of Mormonism. Of course at that time political involvement of the elite "inner circle" was an almost foregone conclusion, as the majority of settlers congregating in the Great Basin were Latter-day Saints.

Why would they not attempt to establish a system of self governance? After all church members had fled the United States hoping to build a country of their own. Regardless of actions taken by generation after generation of early adherents to the Mormon faith, the truth we should be seeking for is not to be found in the history of a past era, but whether or not the ruling hierarchy of The Church of Jesus Christ of Latter-day Saints is still actively involved in politics today.

In an attempt to call off the dogs, the Mormon hierarchy issued another manifesto, but unlike the previous manifesto, this one dealt solely with the subject of politics. Far from the official stance taken by The Church of Jesus Christ of Latter-day Saints, a "Political Manifesto" was issued on April 6, 1896, at the General Conference of the Church held in Salt Lake City. This manifesto dictated that all members with positions of authority of must first obtain permission of the church leadership before running for office or accepting a nomination for political office.

As a condition of statehood Utah was forced to dissolve the Church run political party and support either of the two national parties. How did the Church react to this condition? In a bizarre twist of fate, elite authorities within The Church of Jesus Christ of Latter-day Saints, pushed its members to become registered Republicans and support that party's political platform. Joining the political party that caused the greatest amount of suffering to Latter-day Saints seems like it would have been the last thing the

General Authorities of the Church would have done in the 1890's, but that is exactly what they did. Droves of Mormons voters, at the behest of incredibly persuasive church authorities, wholeheartedly joined the Republican party. Why would any Mormon willingly join forces with the same political party who doggedly pursued the passing of anti-Mormon legislation? Go figure.

At a time when the Democratic Party was heavily favored among Mormons of voting age, the LDS Church jumps feet first into the fire and purposely steers its members right into the mouth of the waiting lion. What could Church leaders have possibly gained from handing over such a large voting bloc to the Republican Party? At the very least, the rapidly unfolding political drama would be quite interesting to watch.

Intended to be a benchmark for all to see, Church leaders used the so-called Political Manifesto as a touchstone to prove they were intentionally divesting themselves of political power. The message of the Political Manifesto of 1896, was instantly assumed to be the de facto rule for all Mormons engaged in politics. The Manifesto emphasized religious duty to the Church over that of political appointments, which would have been a grand gesture of goodwill had it really been that simple. In reality, the Political Manifesto made it possible for the First Presidency to gain even more control over their members. The highest ranking members of the church elite could now claim revelation from God as a reason why permission was withheld from a church authority seeking political office. If you did not play ball with the head honchos you were essentially out of luck.

To quote Mel Brooks, "It's good to be the king."

Case in point, the so-called political rule which was to be applied equally throughout the Church was extremely lax in regards to members who supported the right-wing platform and sought to gain political power as a member of the Republican Party. Whereas those Mormons who dared defy Church leaders and support the Democratic Party soon found the full weight of the church upon them. Church authorities heavily encouraged support for the Republican Party by its members. In 1896, two General Authorities of the LDS Church discovered firsthand what was at stake for daring to oppose Church policy. Elder B. H. Roberts and Elder Moses Thatcher were both severely chastised for accepting political nominations from the Democratic Party without seeking permission from the First Presidency of the Church. Initially both openly disagreed with the Church's stance on politics and refused to sign the Political Manifesto of 1896, stating it was their right as citizens to seek election to any office they chose. Faced with expulsion from the church, B. H. Roberts eventually caved under the enormous pressure being exerted on him and capitulated to higher authorities. Elder Moses Thatcher on the other hand, who stood by his convictions, was removed from his position as a member of the Quorum of the Twelve Apostles.

How can a church which coerces its members to switch political affiliations, claim to be neutral? Dismissing elders from their calling as General Authorities, for actions taken in the political arena, and threatening members in good standing with excommunication if they do not cede to Church authority, certainly does not sound like the actions of a religious organization that is politically neutral. How can a General Authority that was ordained through revelation from God be so easily replaced? That certainly gets me thinking about the validity of other church teachings.

With all their rhetoric and double-talk, it is no great surprise the majority of Mormons still do not understand their church leaders official standing on politics. On the one hand church authorities claim a distinct separation of church and state, yet they also encourage political participation. Which is not a huge issue in and of itself, but it does bring to light some interesting questions.

Where does the LDS Church draw the line in matters of political participation? Is the question we should be asking.

Brigham Young, the second President of the LDS Church, proudly proclaimed his church cared nothing for politics, but in reality he was heavily invested in politics as both the first governor of the Utah Territory and Church President. He also continued to keep a hand in politics for the remainder of his life and was a staunch supporter for establishing the "Political Kingdom of God." Can we afford to trust Latter-day Saints who constantly talk out of both sides of their mouth?

> *"As for politics, we care nothing about them one way or the other, although we are a political people.... It is the Kingdom of God or nothing with us"*
>
> *Remarks by Brigham Young Recorded in The Latter-day Saints' Millennial Star, Vol. 31, Published by A. Carrington, 1869, page 573*

When it comes to a citizen's right to cast a vote on matters the Church considers to be a "moral" issue, their self-righteous indignation comes out of the closet in full force. To think a handful of stogy old men are the only ones who know what is right in the sight of the Lord, is an insult to the intelligence of their world-wide membership. It appears as if the elite hierarchy, ensconced in their ivory towers, do not think all that highly of the congregations they lead.

When an opportunity to cast votes on a "moral" issue appears on the horizon, the General Authorities of The Church of Jesus Christ of Latter-day Saints never seem to be able to shut up. For being politically neutral, the Church sure does spend an inordinate amount of time and an exorbitant amounts of money attempting to influence the voting outcome. Church leaders appear to want to have their cake and eat it too.

Reed Smoot Hearings

As a concession for curtailing their religious practice of polygamy, the American political system secretly shared power with the Mormon Church. With this power sharing agreement came the certain knowledge Latter-day Saint candidates would be granted at least two seats in the U.S. Senate, that was until 1916. With the ratification of the Seventeenth Amendment in 1913, senate seats would be filled by an election of popular vote. Thus entirely removing Church leaders from direct control over who served as their representatives.

Prior to suffering this loss of leverage in the political arena, Church authorities were very much involved in the political battles of the day. A prime example was when members of the 58th U.S. Congress attempted to prevent Reed Smoot, a General Authority within the Latter-day Saint community, from participating as an elected official. During his trial, the highest ranking members of The Church of Jesus Christ of Latter-day Saints — including the Prophet and President of the Church — appeared before the U. S. Senate to testify on behalf of Reed Smoot who was being denied his duly elected Senate seat.

Despite the strict Mormon creed of obeying and honoring the laws of the land, three LDS Apostles stubbornly refused to honor their subpoenas and testify at the hearing. John Taylor, one of the three apostles who failed to appear, chose to flee to Canada instead of appear before the United States Congress.

As a result of Church involvement, the political aspect of the Kingdom of God received a considerable amount of scrutiny and press during the Reed Smoot hearings of 1904-1907. The writings of Apostle Orson Pratt, brother of Parley P. Pratt an early church leader, were of considerable interest during the three years of Senate hearings. The most damning statement of all introduced was an excerpt from a book entitled *Orson Pratt's Works.*

The daring words of Apostle Pratt, expressing his admiration of and fealty to the Kingdom of God, were used as evidence against Senator Reed Smoot during his Senate hearings.

> *The kingdom of God is an order of government established by divine authority. It is the only legal government that can exist in any part of the universe. All other governments are illegal and unauthorized. God, having made all beings and worlds, has the supreme right to govern them by His own laws, and by officers of His own appointment. Any people attempting to govern themselves by laws of their own making, and by officers of their own appointment, are in direct rebellion against the kingdom of God.*
>
> *Orson Pratt's Works, Published by George Q. Cannon & Sons Company, Salt Lake City, 1891, page 41*

Uproar surrounding the election of Smoot to the 58th United States Congress was greatly focused on whether or not a member of the Quorum of the Twelve Apostles was eligible to serve in the Senate. A huge part of the debate centered around Mormonism's discounting of the laws enacted by man in favor of those revealed by God. This controversy convinced many Americans a Mormon apostle could not serve in both capacities and therefore because of his membership in the church hierarchy, Reed Smoot should be summarily disqualified from serving as a U.S. Senator.

As the controversy escalated, Apostle Smoot found himself answering charges based on the religious beliefs and practices of the Mormon Church. After nearly four years of investigation, including three years of exhaustive Senate hearings, little verifiable proof was offered to refute the many charges brought against Reed Smoot and the Mormon Church. More than three thousand five hundred pages of testimony were recorded as the sworn statements of one hundred witnesses who appeared before the Senate committee. In the end, no majority decision could be achieved regarding the charges leveled against the Mormon Church and their temple rituals.

Five of the U. S. Senators attending the hearings commented the testimony gathered was vague, limited, and utterly unreliable because of the disreputable character of the many witnesses. Although the majority of the committee members recommended Smoot be removed from office, he was allowed to retain his seat in Congress by a narrow vote.

Unlike his unfortunate predecessor B. H. Roberts, who was an active polygamist and was never seated as a member of the House of Representatives, Apostle Reed Smoot avoided defeat and did not lose his seat. Among his contributions to government affairs, Senator Smoot co-sponsored the Smoot-Hawley Tariff in 1830, which raised import tariffs on more than twenty thousand taxable products. While serving as the Chairman of the U. S. Senate Committee on Finance, Reed Smoot's actions nearly crippled our economy. Designed to protect wealthy American business owners, the net effect of his legislation wreaked havoc on the economy and greatly exacerbated the financial hardships of our country during the Great Depression. Most economists cite the passing of the Smoot-Hawley Tariff as the beginning of the downward spiral from a recoverable recession, following the stock market crash of 1929, into a full scale depression.

Successfully completing five full terms in office as a United States Senator, Reed Smoot served for thirty years simultaneously as both a member of Congress and an Apostle of the Mormon Church. Upon his eventual defeat in 1932, Brother Smoot returned to Salt Lake City and devoted the remainder of his life as a dedicated member of the Quorum of the Twelve Apostles.

Do you still believe the Mormon church has no political agenda or ambition to influence American politics?

Political Troubles Continue

Although LDS Church leaders had paid lip service to abandoning the principle of polygamy by stating no future plural marriages would be officially condoned by the Church, members of Congress were not yet convinced of their sincerity. In addition to announcing the end of polygamy, the Church hierarchy further declared the practice of celestial marriage would not be solemnized in any of their Temples or Endowment Houses. Despite the apparent efforts of church leaders to comply, this may have been a case of too little too late — at least for some representatives seated in the 56th Congress. In 1898, eight years after the President of the Mormon Church issued the first Manifesto banning plural marriage and a mere two years since Utah had become the 45th state, the U.S. House of Representatives refused to seat Brigham Henry Roberts, the elected Democratic representative, due to his involvement with polygamy.

What members of Congress did not know for an absolute certainty was whether or not the practice of plural marriage had in fact been abandoned by the Mormon Church. More than a few members of congress may have suspected subterfuge by church leaders, but nobody knew for certain. Not to belabor the point, but it would be more accurate to say no one had any concrete evidence against the LDS Church at that time. Although polygamy was publicly denied as a relic of the past, General Authorities within the Mormon Church were still secretly performing and authorizing the sacrament of celestial marriage. The practice of plural marriage, although supposedly banned by The Church of Jesus Christ of Latter-day Saints, was still very much alive.

For the next fourteen years three different Church Presidents authorized and gave their consent for numerous plural marriages to be performed. Naturally all of the illegal unions were kept strictly confidential. In spite of a concerted effort among the Church hierarchy to publicly distance themselves from the practice, those church members who were already engaged in polygamous relationships refused to abandon their spouses. Thus the pretense of polygamy being a relic of the past was not readily accepted by the watchful eye of Congress.

Although polygamy was publicly shunned by the Church, more than sixty-eight documented plural marriages were solemnized by the highest ranking Church Authorities between October of 1890 and September of 1904. Continued practice of the principle and an increasing amount of scrutiny from Congress necessitated further action by The Church of Jesus Christ of Latter-day Saints.

To answer the growing tide of mistrust, the First Presidency issued a second more forceful edict in 1904, which seems to have only compounded the problem. A vast majority of Latter-day Saints who wished to remain loyal to the covenant of celestial marriage believed the further ruling by Church leaders — which was intended to be the final word only on the subject of polygamy — only applied to Saints living in the United States.

Polygamy was turning out to be much harder to cast off than the General Authorities of the Church had anticipated.

Polygamy Flourishes in Mexico

To better understand why Mormons willingly endured the hazards of traveling long distances from their home in order to engage in the practice of polygamy, you have to understand a few key points of Mormon theology.

So let's get started...

According to the religion of Mormonism, God was born a man — mortal if you will, just like you and I — and through a series of "earthly" tests, trials and tribulations, demonstrated his unwavering obedience to his Father's teachings. Elohim, the name of God as taught in the Mormon temples, was found to be a righteous soul and therefore was deemed worthy of an exalted place in heaven. At the time of his mortal passing, Elohim stood before God, his Father, to receive his final judgement and thus was elevated to the status of godhood.

As a newly exalted God, our heavenly Father set about the busy work of planning the miraculous event we call "Creation." Elohim is the grand architect and mastermind behind the "Heavens" and the "Earth." All of the known universe is His creation.

In order for God to populate his newly created "earth" he had to marry hundreds and thousands of wives in the celestial kingdom to bear him spirit children, who would later be sent to earth to undergo their own spiritual tests. Our brother, Jesus Christ is an example of such a man who came to earth and through righteous living was exalted to the status of God.

Latter-day Saints teach every man, woman and child on earth are all literal brothers and sisters, born from the sexual union of God and his many wives. Our heavenly mothers gave birth to us the same way women on earth experience birthing a child.

Within the walls of their sacred temples, worthy Mormons are taught the greatest potential available to them is to become like

God. After a lifetime of devotion and righteousness, worthy males and their wives will one day create and populate new worlds with billions of their own spirit children. The process begins here on earth in a Mormon Temple where plural marriages are sanctioned. Worthy male Mormons of age could be "sealed" in a sacred ritual for all eternity to as many women as they chose.

There you have it, that's pretty much the whole ball of wax. Unquestioning loyalty and blind obedience to the ruling Mormon hierarchy will pave the way for your eternal blessing as an exalted "God" in the celestial kingdom.

Now that we have our very basic and rudimentary lesson on "Early American Religion" out of the way, let us engage in a candid discussion regarding the real issue of polygamy in America. Contrary to popular belief, lawmakers in our nation's capitol did not draft criminal codes and subsequent penalties, nor did they pass laws against those who were engaged in polygamy, cohabitation and bigamy solely to persecute members of the Mormon religion. American society has never condoned the act of polygamy, it simply was not tolerated by our social customs of the day. Nor is it tolerated in American society today.

Let me also be very clear about this next point. Polygamy or plural marriage as it is often referred to, is not unique to Mormonism. If that were the case, the laws against polygamy would not have existed prior to Joseph Smith and the LDS Church receiving so much attention.

Polygamy is not even a uniquely American issue. I want to be very clear and set the record straight, once and for all. State legislatures have enacted laws against anyone involved in polygamous activities since the 1830's. Penalties levied against anyone convicted of polygamy have ranged from two years imprisonment and a one thousand dollar fine to a simple two hundred dollar fine. Bigamy, cohabitation, polygamy and polygamous marriages were deemed an illegal act in each and every one of the states where Mormons later took up residence. Latter-day Saints were not singled to harass or victimize, polygamy was never condoned by American society. Notwithstanding secretive plural marriages were sanctioned and performed by the Prophet Joseph Smith and his Apostles.

The only legitimate argument The Church of Jesus Christ of Latter-day Saints could ever put forth regarding the legal status of plural marriage is this one. The legality of polygamy was at best a gray area and could be seen as being unresolved from the time the first Mormons entered the Great Basin territory until the summer of 1862. To be precise, the land that would in due course become the State of Utah was Mexican territory when the Brigham Young entered the Salt Lake Valley. Mormon pioneers were hoping to build a kingdom free from the reach of U. S. lawmakers, but within months of their arrival the government of Mexico would cede Utah to the United States. All total more than five hundred thousand square miles of land north of the Rio Grande river was acquired as part of the Treaty of Guadalupe Hidalgo. It was beginning to look as if the sanctuary and freedom Latter-day Saints were seeking would never be realized.

Without going into the complex issue of jurisprudence, I will stipulate U.S. territorial law in the late 1840's to the early 1860's was not so cut and dry nor were the interpretation of laws within each territory an easy task. Each territory faced their fair share of issues regarding the application of laws. Apparently the nature of territorial law in the late 1840's was sufficiently ambiguous in nature to support a few differing legal opinions, but that is an issue I will leave for historians and law professors to argue.

Nevertheless, President Abraham Lincoln signed the Morrill Anti-Bigamy Act into law on July 8, 1862, thus effectively ending the discussion. From that day forward, anyone engaging in plural marriage was clearly breaking the law.

After years of conflict with the U.S. legal system, numerous arrests of high ranking church members and countless hours of court room appearances, the practice of polygamy was still not dead. While disavowed publicly by church apostles, the principle of celestial marriage was very much alive. In fact, the practice of polygamy had not been abandoned at all by members of the LDS Church, it had merely been forced underground.

As early as 1885, prior to the 1890 Manifesto issued by Wilford Woodruff, the Church Presidency under the direction of John Taylor started organizing Stakes in the northern parts of Mexico. Initially "colonies" as they came to be known were established in Chihuahua and Sonora, Mexico. Six polygamous colonies were created by the Mormon Church in Mexico during the year of 1885. Each of these colonies, set-up at the behest of the First Presidency, were operated with the express purpose of furthering the practice of plural marriages. Wilford Woodruff, George Q. Cannon and Joseph F. Smith oversaw the construction and daily operations of these polygamous communes.

In February of 1886, agents for the Mormon Church signed contracts to purchase one hundred seventeen thousand acres of prime Mexican real estate in three separate districts. LDS President John Taylor, Trustee-in-Trust for the Church, handed over twelve thousand dollars of church money to secure the purchase. In today's economy that would be the equivalent of slightly less than fifteen million dollars.

Under the watchful eye of the First Presidency of The Church of Jesus Christ of Latter-day Saints the Mexican Colonization and Agricultural Company was incorporated in the state of Colorado for the sole purpose of purchasing land suitable for building colonies that could support Mormon families dedicated to furthering the outlawed practice of polygamy. Residing in Mexico, just beyond the reach of U.S. laws, Latter-day Saints felt a sense of relief.

It will thus be seen that the early Mormon colonists in Mexico held property under the same restrictions as did the early settlers of the Great Basin. In both cases only the devotees of the Mormon Church in full standing were entitled to possession and in both instances possession merely implied a stewardship-the titles being held by the Church while the tiller of the soil held his concession only during good behavior.

Thomas Cottam Romney, The Mormon Colonies in Mexico, Desert Book Company, 1938, page 63

It would appear the United Order was in fact the perfect system of communal living — as long as you did what you were told and never questioned God's appointed ministers. It is no wonder that more people did not want to join. I guess the Mormon Church really did believe in the golden rule and absolutely took it to heart. That is as long as you believe, "He who has the gold makes the rules." What a great way to control your followers.

Under the sanction of members of the Quorum of the Twelve Apostles, Latter-day Saints began to set-up colonies in Mexico and Canada where they erroneously believed polygamy was legal and therefore beyond the punitive punishment of U.S. lawmakers. Plural marriages were even solemnized aboard ships in international waters. All of this deception took place to avoid detection and interference from the United States government.

After the 1890 Manifesto, which supposedly ended the Mormon practice of polygamy, more than three thousand members of the Mormon Church immigrated to Mexico to support the ongoing and continued practice of plural marriage. Over the next fourteen years, a number of Apostles of The Church of Jesus Christ of Latter-day Saints officiated at, performed and tacitly sanctioned thousands of plural marriages. Believing polygamy to be a holy sacrament, Latter-day Saints defiantly ignored the laws of man.

> *To indicate the desire on the part of the Church Presidency to keep these marriages secret and even to maintain secrecy as to the practice of polygamy, my father told me, "almost in the same breath, George Q. Cannon said, 'Now Brother Ivins, if you have occasion to meet Porfio Diaz, President of Mexico, we want you to tell him that we are NOT practicing polygamy in Mexico."*
>
> *H. Grant Ivens, Polygamy in Mexico as Practiced by the Mormon Church, 1895-1905, Typed Manuscript, page 2*

Despite "official" proclamations and continued assertions by The Church of Jesus Christ of Latter-day Saints they were no longer engaged in nor condoned the practice of polygamy, the First Presidency continued sending citizens of the United States across the Mexican border to be "sealed" in celestial marriages. Between October of 1895, and September of 1904, three separate Prophets of the Church sent citizens of the United States to Mexico for the express purpose of being "sealed" in celestial marriage.

So common was this practice of hopping the border, that the couples entering into the covenant of plural marriage rarely stayed in Mexico. Almost all of the newly "sealed" couples immediately returned to the United States upon completion of the ceremony. The First Presidency of The Church of Jesus Christ of Latter-day Saints was so confident American authorities would never find out they were instructing Mormon couples to cross international borders and surreptitiously engage in the illegal act of polygamy, the practice continued unfettered for nearly eighteen years.

> *The story of my father's part in the practice of polygamy while he was in Mexico must begin with his interview with the Church Presidency when he responded to their invitation to meet with them. This meeting took place on October 5, 1895 in Salt Lake City. After perfunctionary instruction as to the general duties of the Stake President he was told that occasionally the Presidency*

would send to him in Mexico a couple bearing a letter instructing him to marry them. He was informed that he would have the authority to perform this ceremony "for time and eternity" although this "sealing" was usually performed in one of the temples of the Church. This unusual authority was, no doubt, delegated to him because of the great distance of the Mexican colonies from any temple. It was plainly understood that these marriages were to be performed in Mexico because it would be against the law to perform them within the borders of the United States.

H. Grant Ivens, Polygamy in Mexico as Practiced by the Mormon Church, 1895-1905, Typed Manuscript, page 2

Of all the polygamous marriages performed in Mexico less than five percent were solemnized for residents living in the colonies. Mormon couples deemed worthy of entering into the sacred covenant of plural marriage would arrive in one of the Mexican colonies with a letter signed by a member of the First Presidency authorizing a priesthood holder to perform the ceremony.

It is perfectly clear from the following statement, the highest echelon of church leaders not only knew what was taking place in the colonies, but actively gave their approval. In the end, what this all boils down to is simple. The highest ranking priesthood members of The Church of Jesus Christ of Latter-day Saints knowingly made false statements and habitually disregarded laws of three sovereign nations.

A further evidence that my father's activities in the performance of marriages were approved by the general authorities of the Church may be found in the fact that in October, 1907, he was made a member of the Council of Twelve. The appointment was made by Joseph F. Smith who had issued the proclamation doing away with plural marriages throughout the entire Church and who had asked John W. Taylor and Mathias F. Cowley to resign from the Council in October 1905 because they refused to conform to his pronouncement of 1904. President Smith, with many other members of the Presidency and the Council had long been aware of what was taking place in Mexico, and the fact of my father's appointment seems positive proof that the part he played met with their approval. He was later appointed to the First Presidency of the Church.

H. Grant Ivens, Polygamy in Mexico as Practiced by the Mormon Church, 1895-1905, Typed Manuscript, page 4

Despite more than two decades of collusion, public deception and circumventing polygamy laws in the United States, time finally ran out for Latter-day Saints. While the LDS Church secretly continued its practice of polygamy abroad, the outbreak of civil unrest was pretty much the final nail in their coffin. Continued escalation of the Mexican Revolution essentially brought an end to the large scale colonization efforts of the Mormon Church in northern Mexico. By the time most of the Mormons fled back to the United States in 1912, the LDS Church owned more than two hundred miles of Mexican real estate.

The Church of Jesus Christ of Latter-day Saints currently owns and operates twelve temples in Mexico. Ground was broken in Tijuana on August 18, 2012, for a thirteenth temple. The latest Temple in Tijuana, Mexico is expected to be completed and operational by 2015.

Second Manifesto

In order for The Church of Jesus Christ of Latter-day Saints to continue growing and truly flourish in the twentieth century, free of watchful, prying eyes and unmolested by government agencies, church leaders knew they would have to put the past behind them. A decision had to be made to remove any and all teachings regarding the sanctity of plural marriage from the ever evolving theology of Mormonism. Polygamy must come to an end, if the Church was to survive

Despite the revelation of 1890 and manifesto issued by the fourth Mormon Prophet, Wilford Woodruff, the practice of polygamy continued among Latter-day Saints to such a degree it was necessary to issue a second manifesto in 1904 which officially ending the practice of patriarchal marriage.

A church wide edict enacted by President Joseph F. Smith, sternly warned that any and all church members who continued to engaged in polygamy would be excommunicated. The situation was serious and much too dangerous for the Church to ignore any longer. After fourteen years of secretly keeping the practice of plural marriage alive, Joseph F. Smith threw in the towel.

The Church had failed to effectively hide the continued practice of polygamy from prying eyes. General Authorities realized Mormons could no longer violate the laws of the land if they wished to keep the church intact. Drastic action would be required. During the early days of the U. S. Senate hearings involving Brother Reed Smoot, church leaders quickly realized two of their precious doctrines were once again being attacked.

Polygamy and the political might of the growing Latter-day Saint community. The Church of Jesus Christ of Latter-day Saints desperately needed to shake off the pall of polygamy and bury the past — it was time to leave it behind once and for all. The Church, as a whole, could no longer afford to be connected with the "detestable" practice of plural marriage.

Unwilling to cede their political endgame, high ranking General Authorities sacrificed the principle of plural marriage, even though it was given through divine revelation as a necessary step toward entering the Eternal Kingdom of our Heavenly Father. According to the teachings of Mormonism, celestial marriage was a sacred ordinance. God had explicitly commanded the faithful priesthood holders of the Mormon Church to honor the practice of plural marriage, but like so much child's play the ruling elite of the Church abandoned their royal road to exhalation in order to hold onto their political capital.

Apparently sacrificing essential elements of Mormon theology was preferable to throwing away the possibility of a future full of political power. The butcher's bill was due and it would seem there was no price that was too high to pay. Preserving the cash cow of Mormonism had become a top priority.

The Second Manifesto was announced by President Joseph F. Smith at a General Conference of The Church of Jesus Christ of Latter-day Saints on April 6, 1904. Reading his edict aloud before a gathering of Latter-day Saints, President Smith presented an "official statement" to all church members who were in attendance at their semi-annual meeting. The document Joseph F. Smith read to the assembled congregation became official Church doctrine from that time forward.

The subject was now closed to discussion.

> *Inasmuch as there are numerous reports in circulation that plural marriages have been entered into, contrary to the official declaration of President Woodruff, of September 26, 1890, commonly called the Manifesto, which was issued by President Woodruff and adopted by the Church at its general conference, October 6, 1890, which forbade any marriages violative of the law of the land; I, Joseph F. Smith, President of the Church of Jesus Christ of Latter-day Saints, hereby affirm and declare that no such marriages have been solemnized with the sanction, consent, or knowledge of the Church of Jesus Christ of Latter-day Saints, and I hereby announce that all such marriages are prohibited, and if any officer or member of the Church shall assume to solemnize or enter into any such marriage he will be deemed in transgression against the Church and will be liable to be dealt with according to the rules and regulations thereof, and excommunicated therefrom.*
>
> *Joseph F. Smith,*
> *President of the Church of Jesus Christ of Latter-day Saints.*
>
> *Seventy-Fourth Annual Conference of The Church of Jesus Christ of Latter-day Saints, The Deseret News, Salt Lake City, 1904, page 75*

Immediately following the somewhat terse speech by Joseph F. Smith, Francis M. Lyman, President of the Quorum of the Twelve Apostles, presented the following resolution of endorsement and called for its official adoption.

RESOLUTION OF ENDORSEMENT

Resolved that we, the members of the Church of Jesus Christ of Latter-day Saints, in General Conference assembled, hereby approve and endorse the statement and declaration of President Joseph F. Smith, just made to this Conference concerning plural marriages, and will support the courts of the Church in the enforcement thereof.

Seventy-Fourth Annual Conference of The Church of Jesus Christ of Latter-day Saints, The Deseret News, Salt Lake City, 1904, page 76

Several Stake Presidents and a number of prominent Elders of the Church seconded the motion and resolution put forth by Quorum of the Twelve President, Francis M. Lyman. Moments before Church members attending the seventy-fourth semi-annual General Conference was asked to vote for the resolution, Apostle B.H. Roberts added the following heart-warming words of wisdom:

In seconding the resolution that has just been read—which I most heartily do—I desire to state at least one reason for doing it. As remarked by the president, the Church of Jesus Christ of Latter-day Saints has been accused of being covenant-breakers with this nation. Of course, there never was, and could not be, any compact between the Church and the general government of the United States. But there could be a compact between the State of Utah and the United States, and there was such a compact made in the Constitution of our state, by and through the Constitutional Convention. And now I am pleased with the opportunity of the Church saying in its official capacity that the Latter-day Saints not only now are, but have been, true to the compact between the State of Utah and the United States, and that they are true to the Constitution of the state, which, by express provision, forever prohibited plural or polygamous marriages, and made that irrevocable, without the consent of the United States. The adoption by the Church of this resolution should put to silence those who have accused us of being covenant-breakers.

Seventy-Fourth Annual Conference of The Church of Jesus Christ of Latter-day Saints, The Deseret News, Salt Lake City, 1904, page 76

So there could be no future possibility of church members misunderstanding or misinterpreting his position on the subject of polygamy, President Smith's official statement was further published in the official church magazine, *Improvement Era* for all Latter-day Saints to read.

The Church's attitude on the subject of polygamy was clear, but once again it would not be that simple. The Church of Jesus Christ of Latter-day Saints had formally put an end to the practice of polygamy, yet unlike the 1890 Manifesto issued by President Wilford Woodruff the church hierarchy never officially canonized the statement by Joseph F. Smith.

Did the church hierarchy cleverly sneak in a loophole for future generations to exploit? Hopefully this entire polygamy nonsense is nothing more than a bad dream remembered. Only time will tell what The Church of Jesus Christ of Latter-day Saints will do.

Despite the Church's newfound resolve to stand firmly against the future practice of plural marriage, several General Authorities persisted in open defiance of their prophet. As a result of their opposition to the Second Manifesto, Apostles John W. Taylor, son of the third Church President, and Matthias F. Cowley were expelled from the Quorum of the Twelve Apostles and stripped of their church duties in 1906. John W. Taylor was eventually excommunicated from the Church in 1911, because of his stubborn opposition to President Joseph F. Smith.

Having taken our first few tenuous steps into the twenty-first century, you would certainly think the time is nigh to pierce the veil of secrecy and finally reveal the truth about polygamy. One hundred twenty-two years has elapsed since the Mormon Church first called for an end to the practice of plural marriage. At the very least, it has been one hundred years since the putrid stench of polygamy wafted from the corridors of Latter-day Saint temples. A few years longer if you are inclined to believe the Church's rhetoric and timetables. So, here is the question. Why do we still not know the entire truth of the matter?

What could The Church of Jesus Christ of Latter-day Saints possibly still be hiding? I am not sure I actually want to know the answer to that last question. However the question does deserve its fifteen minutes of fame. Maybe one day all of our lingering questions will be answered.

In the meantime, we continue...

No longer can the ruling elite of The Church of Jesus Christ of Latter-day Saints claim they are in hiding to avoid prosecution from unjust laws and an overzealous government bent on their destruction. The passing of time has been kind to the Mormon Church. No legal repercussion whatsoever could possibly be levied against the Church's current hierarchy for spilling the beans and telling the truth. Criminal prosecution is not even remotely feasible. Any statute of limitation expired ages ago. The time to come clean about their sordid past is now.

What is the Church waiting for? We want to hear the truth, the whole truth and nothing but the truth.

Mormon Financial Legacy

While proud American soldiers were embroiled in battle during World War II, a handful of elite Church leaders were busy lining their pockets by laundering millions upon millions of dollars as a favor to notorious gangster Bugsy Siegel and fellow crime boss Meyer Lansky. Utilizing a network of privately held Mormon owned banks, money generated from illicit mob activities were passed through a series of back channels and deposited into the hands of legitimate business interests controlled by ruthless mafia syndicates. All of this was done in an effort to avoid unwanted attention from the prying eyes of federal authorities. After decades of close scrutiny, the Mormon Church had certainly learned how to effectively evade detection by law enforcement agencies when it suited their purpose.

This ploy was so successful Bugsy Siegel was able to complete construction of The Flamingo Hotel in 1946, which would forever establish a mafia presence in Las Vegas. Once the mafia, with considerable financial help from the Mormon Church, asserted its presence in the "City of Sin" there was no turning back. Over the next few decades a syndicate of crime families established an ironclad stranglehold on the hotel and gambling industry which has never been relinquished. Despite the suspicious nature of these highly irregular money transactions, federal authorities never caught on to the game and east coast crime families were able to skim billions of dollars off the top of legitimate gambling revenue.

Post-war America quite naturally blossomed into a bountiful vineyard, overflowing and ripe for the picking by unscrupulous individuals. The boom years between 1952 and 1957, saw continuous construction of gambling palaces owned by organized crime families. Climbing into bed with the Teamsters Union, the ruling Mormon hierarchy supervised the lending of large sums of money to mafia front men — ultimately financing the construction of the Sahara, Sands, Royal Nevada, Showboat, The Riviera, The Fremont, The Tropicana and the renovation of Benny Binion's Horseshoe casino, formerly the Apache Hotel.

Operating under the protective veil of legitimate corporations, an unlikely cadre of faithful Mormon elders joined forces with individuals tied to organized crime in order to provide political protection and an air of legitimacy. This joint venture was so successful billions of dollars of unreported income was secretly funneled to underworld figures such as Meyer Lansky. Under the watchful eye of their Mormon overlords, hotel management transformed these crime hotels, as they came to be known, into hot beds of entertainment. Las Vegas was fast becoming the Mecca of gambling enthusiasts.

In their own unique way each of these entertainment venues became successful, almost to the point of establishing a cult following. Despite millions of patrons passing through their doors and depositing piles of cash into their respective coffers, half of these gambling bastions eventually succumbed to financial pressures. Is this the legacy The Church of Jesus Christ of Latter-day Saints wants to leave the world?

I find it a little bit ironic — and more to the point extremely hypocritical — that a church which forbids its adherents from participating in activities that would lead to adultery, consumption of alcoholic and caffeinated beverages, gambling, pre-marital sexual activity, tea, tobacco and the viewing of pornographic material would spend millions of dollars financing an entertainment empire known as "Sin City."

Now that I have your full attention, aside from a quick history lesson, let me tell you why we are discussing this in the first place. My purpose in bringing this topic out into the light of day is to show the real religious conviction of The Church of Jesus Christ of Latter-day Saints is not to spread the restored gospel of Jesus Christ as Mormon priesthood leaders claim, but the accumulation of money and political power on a global scale.

The Religion of Money

To understand the intricate financial structure of the Church, it is important we start at the very top and work our way down. The Mormon Church is owned and run by what is called the Corporation of the President of the Church of Jesus Christ of Latter-day Saints. This entity is a "corporation sole," which is an obscure legal body owned entirely by one person. In the case of the Mormon Church, that person is Thomas S. Monson, the current Prophet and President of the Church.

You also need to know the Mormon presidency is not an elected position. Although the President of the Church is considered a prophet, it is not a direct appointment revealed by God. When the presiding prophet dies, he is replaced by the longest-serving member of the Quorum of the Twelve Apostles. Each new president handpicks two trusted counselors to help him lead the Mormon Church. This three-man team is called the First Presidency.

The ruling elite of the Mormon Church are known as General Authorities. Numbering more than one hundred, they consist of the First Presidency, the Presiding Bishopric, the Quorum of the Twelve Apostles, and two other priesthood groups known as the Quorums of the Seventy.

Although the LDS Church is largely run by lay clergy, General Authorities work full-time and receive salaries from the Corporation of the President. Until the 1960s, salaries were based on hierarchy, with the presiding prophet always receiving top dollar.

And so with that little tidbit of information tucked neatly under your belt, let us continue with our exposé on Mormonism...

Inviting the Devil to Dinner

President David O. McKay, 9th President of The Church of Jesus Christ of Latter-day Saints, vehemently opposed the Mormon Church or any of its subsidiary businesses accepting any type of government aid. Ezra Taft Benson, 13th President of the Church, also opposed accepting federal subsidies in regards to education and textbooks. Both men feared the inevitable government interference that would surely follow any type of financial aid. Neither of these Church Prophets felt the risk of getting into bed with the United States Government was worth the financial gain. Apparently their successors did not feel the same way.

I don't want to be too harsh, but the policies of the Mormon Church and particularly the decisions of the hierarchy charged with enforcing those policies have historically been swayed with huge cash infusions. Why would later Church leaders risk the relative autonomy of their private school by accepting federal grants? One possible reason which comes to mind is this. Beneath the pleasant veneer paraded out to the public, a cleverly devised ruse is being perpetrated under the guise of religion. Lurking behind the mask of religion, the Corporation of The Church of Jesus Christ of Latter-day Saints is pursuing its real political agenda which is once again the accumulation of money and global power.

You would not think a corporation with billions of dollars in assets would need to accept financial aid in the form of grants, but maybe current Church leaders have another reason for accepting an invitation to dine with the devil. This reminds me of an apropos adage by Sun-Tzu, the great military strategist of ancient China, "Keep your friends close, and your enemies closer."

> *"As a matter of general policy, the BYU Board of Trustees has long adhered to a position opposed to general federal aid to education. We have always objected to the Church or any of its branches or agencies receiving any subsidy or "gift" from the government... We have steadfastly refused to participate in any federal education program which is based upon the subsidy principle."*
>
> *Deseret News, Nov. 2, 1964*

> *Brigham Young University added to its area studies expertise on Asia, Europe and the Middle East with the recent receipt of three prestigious grants from the U.S. Department of Education totaling several million dollars, putting BYU in the company of Harvard, NYU, Columbia, UC Berkeley and the University of Washington.*
>
> *Brigham Young University, News Release, August 3, 2010*

Money Laundering in the 21st Century

While The Church of Jesus Christ of Latter-day Saints appears to have learned the fine art of successful banking, their legal problems with money just don't ever seem to go away. Despite owning and operating commercially successful banks since 1873, the LDS Church appears to have been uniquely ordained to be caught with their hand in the proverbial cookie jar.

On February 12, 2011 The Salt Lake Tribune reported federal agencies fined Zion's Bank an $8 million dollar penalty for issues relating to anti-money laundering laws.

> *The Office of the Comptroller of the Currency on Friday said it imposed an $8 million penalty against Zions for shortcomings in its anti-money laundering controls — violations of the Bank Secrecy Act and the USA Patriot Act.*
>
> *The Salt Lake Tribune,*
> *February 12, 2011*

Under the supervision of the Treasury Department, one of its agencies the Financial Crimes Enforcement Network also fined the Salt Lake City based bank an additional fine of $8 million dollars. The Financial Crimes Enforcement Network was created to fight money laundering.

> *"These suspicious activities involved, among other things, sequentially numbered travelers checks, possible black market peso exchange, transactions involving entities and accounts alleged to have been involved in drug trafficking activities and unusual wire transfers," the Financial Crimes Network said in a document released Thursday.*
>
> *The agency said Zions processed money transfers that indicated patterns commonly associated with money-laundering, such as the nature of the business, originators and beneficiaries in "high-risk" locations and lacked any apparent business or legal purpose.*
>
> *The Salt Lake Tribune,*
> *February 12, 2011*

With the advent of Citizen's United, could any of the illegally transferred money have been earmarked for political campaigns?

Continuing the Legacy

For more than one hundred fifty years Latter-day Saints have repeatedly referenced the Church's official position of adopting a stance of neutrality in regards to political involvement, yet despite their vocal and often vehement protests, we know — without exception — every level of government has been infiltrated by faithful Mormons who actively support and seek guidance from their beloved prophet. But, and I emphasize that word strongly, we must remember I am not speaking about a group of American citizens who merely desire to be involved in the political process of drafting laws and regulations which will govern their daily lives, but a small contingency of religious zealots who most assuredly wish to curtail, and in some cases, obliterate your sovereign rights because they simply do not match the strict ideals as set forth in their own religious creed.

We have spoken at length regarding The Church of Jesus Christ of Latter-day Saints' assertion their ordained leaders remain politically neutral and do not use their position of authority to influence local, state or national policies, yet their actions in the political arena — well documented this past century alone — are evidence that another agenda just might be in play. Before you dismiss the previous statement as pure conjecture or wishful thinking, let me remind you once again about the Political Manifesto of 1896, also known as the political rule, issued by Church President Wilford Woodruf. As you are now aware of, the Political Manifesto issued by the Mormon Church sought to impose strict authority over Latter-day Saints who desired to run for political office. In essence the manifesto curtailed all political activity not sanctioned by the elite hierarchy of church authorities.

Just in case you might be thinking the Political Manifesto of 1896, was a relic of the past, set aside, abandoned and no longer adhered to, let me remind you of an occurrence that happened in my father's lifetime. You and I are not so far removed from the days when church authorities were brazenly open and proud of the political power they wielded, but more to my point, The Church of Jesus Christ of Latter-day Saints still to this day remains very much politically active — despite any protest to the contrary.

Case in point. Before accepting a political appointment as a cabinet member of the Eisenhower administration, Apostle Ezra Taft Benson sought out and obtained explicit permission from David O. McKay who was at that time the ruling Mormon Prophet. Elder Benson, who would later be ordained as the 13th president of the LDS Church, served as United States Secretary of Agriculture under President Dwight D. Eisenhower from 1953 until 1961, while simultaneously serving as an active member of the Quorum of the Twelve Apostles of The Church of Jesus Christ of Latter-day Saints. Once again we are witnessing a clear bias on the part of the Mormon Church, favoring a Republican sponsored agenda versus that of their Democratic leaning members.

A rousing and engaging public speaker, Ezra Taft Benson repeatedly addressed young impressionable students and faculty of Brigham Young University throughout his tenure as an Apostle of The Church of Jesus Christ of Latter-day Saints. Eventually serving as the President and Prophet of the Mormon Church, Ezra Taft Benson gave more than twenty-five devotional talks on the campus of Brigham Young University. Addressed to Latter-day Saints world-wide, many of the remarks by this elder statesman were earmarked for Mormon youth.

On December 1, 1952, in one of his devotional talks entitled, "The LDS Church and Politics," Ezra Taft Benson mentions that no man-made honor can compare to the exquisite honor of being ordained into a high office in the "Political Kingdom of God." Benson also remarked saying, "Men's ways are not God's ways" and how God will continue to direct His Church in the future. Quoting from a transcript of a devotional talk Elder Benson delivered at Brigham Young University on October 25, 1966, I offer you the words of a man who would later take hold of the reins of The Church of Jesus Christ of Latter-day Saints as their President and Prophet. Excerpts are arranged in chronological order.

> *"No greater immediate responsibility rests upon the members of the church, upon all citizens of this republic and of neighboring republics than to protect the freedom vouchsafed by the Constitution of the United States."*
>
> *"Efforts are being made to deprive man of his free agency — to steal from the individual his liberty.... There has been an alarming increase in the abandoning of the ideals that constitute the foundation of the Constitution of the United States."*
>
> *The fight for freedom cannot be divorced from the gospel — the plan of salvation.*
>
> *At this particular moment in history the United States is definitely threatened and every citizen should know about it. The warning of this hour should resound through the corridors*

of every American institution – schools, churches, the halls of Congress, press, radio and television...

Our Republic and Constitution are being destroyed while the enemies of freedom are being aided.

One regrettable development is the increasing number of government programs embracing our youth.

"Our government with its liberty and free institutions will not long survive a government trained and supervised youth.... Such a youth can be a revolutionary machine."

One of the main thrusts of the Communist drive in America today is through the so-called civil rights movement.

The man who is generally recognized as the leader of the so-called civil rights movement today in America is a man who has lectured at a Communist training school, who has solicited funds through communist sources, who hired a Communist as a top-level aide, who has affiliated with Communist fronts, who is often praised in the Communist press and who unquestionably parallels the Communist line. This same man advocates the braking of the law and has been described by J. Edgar Hoover as "the most notorious liar in the country."

Think of the impact for good we could have if we all united behind the prophets in preserving our Constitution. Yet witness the sorry spectacle of those presently of our number who have repudiated the inspired counsel of our prophet when he has opposed federal aid to education and asked support to the right to work laws.

For years we have heard of the role the elders could play in saving the Constitution from total destruction. But how can the elders be expected to save it if they have not studied it and are not sure if it is being destroyed or what is destroying it.

Now Satan is anxious to neutralize the inspired counsel of the Prophet and hence keep the priesthood off-balance, ineffective and inert in the fight for freedom. He does this through diverse means including the use of perverse reasoning. For example, he will argue, "There is no need to get involved in the fight for freedom – all you need to do is live the gospel." Of course this is a contradiction, because we cannot fully live the gospel and not be involved in the fight for freedom.

Let me give you a crucial key to help you avoid being deceived. It is this – learn to keep your eye on the Prophet. He is the Lord's mouthpiece and the only man who can speak for the Lord today. Let his inspired counsel take precedence. Let his inspired words be a basis for evaluating the counsel of all lesser authorities. Then live close to the spirit so you may know the truth of all things.

The Prophet Joseph Smith is reported to have prophesied the role the Priesthood might play to save our inspired Constitution. Now is the time to move forward courageously – to become alerted, informed and active. We are not just ordinary men. We bear the priesthood and authority of God. We understand the world and God's divine purpose as no other men.

Will we of the priesthood "arise and shine"? Will we provide the "defense" and "refuge"? Now is our time and season for corrective and courageous action.

"No greater immediate responsibility rests upon the members of the church, upon all citizens of this republic and of neighboring republics than to protect the freedom vouchsafe by the Constitution of the United States."

"Our Immediate Responsibility," a devotional sermon given by Apostle Ezra Taft Benson at Brigham Young University on October 25, 1966

At a time when leading Church authorities began to tone down the rhetoric and carefully censor their words, Ezra Taft Benson threw caution to the wind and ran headlong into the fray. Elder Benson was one of the most outspoken members of the Quorum of the Twelve Apostles, especially when the subject of politics was placed on the table. Of the more than one hundred seventy-seven devotional talks and addresses Ezra Taft Benson delivered to Latter-day Saints throughout the world, a full sixty percent were overtly political in nature.

Apostle Benson was clearly an asset to church leaders seeking political power, but many found his rhetoric difficult to control. Notwithstanding the Mormon Church's attempt to publicly distance itself from the John Birch Society in January of 1963, Ezra Taft Benson, a life-long Republican and avid supporter of the John Birch Society, claimed the ultra conservative political organization was, "the most effective non-church organization in our fight against creeping socialism and Godless Communism."

Apostle Benson's son Reed, a retired professor of religion who taught at Brigham Young University, was an active member of the John Birch Society. Reed Benson, much like his father, was known for his extreme political views. Rising above and beyond his considerable skill as an orator, Ezra Taft Benson was also known throughout the Mormon community as a prolific writer. A few of his celebrated works published by the Mormon Church are:

The Red Carpet (Bookcraft - 1962)
Title of Liberty (Deseret Book Co. - 1964)
An Enemy Hath Done This (Deseret Book Co. - 1969)

In his book *An Enemy Hath Done This* Apostle Benson advocates the complete dissolution of all government "welfare" programs, which he likens to a growing cancer that must be surgically removed from a diseased body. To his credit, Ezra Taft Benson, does at least acknowledge the economic and social calamity that would befall our nation should all "welfare-state programs" be instantly dismantled. Under his plan, which Benson labels as practical and prudent, Congress would accomplish this colossal feat by adopting a three pronged approach:

1. Restore the limited concept of government and freeze all welfare-state programs at their present level, making sure that no new ones are added.
2. Allow all present programs to run out their term with absolutely no renewal.
3. Gradually phasing-out programs which are indefinite in their term.

There you have it, how to get off the government tit in less than ten years. No doubt supported by years of scholarly research, Ezra Taft Benson shows us exactly how The Church of Jesus Christ of Latter-day Saints would eradicate needless government spending by simply cutting social services to the poor and needy.

Under Brother Benson's carefully crafted plan, within a time frame of no more than twenty years max, Congress would no longer be authorized to spend one thin dime on helping the less fortunate should we as responsible citizens be so inclined to elect candidates who would support these types of social measures. If it was not so sad, it would be laughable. For a prophet of God, who professes a desire to care for those poor souls in need, Ezra Taft Benson certainly had a peculiar way of demonstrating his understanding of supporting American citizens.

Although not a member of the Church's ruling hierarchy, Mormon author H. Verlan Andersen peels back the heavy curtain and exposes a great many of the disturbing political ideals held among Latter-day Saints. In his book *The Great and Abominable Church of the Devil*, originally published in 1972, Andersen claims God, or the Lord as he writes, is involved in our daily political affairs. It would appear that the Lord is busy establishing governments and choosing political leaders to whom He will reveal which laws He wants enforced among His children.

Andersen quotes liberally from Mormon scripture and cites the numerous talks of past Church Presidents including Heber J. Grant, David O. McKay, Joseph Fielding Smith and of course our good buddy Ezra Taft Benson. He also references the extensive work of LDS Apostles Marion G. Romney and J. Reuben Clark, Jr. in support of his hypothesis.

Andersen goes on to further state our Creator judges us not solely on the basis of our moral conduct. Apparently our inevitable accountability in the after-life extends far beyond any moral code we live by and into the political arena. According to H. Verlan Andersen, God judges us by who we vote for. Surprise, surprise! Well, I guess the cat definitely is out of the bag. If, for even the slightest moment, you were lead to believe the Church and its Latter-day Saint adherents advocate a separation of church and state, you can throw that notion right out of the window.

> *If the world be the Lord's, He certainly has a right to govern it; for we have already stated that man has no authority, except that which is delegated to him. He possesses a moral power to govern his actions, subject at all times to the law of God; but never is authorized to act independent of God; much less is he authorized to rule on the earth without the call and direction of the Lord; therefore, any rule or dominion over the earth, which is not given by the Lord is surreptitiously obtained, and never will be sanctioned by him.*
>
> *The kingdom of god, as I have already stated, is the government of God, whether in the heavens or on the earth.*
>
> *John Taylor, The Government of God, Published by S. W. Richards, Liverpool, 1852, pages 58 & 83*

Although early Church leaders were extremely careful not to divulge their true goals, for fear of public reprisals, more than a few modern day Mormon historians have not only alluded to the secretive doctrine of global political domination, but have actually openly discussed it — thinking no one was still listening. As you can clearly deduce from the following passage, the Mormon plan of creating a theocratic state ruled by LDS Church leaders for the purpose of wielding religious and political power over all of the inhabitants of earth has never ceased to exist.

> *In an attempt to live in the world, the Mormons were forced to modify their ideas of a political kingdom and to relegate them to the uncertain period of a future millennium, a context in which aspirations of world government would cause little alarm to suspicious Gentiles. In a logical attempt not to arouse the already excited non-Mormon world further, Church leaders thought it wise to publicize their true aims regarding the political Kingdom of God as little as possible. At times, the leaders felt it necessary to flatly negate political aspirations.*
>
> *Klaus J. Hansen, The Theory and Practice of the Political Kingdom of God in Mormon History, 1829-1890, Master's Thesis, Brigham Young University, Department of History, 1959, pages 15-16*

In today's environment of instant gratification most American citizens cannot fathom the patience required to hatch a plan which would by necessity have to be bequeathed to generation after generation. Church founders knew surprisingly well the task they set before their faithful followers could only be accomplished over hundreds of years. With the possible exception of Joseph Smith, never once did the early Church leaders actually intend to witness the birth of their brain-child — at least not in their own lifetime. Those early pioneers set aside their own agendas for the greater good, knowing full well they were being called upon to lay the foundation stones later generations would stand upon.

I have to respectfully disagree with those faithful Mormons who are so eager to ignore that which is painfully obvious. By subscribing to the point of view that church history of days past is no longer relevant and not an accurate or fair indictment of current church policy, they do a great disservice to themselves and their faith. A sleek new exterior with gleaming surfaces may have been erected to obfuscate the crumbling old edifice, but the foundation laid by Joseph Smith over a century and a half ago is still supporting the Church today.

We are often reminded of Latter-day Saints who stubbornly refuse to let go of memories of ages long past, yet when it appears to be more convenient for their own purposes, Church members are quick to set the past aside. For a seemingly tight-knit group who tenaciously cling to the vestiges of past eras, Mormons certainly are willing to forget their own history should it prove embarrassing. I find it curiously interesting how Mormonism has changed over the years

Great pains were taken to conceal the true aims of Church leaders from its rank and file membership, so it should come as no surprise a large percentage of Latter-day Saints have yet to recognize the political end game the Church is running. I would be willing to wager everything and bet the farm that of their nearly sixteen million members scattered across the globe, the largest part of its world-wide congregation are completely in the dark regarding the LDS Church's political goals.

I would encourage star-struck, doe-eyed converts to revisit the eloquent words written by the hand of one of their own General Authorities, before causally dismissing the past as less than relevant while referencing the Church of today. A hidden agenda is by no means a forgotten or dormant scheme. I would even go so far as to postulate the exact opposite is true. The gears of the machine are greased and ready to roll. Apostle Bruce R. McConkie clearly states in his seminal work *Mormon Doctrine*, the Kingdom of God as established by the Council of Fifty in 1844, is very much alive and actively working toward total domination of world-wide politics.

> *The Church of Jesus Christ of Latter-day Saints is the kingdom of God on earth; it is the kingdom which shall never be destroyed or left to other people; it is the kingdom which shall break in pieces and consume all other kingdoms; and it shall stand forever. But for the present it functions as an ecclesiastical kingdom only. With the millennial advent, the kingdom of God on earth will step forth and exercise political jurisdiction over all the earth as well as ecclesiastical jurisdiction over its own citizens.*
>
> *Bruce R. McConkie, Mormon Doctrine, 2nd Edition, Bookcraft, 1966, page 499*

The above statement flies in the face of the LDS Church's often repeated stance regarding the separation of church and state. Unless you have your head buried in the sand, it can't possibly get much clearer than that. Wake up and read the writing on the wall. The Church of Jesus Christ of Latter-day Saints, firmly and unequivocally intends to wield political power over the entire planet, subjecting American citizens to their own personal interpretation of God's law much in the same way Islam controls Muslim countries by enforcing Sharia law.

Mormon Doctrine: A Compendium of the Gospel, originally published in 1958, by Apostle Bruce R. McConkie, was instantly criticized by higher ranking church members. Primarily because Brother McConkie failed to receive permission from the First Presidency of the Church to divulge sensitive Mormon concepts. Although members of the First Council of the Seventy are equal in priesthood authority as the Quorum of the Twelve Apostles,

McConkie was still brought to task for his audacity. Incensed Church leaders put an immediate stop to the publication and distribution of the book, but not before it received wide circulation.

> *We decided that Bruce R. McConkie's book, 'Mormon Doctrine' recently published by Bookcraft Company, must not be republished, as it is full of errors and misstatements, and it is most unfortunate that it has receive such wide circulation. It is reported to us that Brother McConkie has made corrections to his book, and is now preparing another edition. We decided this morning that we do not want him to publish another edition.*
>
> *LDS Church President, David O. McKay, excerpt from President McKay's official office journal as Prophet of the Church, dated January 8, 1960*

It is hard to imagine a scholarly tome of precisely worded teachings that carefully analyzes and explains important doctrines of the Church not being welcomed by all Latter-day Saints, from the highest to the lowest. McConkie's work would eventually be praised by millions of church members attempting to gain a better understanding of the essential elements and fundamentals of Mormonism, but at that particular time in history the highest echelon of Church leaders did not want church doctrine disclosed to the world. Were they afraid people would learn the truth?

Marion G. Romney, an Apostle of the Church, was assigned the task of reading, commenting and recommending edits to the book. Romney along with Apostle Mark E. Petersen reported their findings directly to Church leaders. Shortly after an exhaustive study of the massive seven hundred seventy-six page encyclopedic volume, more than one thousand changes were recommended to the LDS Church President. I find it a bit troubling that a life-long Mormon, raised in the faith, who had been a General Authority of The Church of Jesus Christ of Latter-day Saints for more than twelve years and who was also married to the daughter of a Church President, was not deemed qualified to write about Mormon doctrine. Why did this one book cause such a stir?

> *"Now, Brother Smith, he is a General Authority, and we do not want to give him a public rebuke that would be embarrassing to him and lessen his influence with the members of the Church, so we shall speak to the Twelve at our meeting in the temple tomorrow, and tell them that Brother McConkie's book is not approved as an authoritative book, and that it should not be republished, even if the errors...are corrected."*
>
> *LDS Church President, David O. McKay, excerpt from President McKay's official office journal as Prophet of the Church, dated January 27, 1960*

I suppose the old adage still holds true today, it is impossible to un-ring a bell. The cat was already out of the bag, which placed Church leaders in a particularly precarious position. The subject was at hand and now it had to be dealt with. Although chastised for the initial publication, obviously for spilling the beans about subjects the LDS Church would rather not openly discuss, author Bruce R. McConkie was asked by Church President David O. McKay to revise the text with the editorial help of Spencer W. Kimball, who would later become the twelfth President of the Church. The second edition of *Mormon Doctrine* released in 1966 saw dramatic changes to the overall context and tone of the book.

After being reprinted forty times over the course of fifty years and despite being one of the all-time best-sellers for Mormon related studies, Deseret Books cited poor sales as a justification to cease printing of the *Mormon Doctrine*. Almost overnight publication came to an abrupt halt early in 2010. Curiously though, sales rankings from online book behemoth Amazon.com were reported as being far higher than almost any other book title referencing The

Church of Jesus Christ of Latter-day Saints. Of course we might just be overlooking the obvious. The decision of the Mormon Church to pull the *Mormon Doctrine* from circulation came just in time to allow it to fade from public memory as American voters prepared for the 2012 presidential race.

Who are You Voting For?

Ecumenical leaders are constantly referencing the rapid decay of our moral fabric, while warning us to get right with God. Preachers and ministers of all faiths love to proclaim to anyone willing to listen, "His judgment is nigh at hand." When you begin to seriously contemplate the current state of affairs in American politics, with all of its corruption and back-alley deals, you might just wonder if any of the candidates are trustworthy. It is easy to become frustrated when you are constantly hearing, "I might as well stay home on election day. There is nobody to vote for." I for one will never give up my right to vote. Nobody will ever take that privilege from me and besides I do believe there are a handful of dedicated, kind, caring individuals who are working tirelessly behind the scenes to strengthen America and fortify our future.

Without being too presumptuous, let us stipulate the previous statement is one hundred percent correct. Electing a Mormon candidate may seem like the perfect choice for a variety of reasons in today's political climate. We can affirm with clear confidence an elected official who just happens to be faithful to LDS teachings would abstain from alcohol, coffee, drugs and the use of tobacco. The possibility of extramarital affairs would be thrown right out of the window and you could be fairly certain they would give broad support to any legislation involving family values. Which brings me to the final point on our checklist — a strong commitment to family and faith. Sounds almost too good to be true.

Naturally it goes without saying, the above scenario would for all intents and purposes hold true of a Mormon candidate who strictly adhered to the doctrines of their faith. In these troubling and uncertain times, we as American citizens need to be extra careful when we go to the polls to cast our votes. We should do our research, learning as much as possible about the candidates and how they plan to govern us. What are their long term plans for America?

I have listed a number of qualities most American citizens would consider positive virtues when deciding who to cast a vote for, but remember a lot can happen in four years. Can voters trust a candidate who is devoted to a religion that openly references organizing the political kingdom of God? Will the political kingdom of God be given a higher priority than the government of the United States? I hope the answer to that question is never part of our future.

> *On 11 March 1844 a council meeting was held in Nauvoo to organize the political kingdom of God in preparation for the second coming of Christ. Now that the Prophet was a candidate for high political office, the time seemed right to inaugurate this body which would also serve as a committee to direct his campaign.*
>
> *Church History in the Fulness of Times, Student Manual, Published by The Church of Jesus Christ of Latter-day Saints, Salt Lake City, 2003, page 270*

The White Horse Rides Again

I am certain we are all familiar with the adage attributed to Benjamin Franklin, "In this world nothing can be said to be certain, except death and taxes." To that I might add this little tidbit of wisdom, "You can rest assured the subject of the infamous

White Horse Prophecy will rear its notorious head whenever you have a Mormon candidate running for President."

I can barely remember a Mormon candidate who in some fashion did not have to answer questions about the statement "you will see the Constitution of the United States almost destroyed; it will hang by a thread" allegedly uttered by Joseph Smith.

> *The Church of Jesus Christ of Latter-day Saints is politically neutral and does not endorse or promote any candidate, party or platform. Accordingly, we hope that the campaign practices of political candidates would not suggest that their candidacy is supported by or connected to the church.*
>
> *"The so-called 'White Horse Prophecy' is based on accounts that have not been substantiated by historical research and is not embraced as Church doctrine.*
>
> *Kim Farrah, spokeswoman for LDS public affairs, December 24, 2009*

As evidenced by the above statement, let me once again reiterate my previous remark by asserting the "White Horse Prophecy" is not recognized by the First Presidency or General Authorities as ever being part of official Church doctrine. Notwithstanding the often repeated declarations of contemporary Latter-day Saint authorities as to the "official" status of the "prophecy" within the greater context of accepted Mormon theology, it is very much a part of the Church's folklore and cannot be so easily ignored.

It is not too hard to understand why this mythical document keeps reappearing. Latter-day Saints obviously feel drawn to its message and it is easy to see why. The "White Horse Prophecy" explicitly praises the Saints for their dutiful devotion to maintaining God's principles, as well as assuring the stalwart legions of God's faithful army of their preeminent position in the newly formed governing body. If you were a Mormon, I bet you would want to be reminded of the lofty treasure that awaits you after years of sacrifice and service. More importantly, I believe the possibility of such a dream coming true was the impetus for a number of Mormons entering the political fray.

> *Steve Olsen, the Democratic candidate for Utah's First Congressional District, told me that Smith's vision inspired him to run. According to Mr. Olsen, a party official persuaded him to throw his hat into the ring by alluding to the prophecy. "You owe it to the Lord and the people to run," Mr. Olsen was told by Larry Daniel, chairman of the Iron County (Utah) Democrats. When Mr. Daniel noted that "our Constitution is more under attack by the Republicans than by outside forces and you are one of the elders of Israel who can help save it," Mr. Olsen says he was moved.*
>
> *Wall Street Journal, November 3, 2006*

While interviewing Republican Senator Orrin Hatch on his program which aired November 4, 2008, Glenn Beck mentions the threat to America. Within minutes of beginning his interview, Glenn Beck mentions an audio recording from the 1960's of LDS Church President Ezra Taft Benson talking about the evils of socialism. Continuing with his rank he proclaims, "We're at a point to where our country and our Constitution is slipping through our fingers." Beck manages to mention the Constitution no less than three times in less than twenty minutes and finally succeeds in prompting Senator Hatch to say, "I believe the Constitution is hanging by a thread."

Have you ever wondered why the Mormon Church owns and operates so many radio stations, television stations, newspapers and magazines? Maybe their goal is to inundate naive American citizens with their fastidious brand of propaganda through an onslaught of media outlets.

In deference to *Washington Post* columnist Dana Milbank's astute comments regarding Glen Beck's thinly veiled coded message on Fox News, I believe it will take more than a handful of cleverly placed and seemingly unassuming remarks to rally non-Mormons in support of The Church of Jesus Christ of Latter-day Saints "secret agenda." This is especially true since the LDS Church has taken great pains to conceal their long term plans from American citizens.

Throughout all of Mormondom you can hear whispered discussions about the impending collapse of our governing body, how the faithful need to be prepared for the coming hardships and to be ready to take up arms at a moment's notice. Of course all of this chatter is taking place outside of the Church's official lines of communication, but a vast majority of church members unquestionably believe the time is fast approaching when the elders of the church will step in to "save" America by rescuing the Constitution from the clutches of "evil."

On that fateful day in May of 1843, when the Prophet Joseph Smith, Jr. raised his glass to toast the overthrow of the mobocrats, he was not only referring to those who had gathered in force to supplant his vision of creating a theocratic government, but he was also making a clandestine threat against those in power. On more than one occasion Apostles of The Church of Jesus Christ of Latter-day Saints have used the term "mob" to reference the ungodly members of Congress who dared to interfere in their divine right of leadership.

It is remarkably fascinating to observe the sphere of influence an "unofficial" doctrine has upon members of the Mormon Church. Point in fact. Despite being relegated to a non-official status, which means it is never discussed openly at Church meetings nor is it considered a living doctrine, the staying power of this particular prophecy is exceptionally strong — much like an urban myth that refuses to die. Why? I suppose one possible reason could be the majority of Latter-day Saints furtively want the "White Horse Prophecy" to come true, although I doubt many would candidly admit their belief in the prophecy if you were to ask them about it directly. Frankly, most Mormons in America do pay homage to the message regardless of the fact it has never been canonized by the First Presidency. An unrealized dream is still a dream.

In the words of Glenn Beck himself, "If you take what I say as gospel, you're an idiot." So there you have it folks, straight from the horses mouth. Lies, lies and more lies. I wonder where Brother Beck received his schooling in the art of lying. His show on *Fox News* is yet another example of purposeful deceit.

It seems almost pathological how apparently good hearted, faithful people have been unwittingly programmed to lie. It is so entrenched into their psyche they unconsciously lie about the faith they profess to love so much. Members of the LDS Church rationalize their lying to non-members, friends and even family because they honestly believe those outside of the Church would not understand the highly spiritual concepts of the Gospel. As if Mormons are any more capable of understanding religious precepts than anyone else. Oh, that is right — they are imbued with the Spirit of the Lord. Please forgive me. It would appear that members of the LDS Church are capable of perceiving what us mere godless heathens cannot possibly comprehend. At least that is what they like to believe.

The truly sad part is that most Mormons do not have the slightest clue they are mindless actors on a global stage, reciting rhetoric from an unwholesome script. A script which has been handed down from director to director for the sheer purpose of subverting any and all analytical thinking of those within the fold.

Which leads us into our final section.

Unwavering Loyalty is Essential

Indoctrination into Mormon theology plays such a critical role it often begins at birth, at least that is for those fortunate enough to be born into the faith. I am going to put my neck on the chopping block and will be so bold as to state with unequivocal certainty, the highest echelon of the Mormon hierarchy has in the past surreptitiously subverted the innate human tendency of Church members to question their authority. Not only were the faithful followers of Joseph Smith psychologically manipulated into believing God would seek retribution and punish anyone who dared to question Church theology, but they were conditioned to believe in a celestial reward for following God's plan.

So there you have it, reward or punishment — a near perfect example of B. F. Skinner's operant conditioning. What makes this practice so deceptive and vile is many Mormons actually believe they are consciously making "free will" choices. Indulge me just for a moment as we look at the structure of this type of psychological conditioning, especially in connection with Mormon theology. Without going into a detailed analysis of the four points that must occur in order for the programming to be effectively received and ingrained into the subconscious mind of the subject, allow me to provide you with a more than plausible scenario. In fact, the following is a prime example of how Latter-day Saints are taught to accept Mormon theology.

1. In order to be worthy to attain entry into the Celestial Kingdom and thus achieve your own highest divine potential, you must adhere to the strict principles of the Gospel as revealed by God to Joseph Smith or one of his legitimate successors.

2. Priesthood holders who have been appointed to care for and watch over their congregation, namely Elders and

High Priests, interview hopeful candidates to determine if they are worthy to receive God's blessings, i.e. Baptism, Confirmation, Ordination into the Priesthood and entry into a LDS Temple where they can participate in further ordinances such as Endowment Ceremonies, Sealing's or Baptism for the Dead.

3. By voluntarily paying a full tithe of ten percent annually to the Church, regularly attending Church services, remaining sexually pure, obeying the guidance and dictates of the General Authorities, abiding by the Word of Wisdom (abstaining from alcohol, tobacco, drugs, coffee, tea or other caffeinated drinks) and professing a burning testimony of the Fullness of the Gospel — including supporting the President of the Church as God's appointed representative on earth, you are deemed worthy to hold Priesthood offices and attend Temple ordinances.

4. Should you find yourself doubting the truth of God's words as revealed by his prophets and choose not to abide by his precepts such as imbibing in the use of alcohol or drugs, being sexual promiscuous, etc. you would be called before your Bishop and reprimanded with an admonition to repent. You could also receive a formal probation which may suspend you having the right to partake of the sacrament, hold a church calling, exercise the priesthood, or enter the temple. If by chance the offense is considered grievous enough, you could possibly face disfellowshipment. Once disfellowshipped a disciplinary council must be convened to reinstate your membership — usually in one year's time. In the event you decided to publicly criticize Church authority

either by challenging official doctrine or questioning its leadership you could be excommunicated.

The Church of Jesus Christ of Latter-day Saints has created a fairly remarkable and sophisticated system of checks and balances to deal with its world-wide membership, but in the end it all comes down to reward and punishment. Here is a cute little Mormon axiom you might find interesting. "When our leaders speak, the thinking has been done." I am not going to include the entire statement verbatim, but if you would like to read it in its entirety you can find the referenced material by doing an Internet search on *June 1945 Improvement Era "Sustaining the General Authorities of the Church."*

> *When our leaders speak, the thinking has been done. When they propose a plan–it is God's plan. When they point the way, there is no other which is safe. When they give direction, it should mark the end of controversy. God works in no other way. To think otherwise, without immediate repentance, may cost one his faith, may destroy his testimony, and leave him a stranger to the kingdom of God.*
>
> *The Improvement Era, Volume 48, Number 6, "The Voice of The Church," Published by The Church of Jesus Christ of Latter-day Saints, Salt Lake City, June 1945, page 354*

Throughout the entire history of Mormonism we find these types of short adages proffered by the Prophet or one of his General Authorities. What is their purpose you might ask? You could surmise, from the above statement Church leaders do not condone members questioning their authority. Of course, apologists for the Mormon faith contend there is an entirely different meaning lurking behind those words. I invite you to decide for yourself.

From time to time, the First Presidency of The Church of Jesus Christ of Latter-day Saints obviously believe it is necessary to remind church members of their duty to uphold the authority of God's one, true church. Now don't get me wrong and instantly jump to conclusions. I am not saying members of the Mormon Church are being brainwashed, nor am I implying they are stupid or lack critical thinking skills — yet there remains little wiggle room for their followers to question the decisions made by the Church's elite hierarchy.

> *Now, does the office of the President of the Church embrace the right to identify for the whole membership of the church, and all the peoples of the world for that matter how the Lord would desire that we vote on certain matters? Certainly it does! Who would dare to proscribe God?*
>
> *LDS Stake Bulletin, Renton Washington Stake, Fall, 1976*

So far I have offered you considerable evidence on the subject of The Church of Jesus Christ of Latter-day Saints and their political agenda, but I also think it is essential to this discussion that we not overlook how they have accomplished their goals thus far. Quite frankly the LDS Church would not be a global force with billions of dollars in resources if they did not authoritatively exercise power over their own congregations, but this goes much deeper than winning over the hearts and minds of a few million souls seeking spiritual truth.

I believe most Americans would agree all of the major religions, to some degree or another, employ their own subtle machinations when it comes to attracting new converts into the fold. Of course this is all well and good. Humans yearn for social interaction, there is a deep psychological desire to gather together and form groups of like minded people. We simply want to feel a sense of belonging and religion affords us that opportunity.

Sometime between 1985 and 1994, LDS Church President Ezra Taft Benson proudly exclaimed the Mormon Prophet should be involved in politics, he went on to further explain his position by proclaiming, "The Prophet is above all humanity, above all scripture, above all the other prophets, above scientific knowledge and Must Be Obeyed." Which leads us to yet another question. Where do we draw the line? It is a perfectly reasonable to assume most humans tend to avoid embarrassing situations. Nobody likes to be humiliated. Is it permissible to lie to conceal a shameful act committed in the past? I suppose most of us have at one time or another uttered a little white lie to avoid an embarrassing moment. Giving into a momentary weakness is one thing, but persistently subsidizing a campaign of subterfuge and deceit is in my opinion going way too far. Why would a church want to purposefully mislead its members? To maintain loyalty among members who may otherwise doubt and question the veracity of their beliefs.

> *It is also my conviction that God desires everyone to enjoy freedom of inquiry and expression without fear, obstruction, or intimidation. I find it one of the fundamental ironies of modern Mormonism that the same general authorities who praise free agency, also do their best to limit free agency's prerequisites—access to information, uninhibited inquiry, and freedom of expression.*
>
> *D. Michael Quinn, quoted in Faithful History: Essays on Writing Mormon History, Edited by George D. Smith, Signature Books, Salt Lake City, 1992, page 95*

A letter sent from the Europe Area Presidency of The Church of Jesus Christ of Latter-day Saints on April 10, 2012 to Bishops, Branch Presidents, Stake Presidents and Mission Presidents addresses the issue of helping those members who may have reason to doubt their faith find their way back into the fold. Accompanying the letter was a second document entitled "Assisting Members

Who Struggle with Faith and Testimony" which lists nine specific points for helping wayward members either obtain or regain a strong testimony of Joseph Smith as a Prophet of God. Five of the nine points are precise instructions on what to do when a members expresses doubt. Referencing scripture and Handbook 1 "material on Apostasy" the letter further indicates a priesthood holders duty to take disciplinary action against members who publicly oppose the Church and its leaders.

You have just got to love that! Shape up and shut up or get out. I could be wrong, but I do not feel that is a very compassionate response to a crisis of faith. What do you think? In response to this letter, Christopher Ralph earnestly asked, in a very respectfully manner I might add, for answers to some of his nagging questions. I have reprinted a small section of Chris's more than three thousand word letter. The truth is out there.

> *Do we still place value upon the title Truth which the Saviour took to himself? Can it justifiably still be claimed that truth is the common currency of the LDS church in 2012? If so, then surely there must be a respectable place within the LDS church for those of us who love transparency enough to speak it, and share it, and stand for it, even though some of us have hitherto been despised and misunderstood for doing so.*
>
> *Sadly, too many faithful advocates of historical truth have been shunned and discarded over the years, simply because they cared enough to question that which, although not of their own making or choosing, was nevertheless right there before them. What else could they do if they valued their integrity? It has long been a puzzle to me how we, as a church, might teach that the glory of God is intelligence, while, at the same time promoting the idea that when it comes to historical realities, ignorance is accounted a virtue. This, surely, is a contradiction which needs to be reconciled in the eyes of a quizzical world.*

> *The concern extends beyond routine circumvention of intellectual discomfort however, to the weightier matter of commissioned institutional misrepresentation. The charge we, as Latter-day Saints of all levels of understanding, must confront is that the church has actively sought to replace authentic narratives of its history with deceitful mythologies.*
>
> *Signed, Christopher Ralph*

So where does that leave us?

The purpose of this particular argument is not to find fault with The Church of Jesus Christ of Latter-day Saints, but to point out the inherent danger associated with giving up your God given right to question authority. Where would we be as a nation had our founding fathers never questioned the rules and regulations they were subject to obey?

Just something for you to think about while you contemplate the wisdom of casting a vote for a candidate who espouses the teachings of Mormonism. I will leave you with this quote by an enlightened man whom many people considered to be a great teacher and a champion of human rights.

> *"Nothing in the world is more dangerous than sincere ignorance and conscientious stupidity."*
>
> *-Martin Luther King, Jr.*

Conclusion

Is it alarmist to distrust a religious community which continues to uphold and support the erroneous beliefs of their early church leaders? Forget the scientific evidence, or lack thereof, that clearly repudiates a substantial portion of their core beliefs, even looking beyond the numerous failed prophecies proclaimed by LDS Church authorities and let us take into consideration the passive/aggressive attitude the current Mormon hierarchy exhibits toward our own government. I have said it before and I will say it again. Joseph Smith, Jr. was arrogant, conceited, presumptuous and self-righteous, but he knew how to spread his particular version of propaganda. I can only imagine the audacity it took to teach his followers the United States will crumble and collapse under the weight of its own corruption, only to be saved by God's Prophet and an army of chosen people. Can you imagine how entitled you must feel in order to lay claim to the entire United States as your own personal kingdom?

Should American citizens be worried?

When you study the historical evidence available, it clearly indicates the leaders of The Church of Jesus Christ of Latter-day

Saints made frequent rash, harmful and illegal decisions which resulted in terrible tragedies. How can we trust a clergy who steadfastly refuse to admit any wrong doing? Church historians and apologists alike constantly bend the truth to suit their own needs. Altering the historical record is tantamount to telling a bold face lie, but I guess if you repeat the lie often enough people begin to believe it is true.

A casual reader might not fully grasp the importance and significance of all that has been discussed throughout this book. The religious practices and core beliefs of the LDS Church is just the tip of the iceberg. What lie hidden beneath the calm surface is far more dangerous than most would imagine. You might be inclined to slough off Latter Day Saint beliefs as mere curiosities or oddities of a slightly quirky spiritual movement, but that would be a mistake. To faithful Mormons world-wide, the oaths, obligations and directives of the General Authorities are matters of eternal salvation. The elite members of the First Presidency are accorded a God-like status. In the eyes of a true believer, the declarations of a living prophet are infallible.

It may not have immediately jumped to the reader's attention, nor appeared to be overtly obvious as we persisted on our path to track down the truth, but we uncovered numerous clues in regards to the not so subtle steps leaders of the LDS Church took in the past and continue to take today in order to keep the "silent agenda" of the Mormon Church alive. While the larger picture may still seem unclear to those who are unable to connect the dots, there is enough evidence to support the following conclusion. The Church of Jesus Christ of Latter-day Saints maintains as one of its primary goals the unspoken agendas of past generations. It is not enough to simply recognize the political double talk and carefully worded end runs LDS Church leaders engage in. We must exercise our God given freedom and cast our ballot wisely.

I am not suggesting you shun and avoid your neighbor or co-worker who may just happen to be a member of The Church of Jesus Christ of Latter-day Saints. For the most part members of the LDS Church are descent, hard working people, but the elite hierarchy who run the Church are a different matter altogether. I personally would not chose to elect any Mormon to public office, no matter how good they might sound. Remember the Council of Fifty was a secret organization hidden from all but the most elite members, whose sole purpose was and still is to establish the Political Kingdom of God.

Contrary to their own public statements the leadership of the LDS Church has on numerous occasions violated the spirit, if not the actual word of God, as proclaimed by a line of Prophets since the time of Joseph Smith Jr. Despite the many shortcomings of The Church of Jesus Christ of Latter-day Saints in regards to factual truth and historical accuracy, the faithful still continue to apologize, making excuse after excuse for the behavior of these so-called men of God they so lovingly adore and revere. Are there no men worthy to carry on God's work?

When will The Church of Jesus Christ of Latter-day Saints finally come to appreciate the inherent wisdom of plainly speaking the truth? Their attempts to hide what is so blatantly obvious only makes their faithful followers look naive and gullible.

I do not see any light at the end of that tunnel and would not hold my breath waiting for it to happen anytime soon. How many times do they have to be caught with their pants down before they realize it is in their best interest to come clean. You do not have to be a rocket scientist to understand the honorable course of action would be for the LDS Church to stop lying to its membership. It really is a very simple process. Own up to the past indiscretions, misdeeds and misconduct of early church leaders, including all of their self-proclaimed prophets and blaze a new trail forward.

After all is said and done, there still remains an air of mystery regarding any actual and authoritative teaching of The Church of Jesus Christ of Latter-day Saints on the subject of taking over and suppressing the United States government. Dare we risk to ignore the subtle whispers of revolution? Leaders of the LDS Church cannot afford to, nor will they risk publicly giving voice to words of subversion and subterfuge. For nearly two centuries Mormon fear has kept their "secret agenda" quiet. What fear you might ask? Fear that the ears of an uninitiated bystander may catch a softly whispered phrase or two and spoil their well laid plans. You can bet the house and take this one to the bank. The hard earned political leverage the Church has garnered over the years will never be voluntarily relinquished or abandoned. The real danger lies with the Church elite who hold the power and know how to wield it effectively.

Final Word

Regardless of how many times historians and official spokesmen for the Church attempt to force their revisionist histories upon us, the facts remain the same. There simply is no sane rationalization for the disturbing and callous behavior of The Church of Jesus Christ of Latter-day Saints. Should we allow the actions of God's self proclaimed prophets to taint our opinion of all Latter-day Saints? No, but the First Presidency of the Church must be held accountable for continuing the perpetuation of a lie.

Despite all of the Mormon Church's efforts to spin the truth in their favor, you would be extremely foolish to ignore a couple of cold, hard facts.

1. The hierarchical structure of the LDS Church is surprisingly narrow. Allowing a mere handful of faithful supporters to inherit a place of power.

2. The upper echelon of elite leaders have continually exerted pressure on their followers to do their bidding — using deceit, extortion, murder and subterfuge in order to attain their goal of establishing the "City of Zion" and creating a "Political Kingdom of God."

I cannot, for the life of me, discern the hand of God in any of their insane strategies.

Did the leaders of The Church of Jesus Christ of Latter-day Saints purposefully devise a secret and hidden agenda for the governing of the American people? I believe that question has been satisfactorily answered. Whether or not that agenda is still being pursued is a debate that will surely continue for many years to come, but one fact that cannot be ignored is the historical record is filled with incident after incident of LDS Church leaders either implicitly commanding or tacitly approving civil disobedience among its members.

This leaves but one question to ask. Can we as citizens of the United States afford to have the elite religious leaders of a rapidly growing multi-national corporation masquerading as a religion influence the political aspirations of its members?

Made in the USA
Monee, IL
17 July 2023